RAGE TO PEACE

FROM WOUNDED CHILD TO GANG MEMBER TO PEACE ADVOCATE

IRAN NAZARIO

GREEN HEART
LIVING
—PRESS—

ISBN Paperback: 978-1-954493-60-5

Published by Green Heart Living Press

Cover photography by JCV Freelance Photography LLC

DEDICATION

I dedicate this book to my brother Efrain "Smokey" Nazario who had begun to embrace a change in mindset that would allow him to make better decisions.

He lost his life to the violence we had known all of our lives.

His rage went with him and he was unable to achieve Peace in this life.

&

I dedicate this book to the many people who battle with rage every single day and are engaged in an internal struggle to rid themselves of it.

You can and will do it.

CONTENTS

—·—

"A Warrior sees the possibilities within the chaos, the lessons between the tragedy and the abilities amongst the pain."

– Iran Nazario

— • —

FOREWORD

In 1994, Hartford, Connecticut was experiencing intense gang activity. Drive-by shootings were becoming commonplace and nowhere was it worse than in public housing across the city. This was viewed as the purview of law enforcement to handle until a six-year-old girl, Marcellina Delgado, became a victim of it. The result was an uproar for the city to do something about this scourge on our community.

I was serving as the Director of Youth Services for the city. One afternoon, I was dispatched to a meeting at the Hartford Housing Authority to participate in a discussion on how to address the violence issue in public housing. We were to begin with Charter Oak Terrace where this child had been killed. I wasn't anywhere near a gang expert but had been doing a great deal of research to try to understand it. My area of expertise was youth development and I had been working to bring organizations across the city together to coordinate and collaborate to intercede in and prevent youth problems. This day, John Wardlaw, the visionary Executive Director of the Housing Authority, wanted a different approach to calm the atmosphere within these developments scattered across the city. I was the designated city representative.

I mostly listened during this meeting. It was a time to learn and to identify how we could partner to help John's vision become a reality. When I returned from the meeting, I reported to my director who was the Head of Human Services. When she asked how it went, I told her that only one person in the meeting made sense and it was an Iran Nazario. I'd never met him before that day. I had developed a leadership program for youth who lived in one of the developments and yet,

Iran's and my paths didn't intersect. I heard in him a compassion for others and a realistic perspective that, to me, could help.

I watched, from the sidelines, Iran do his thing. John had taken the controversial action of hiring him, a known and highly placed gang leader, to do work in the projects. After some time, I saw him behind me in a grocery store checkout line. I'm not one that generally approaches others, but I did that day. He didn't remember me. I told him of our meeting and my assessment of those around the table. He thanked me and we went our separate ways. Over time, I continued to watch Iran's work as a mediator, negotiating Peace among warring factions, and how committed he was to improving lives.

In 2000, I was tapped to run a federal project for high-risk youth ages 14-21 with a focus on bringing them into the workforce. It was a bold initiative with five years of funding under the George Bush administration. We were to be part of a national movement called Youth Opportunity. As I sought to put my leadership team together, I was struggling to identify how we were going to do the street work needed to recruit youth. These would not be kids who would join a program just because it promised them a job, especially when they could make so much more through the drug trade.

I had a conversation with a colleague who was still working for the city and who had been one of my staff. I said to him, "I need an Iran Nazario." He replied that he believed Iran Nazario was available so I asked him to reach out and ask him if he would be willing to meet with me. Soon after, Iran and I had our first official meeting to talk about this new grant project and what I believed we needed to get youth engaged.

He was hesitant at first. He had to feel me out to determine if I was for real. I knew what needed to be done but I didn't know how to do it. My intuition told me that Iran would know what to do and if he and I could work together, we could make it happen. He said yes provided he could recruit staff members that he believed could do the work successfully. I agreed, not knowing what I was agreeing to, but trusting my instincts.

The result was a Recruiter Team made up of former gang members, both male and female. Two of the new staff were reportedly two of the "baddest" street gang members around. They had been incarcerated and were known to be violent. I was hesitant but ended up keeping my commitment and working with Iran to provide training and orientation to the project. I did what John Wardlaw had done a few years earlier by trusting Iran and supporting a new gang of recruiters working to pull youth from street life. They were remarkable and I grew to love this staff. I gained such respect for Iran, teaching him what I could, supporting him in his development, and letting him do what he knew had to be done. His staff worked 24/7 at times, weekends and holidays, going to where youth were and building relationships in a way that had never been done before.

From that early first meeting to our working together, a connection bond was strengthened with great respect on both sides. He and my son became best of friends with Iran as a big brother. He became the padrino to my granddaughter. And, along the way, over the span of 25 years, I went from being April to being Mom. My husband became Dad.

I've watched the struggle he'd experienced working to leave the old street life behind. There were always threats against him from the streets. I remember at one point while we were working together I'd received a call from the police department and I was asked to bring Iran into a meeting. The threats on his life were discussed and it was the very first time there was respect given to Iran from law enforcement. Things were changing.

The real demarcation point for Iran was when his brother Smokey was murdered. What would Iran do? Would he retaliate and take revenge as he had been indoctrinated to do? Or, would this so-called man of Peace win out? There was tension across the city, from the streets to law enforcement. Everyone, it seemed, was braced for retaliation and a body count.

People from all corners of Hartford waited, prepared, wondering whether we would see a war break out. This grieving brother, heartbroken, was given the opportunity to demonstrate he wasn't just talk, but truly believed in what he stood for. My husband and I went to the calling hours and when we got to Iran, he and I just hugged and he cried into my shoulder. Time stopped for a bit and I held him and did a mama thing until he was ready to let go. Perhaps that is when I became Mom, showing him the maternal caring that he so desperately needed.

To me, that is the time Iran truly had Peace enter his entire being. He was able to shrug off the pain and indoctrination of his early life and move fully into this new one where he committed himself to the work of Peace. I have been honored, as is my husband and son, to welcome Iran into our hearts and family, and to adopt him as ours. We are grateful he has accepted and become ours.

Iran is an inspiration. His Taurean stubbornness melded with his commitment to his beliefs and this carries him through his days. He shows us people can change when they are open to the possibility. He doesn't give up. There is always a way even if he hasn't thought of it yet. He listens to various viewpoints and integrates them into a fuller vision. He shows us that change is an ongoing struggle but with determination and loving support, it can be done.

One evening a number of years ago we had a conversation. I said to him that God had a plan for him. He shouldn't have been here by then but every time it was needed, an angel showed up in the form of a mentor, an attorney, or a benefactor. It was a clear message that God wasn't done with him yet. He had to know that. I told him, in a very mama way, that he had been given a responsibility to change lives and to never forget that.

He hasn't.

I am honored and grateful to be a witness to the transformation of a rage-filled young man who was hurt and searching, into an honorable man of integrity and Peace. Transformation is possible if you are willing to do the work to become who you are truly meant to be.

Iran is proof of that.

I love you Iran. I am beyond proud of you and your humanity.

Mama April / April Goff Brown

Author, Human Design Specialist, and Intuitive Life Coach

—•—

Author's Note

"I hope that Rage to Peace *inspires readers to believe in their ability to pursue a life filled with Peace, positive purpose, and a passion for their success despite the challenges they have faced. I wrote this book to motivate readers to turn their anger, self-sabotaging actions, and pain into healthy thoughts, forgiveness, healing, and being open to opportunities."*

– Iran Nazario

— • —

PROLOGUE

The dumpster at the side unit of the SANDS housing complex was filled with garbage. It was large enough to fit mattresses from tenants who had moved away. Brown in color and made of heavy steel, the dumpster was easily capable of holding over one thousand pounds of garbage. Shadowing the top of the dumpster was a large tree that stood so tall I believe it could touch the clouds.

As a pre-teen, I could see the dumpster through the blinds of my bedroom window. At night it would disappear into the darkness and reappear when the car headlights drove onto the driveway, coming or leaving the complex. Behind that dumpster was a grassy field, similar to one used for high school baseball. There was a fence that separated the baseball diamond from the street, preventing any baseballs from flying into the oncoming traffic.

The field was facing Main Street in Hartford, Connecticut. Drivers passing by could see the field from any direction they were traveling. To the left of that dumpster was another part of the field, less developed, that led to a man-made path leading to the train tracks behind our complex. I had made my way down that path and traveled along the train tracks on many occasions along with other kids. We would lift up rocks and look for grass snakes to play with.

The view out over the field was my place of solace. I could look through the blinds and escape the noise coming from behind me. A window to Peace. The view smothered the sounds of loud talking, yelling, fighting, music, and the sounds that no child should hear of adults engaged in sexual behaviors.

I could shut it all out by watching the cars and the people passing by. Listening to the sounds of the bats as they smacked the baseball out into the field, listening to fans yelling as they watched the games, or watching the weather during the change of seasons.

I could forget about my hunger, my shame, my fear, my anger, and my pain. I did not know from one minute to the next if chaos would grip the small apartment I shared with my three siblings, my mom, and the many visitors who would stop in to be entertained by my mom.

I looked forward to the moment when I was allowed to or asked to step outside so that I could walk around our apartment building and head toward the dumpster. A couple of the neighborhood kids would climb on top of the dumpster and play king of the castle. There was a mad dash up the side of the dumpster to claim the throne.

Opening the side doors of the dumpster gave me an entry into what seemed to be a playland of garbage. We'd put our feet on the ledge and hurl our bodies in, lying flat on our stomachs atop the mound of junk. We loved it when people threw out their old mattresses. This meant we could stack the mattresses on one another so it could comfort our fall as we bounced off the dumpster.

There were times when we misjudged the jump, flying off the side onto the hard ground. The fall would hurt our agile bodies. The ground was hard with small pebbles of gravel that covered the dirt from constant foot traffic, yet I felt invincible. Flying through the air as if nothing could stop me. I was safe. I was free.

Unlike the loss of innocence I was experiencing within the walls of my apartment, outside, in that dumpster, I felt innocent. I felt like a child. I was in control of the height of my leaps, the depths of my falls, and the way my body could contort itself into any position I chose.

My place of Peace was outside my window. Yet once again I found my Peace disrupted. Peace was stripped from me. There were no longer the sounds of children's laughter, or the sounds of a baseball game and cheering fans.

One afternoon the space around the field and dumpster was silent—free of young children's laughter or cheering baseball fans. Just the sound of cars passing by.

There was a commotion coming from nearby. I could hear loud voices talking but I couldn't see their faces.

That day slowly became night and I never got to go outside. I missed that retreat. I felt trapped inside my apartment. The following day while I was walking outside, I heard rumors from other kids in the neighborhood. Somebody died in the park. They killed somebody by the tree that touched the clouds.

Death.

Once the body was found in the park it no longer felt safe to be there.

This would become just another day in my life that included violence, death, trauma, fear, isolation, criminality, depression, resentment, failure, and no expectation to live beyond each day. This became normalized.

This reality shaped my actions, behavior, thinking, and negative experiences. I needed to dig deeper and fight harder than I ever thought I could to discover that Peace was my passion and that inspiring others to seek Peace was my purpose. Along the way, I discovered myself, my talents, my positive habits, my true desires, my sanity, my hope, my abilities, my value, my heart, my mind, and my calling.

I needed to evolve from Rage to Peace.

1

— • —

BROKEN

JANUARY 13, 2008

I n the early morning hours, I awakened to a normal routine of clearing my
eyes, relieving myself, and washing up. I walked out of the bathroom and
down a small hallway between the doors of our bedrooms. My son, daughter, and
wife were sleeping soundly.

The floors were made of natural wood planks that felt cold to the touch. I liked
feeling the cold floor on the bottoms of my feet. As I headed towards the living
room and into the kitchen, I peered outside the living room window, as I often
had, to see what the weather was like and if there was anything happening outside
the window.

The house sat on about 1/3 of an acre and was surrounded by many old and
tall trees. There was one giant tree in the middle of the front lawn that obstructed
the view of the neighbor's house. I turned towards the kitchen, leaning upon
the kitchen counter, once again, gazing out the window above the kitchen sink.
Looking out into the backyard, I could see the two-car garage that was detached
from the house and could also see through the tree line in the backyard that
separated our property from our neighbors.

The net of the basketball hoop swayed gently due to a light breeze. It was a cold
January day in Connecticut. There was a light rain and the temperature was in
the low 30s.

I poured myself a bowl of cereal with milk and opened my cell phone to see if
there were any messages on my voicemail or any missed calls. Shortly after, my cell

phone battery died. It was unlike me to let my battery deplete. At the time, I was working as a Peacebuilder and was "on call" in the event of a shooting or a violent incident involving a teen in Hartford.

I was expected to answer the phone when the local hospital called so that our team of Peacebuilders could make our way to their emergency room foyer. I was part of a crisis response team charged with engaging the friends and loved ones of teens who were victims of violence and were transported to the hospital for treatment.

I had been at a neighbor's party the night before but for some reason, I did not walk across the street and simply plug the phone into the charger and go back to the party. I finally attached my phone to the charger, waiting until the battery reached three percent charged. Almost immediately upon powering up the phone, the pings started coming in as notifications of missed calls and voice messages were being received.

I took a look at the phone number associated with several of the missed calls. I did not recognize the number. It was not familiar nor was it a saved contact. I assumed I may have been called in error. I kept scrolling through the missed calls and noticed my half-brother's name as one of the missed calls. The calls were made to my cell and, typically, an early morning call meant bad news or someone was reaching out who had partied just a little too hard.

Curious, I punched in the phone icon for "messages" and was directed to voicemail. I punched in my access code and heard the familiar voice of the mobile voicemail prompt. I heard, "You have seven new voice messages."

I asked myself, *What the heck is going on?*

The recording spit out its usual notice, "First new voice message, from -------
received at -------."

"Yo Smurf!!!" A frantic high piercing yell came through the speaker. "Smokey got shot. Yo, call me right now!!!"

My brain could not comprehend what I had just heard. I froze and pulled the phone away from my ear. I felt confused but I had enough experience on the streets to know the caller's tone was serious.

I began to move towards my bedroom, anxious to hear the next messages.

This time, the voice was seemingly angry, with a sense of frustration that they couldn't reach me. "Yooooo Smurf!" they yelled, "Call ME!!! Smokey got shot."

I stumbled into my bedroom to grab my sneakers and clothes. I hurried frantically to the front door and ran to the driveway. While I was running to the car not knowing where to go, I called the number from where the messages were left in the hopes of speaking to whoever was breaking this news to me. No one answered, so I called again. Still, no one answered. I felt helpless and without direction. My brother was reportedly shot and I had nowhere to go to help him or see him to determine if the report was true.

As I hurried to my car, I continued to listen to the messages. Finally, I heard in one of the messages, "Yo Smurf! What the F***??? Call me back. Hurry the F*** up! Smokey is at Hartford Hospital, come down here now!"

I peeled out of my driveway and headed towards the highway that would lead me to Hartford Hospital.

I-91 South was clear. I did not pay attention to the traffic laws. I could feel my desperation as I did all I could do to find the best route to the hospital.

After hearing the last voicemail, I decided to call my half-brother to share the news with him. He answered, and simply said, "Yo, Smokey was shot. He got shot right across the street from my house." He went on to say through his sobs, that he saw him lying on the sidewalk, and at first, he did not know who it was.

I could feel his heartbreak through the speaker on the phone. I asked, "But what happened?"

"I don't know Smurf. I was sleeping when my father woke me up by saying that he believed that someone had been shot across the street and that he thought he heard someone kick the front door of their apartment."

He said that he also faintly heard someone scream Smokey's name, but he wasn't sure. He had jumped up from bed and went to the window to look. It took him a few seconds to see clearly. He then spotted someone lying on the street as the ambulance arrived, performing life-saving efforts. They placed the victim into the ambulance.

It was then that he was able to get a good look at the victim and realized that it was Smokey. He ran outside but the ambulance was gone and the police had taped off the scene. That is when he ran back inside his apartment and called me.

I once again asked him what happened. He once again repeated that he didn't know! He then started to share a little of what he last remembered from his night out with Smokey.

He mentioned that he was at a party with a few people he knew and after a while of being there, he decided to call Smokey and invite him over to the party.

Smokey was at home and took the call. He was excited about the party and decided to meet him at the address he provided. This was an apartment Smokey had visited before. It was a place where a friend of ours lived and where apartment parties were a regular occurrence.

He reported that after a while Smokey arrived and they partied with the crowd together. As the party entered the early morning hours, he decided that he was going to head home. He advised Smokey that he was leaving and Smokey said he would stay with other friends. They parted ways and he did not see anything that concerned him. The next thing he knew he was being awakened by his father.

I continued driving and exited 1-91 and followed Hudson Street to Hartford Hospital.

I pulled into the driveway entrance of the hospital that led to the emergency room entrance. I quickly entered the valet parking area. I ignored the signs for valet and parked my car. I got out of my car and quickly made my way to the emergency room entrance.

I vaguely remember that there were already people gathered on the way to the emergency room entrance. Whoever they were, they knew me and must have known my brother. They stared at me intensely, looking for my reaction. I cannot recall how many steps it was from the valet lot to the emergency room entrance. I cannot recall if I looked at those who were standing there directly in the face or simply saw their shapes and shadows. It is still all a blur.

I arrived at the emergency room nurse's counter and asked about my brother.

"I am here to see Efrain Nazario."

I mentioned to the nurse that I had received a call stating he had been shot. The nurse asked me for his date of birth and asked me what my relationship was to the patient. I told her I was his little brother. She began to type into her computer keyboard and then requested my identification.

I reached into my back-right pants pocket and grabbed my wallet, pulled out my driver's license, and handed it to her. After what felt like 10 to 20 minutes the nurse mentioned that yes, he was a patient and was currently in surgery.

The nurse stated that I could head up to the trauma floor and wait until someone was available to give me an update on his condition. The nurse pointed me in the direction of automatic double doors and allowed me access to the main foyer in the main building of the hospital.

I pushed the button on the wall and activated the double doors to open.

The emergency room lights were a little dim and it was full of patients sitting in the waiting area to be seen. There were also many hospital staff members moving quickly between rooms, offices, and nurse stations.

That area seemed to create more anxiety in me. It felt as if everything I was seeing and hearing was not going to end well for the patients who were waiting to be seen. The faces I can remember appeared to look sick, in pain, and under duress.

As I walked into the main building of the hospital, I noticed the elevators were to my right. This side of the hospital appeared well-lit and clean. It was still decorated for the Christmas and New Year holidays. On the walls, signs were pointing to several departments and the gift shop. I proceeded to the elevators and punched in the up arrow on the panel.

Once the doors opened, several people exited the elevator, I entered the elevator and selected my floor. With each ding, after each floor, I became increasingly more nervous as to what I would find out. I was also more and more uncertain of what to do, who to ask for, and where to go.

I finally arrived on the floor. There was no one in the hallway to my left or right. The walls were a clean, bright white with very little art or decor to be seen. It reminded me of a psych ward from an old movie.

I turned right off the elevator and proceeded down the hallway. I heard nothing and saw no one. I then walked toward the left hallway and saw someone at the end of that hallway. I could hear that person talking and could see they were talking on a cell phone. This person was telling whoever he was speaking with that Smokey was shot.

He was angry and talking very loudly.

One of my deepest fears for my big brother was that he would become a victim of the streets and a victim of violence. This man's words were beginning to confirm these fears.

When this person looked up from where he was standing, it was apparent that he saw me and knew who I was, although I did not know him. Once he realized it was me, he ended his call and walked toward me.

He opened his mouth and said, "I am sorry, Smokey was shot. I am so sorry. I was with him when he was shot. I tried to help him but I was not able to help. I called the ambulance and they brought him here."

I was numb because he was present when it happened and he was able to confirm that my brother was shot. He then said that he was the one who called me. He was my truth.

He asked, "Bro, why didn't you answer the phone?"

I did not answer. I remained quiet while he talked. I do not remember what he said next. I was thinking about my brother, how serious his injury was, and where he was on this floor. I started to walk away quietly and I listened to him as he dialed a number on his phone. I had turned my back to him at this point.

I listened to him say, "Yo, Smurf is here. Yeah, he's here and it's on now!"

He knew me and my reputation on the streets. He knew I had deep connections. He knew that I would defend my brother with my life. He was certain there would be retaliation now that I was aware that my brother had indeed been shot.

On the street, when the blood of someone you love is spilled, the blood of those responsible must also be spilled. He was anticipating the actions we would take for my brother.

Relationships between brothers can be tricky. Even those who are related by blood and have the same parents. There are the usual brotherly arguments, scrums, and fights as young children wanting to win a game, wanting to have something the other one has, one is pranking the other and pride turns it into a fight, or one is impressing a girl and showing off a little too much leading to an argument over how unfair the treatment is. There are also fights that happen over wearing the other's clothes, changing the TV channel, or spending too much time in the bathroom when the other one desperately needs to use it.

The scenarios that lead to these confrontations are many. It felt as if we had been through them all. Our anger would boil up to the surface quickly and in several instances led to a physical confrontation. Smokey was bigger than me, not only due to him being older than me but also due to his physical structure. He was what I describe as beefy or heavy-boned. His hands and body were thick.

He was very much an emotional responder to anything that he felt embarrassed him. I would make fun of him for anything I thought was funny and he would do the same to me.

One day I noticed that my brother was talking to a girl near our apartment building. To me, he was behaving and talking differently than usual. He was leaning into the girl a little bit and he was rocking back and forth slightly. Every once in a while he would tilt his head and smile. It was a little weird to me and funny at the same time.

I continued to watch my brother have this conversation and I realized that he was flirting or hoping to impress this girl. As I watched from the kitchen window I decided to step outside to the landing of the front door.

I started calling his name repeatedly as if I needed him for something. I truly had no reason to call out for him. I knew that if I called his name out enough it would irritate him and it would make me laugh to see him get angry at me.

I stepped off the landing and onto the pathway of the complex. I decided to walk towards where he is talking to this girl. As I got closer to him I begin to tease him. "Smokey, what are you doing? Do you like this girl?" I asked.

I said, "You better stop and go to the house. You are not GQ." (I said this to insinuate that he was not handsome or sexy as the men featured in GQ magazine were made to look.) I called out his name several more times until he responded.

"Iraaaaan," he said in a frustrated tone. "Leave me alone."

I continued to call his name and asked him, "Do you like that girl?"

The girl decided to walk away. Perhaps it was due to my heckling and teasing, or perhaps she was not interested in my brother.

As she walked away it was obvious to me that he believed that she walked away because of me. He began to walk towards me with a look of disgust and disappointment on his face.

As he got closer to me I began to walk away from him. I walked around him to avoid making contact with him.

As he walked past me he murmured, "You're stupid."

I said, "She left you, she didn't like you," in a teasing high-pitched voice. I continued walking towards the field that was in the middle of the housing complex. It is where the kids would play games and the older boys played football. From this field, you could see every building in the complex. I knew I had irritated my brother and I joyfully stepped onto the field.

For some unexplained reason, I decided to turn around and look back to see if my brother had made it into our apartment.

As I made the turn toward our apartment building, I saw something approaching me at a high rate of speed. I was not able to make out what it was but I instinctively ducked my head and leaned away from what was coming at me.

As the item passed by my head, I felt the wind and heard a *whoosh*. That was followed by a thud, a click, and a deep cracking sound. I turned to look at what had just missed my head. As I located it on the ground, I was shocked to see that it was a brick.

It was lying on the ground almost intact. A few chips from the brick could be seen near the rest of it and there was a trail of chalk-like markings on the cement that were left there as the brick scraped against the ground.

I turned towards my brother with a surprised look and realized he had thrown the brick at me in response to my messing up his chance to continue talking to the girl. He sat there staring at me and I just stared back. That brick would have caused major injuries to my head had it made contact with the force he used to throw it.

I know that if I were that angry I would be able to react in the same way. Rage and violence existed in us.

We were a pair of Taurus bulls who were so very similar in temperament and life experience. The Taurus is a stubborn and fiercely competitive zodiac. This included the well-known anger associated with the Taurus sign. Simply put, they are fearless in conflict.

My brother and I were our fiercest defenders. No one anywhere could challenge either one of us without the other one stepping in and risking everything to make sure they were clear that they had made a mistake choosing either one of us. My brother was easy to love when we weren't in a disagreement with each other. He was kind, and funny, and made me feel as if I was safe when I was with him.

He made sure to talk about me to all his friends with genuine admiration and love. I was his little brother and he wanted to make sure everyone thought of me as he did.

My brother and I were separated by 360 days in age. For five days we were the same age. We were both born in May. This meant that for five days every year, we were the same age and he was no longer my big brother. We were even. Like twins. Perhaps that is why I felt him close, always!

His hugs were strong and filled with compassion for me. We greeted each other with a kiss on the cheek and a deep embrace every time we connected because we were truly happy to connect again.

As a child, he had put his body in the way of blows meant for me by one parent or the other. He would take responsibility for things I had done and never told on me even when severely beaten for what I had done.

We cried together, were abused together, were in foster care together, were scared together, and were uncertain together, but we were together.

I paced back and forth in that hospital hallway. It felt similar to the times I had been waiting to be released from prison—time seemed to tick by at a snail's pace. The greatest difference this time was that there was no sense of relief associated with waiting to learn about the condition of my brother as there was when I was waiting to be released from incarceration.

I felt his energy within the walls of this long corridor of the trauma unit. I was once again close to my brother but not in the way that I wanted to be. The walls separated our embrace and as time passed by it felt as if I was being robbed of visually seeing his smile.

2

—·—

THE NEWS

After some time, I re-engaged with the person who was with my brother in the last moments before he was shot. There was no effort on my part to re-engage. It simply happened due to us being the only two people in the hallway during a tense and emotional situation.

He must have felt as if he needed to share information with me or simply needed to talk to someone or maybe even feel me and my intentions out. That is the feeling I had when he looked at me.

While I was pacing the hallway, I could not help but think about this person at the other end of the hallway. *Who is he? What does he know?*

"He's in there," he whispered, motioning with his head toward a door that was embedded into the wall. The door had no lock on the outside, and no handle to pull on. It was a door that was only meant as an exit from whatever space was behind it.

I quietly acknowledged his attempt to share my brother's location. I stood there staring at the door, hoping it would swing open and he would walk out. I gently leaned toward the door and placed my ear on the door nearest to the door frame where there appeared to be some space where I might be able to listen through.

I quieted my heart, my head, and the natural sounds around me. There was nothing. Not a buzz, a ping, a voice and clanking of metal, or any sounds associated with surgery or crisis.

This person watched me closely, perhaps hoping to understand what I was thinking of doing next. "Bro. I don't know why he shot him."

I finally understood he had important information to share with me that might help me understand why my brother was in surgery and who was responsible.

I looked into his face and asked, "Who shot him and where was he shot? Why was he shot? What happened?"

He told me the person's name. I immediately knew who he was referring to. I knew this person as far back as my childhood. My brother has also known him since they were children. What reason would this person have to shoot my brother?

I asked, "Why in the hell would he shoot my brother?"

I was still digesting the name he said was responsible. In seconds I remembered the times we spent together, the times I helped him when he needed me, and the times he visited my home and spent time around my wife and daughter. I couldn't comprehend or come to terms with any reason he would shoot my brother or even have a reason to be in serious conflict with him.

He then began to share the details of the evening that led to the shooting based on his experience and recollection.

It all began after he and my half-brother decided to attend this party. My half-brother and this person knew one another from Hartford. They had spent time at different parties and clubs in the past.

While they were there having a good time, they decided that Smokey would enjoy the party and would also make the party more enjoyable.

Smokey had an infectious personality, a kind smile, and a knack for turning your average party into an all-out bash. His sense of humor and personality attracted the fun crowd.

After Smokey arrived, they simply continued the party, laughing, flirting with girls, and enjoying the music. At some point, a few others joined the party crowd. Among the crowd, he spotted someone he had disagreed with recently. By this time my half-brother had left for the night. He continued to tell Smokey that someone he had a problem with had arrived at the party.

He said that he wanted to clear the air and went to confront one of the individuals. Words turned into yelling and shoving. The tenant asked him and the other participant in the altercation to leave.

He said that at some point it was decided that the conflict would be resolved outside of the apartment.

They decide that a "fair one" (one on one fight) would settle the disagreement. Smokey, this person, and three others ended up on the side of the building away from the main street. This is where this fair one would take place.

Each person squared up in a fighting position and the fight began. After a couple of minutes, he claimed he began to gain the upper hand on the other guy and suddenly felt something or someone striking him on the back of the head.

As he turned to look, he witnessed the girlfriend of the guy he was fighting striking him with her hands and a shoe she had taken off her foot.

He turned toward his girlfriend and pushed her down. At that time everyone watching jumped into the fight to help break it up. The guy who was losing the fight and his girlfriend were upset and declared that they would come back to take care of this.

He claimed that at that time the person who shot my brother yelled out, "This is none of your business."

The guy said to my brother, "Why are you getting in it?"

Smokey responded, "I was only stepping in so no one would be jumped and to make sure the fight was fair."

The person who shot my brother said, "Ok, you should stay out of it."

All three people in that group jumped into a vehicle and left the area. Smokey and this person decided that it was over and that they would return to the party. He claimed that they were there until daybreak and then decided to walk to a place for breakfast they knew about.

After walking outside and reaching the corner they were approached by one of the individuals from the fight who said, "You should not have gotten in the way."

He said the person was holding something near his body. It appeared that he had a gun.

He told me Smokey said, "Yo, I know you. I did not hit anyone; I was just breaking it up. You are not going to shoot me over that. I know you."

Smokey turned to walk away and that is when this person pulled the trigger, striking my brother in the back. He says he had started running when he saw the person with the gun but that Smokey did not run. He says he saw Smokey stumble to the ground. The shooter ran in the opposite direction to a waiting vehicle and they drove away.

He came out to find Smokey crawling on the sidewalk. He appeared to be crawling to my half-brother's house for help. His head faced the townhouse-style apartment where my half-brother lived.

He said he grabbed him and asked him if he was hurt. He said my brother was barely speaking and that he called for the police and medics. He says he remained with Smokey until police and EMTs arrived to provide aid.

After Smokey was taken away, he was able to pull my number from Smokey's phone and call me. He said he tried to reach me so I could help.

Despite this rundown of the events, I still could not believe a man I knew almost all my life would shoot my brother in the back as he was walking away.

I felt a flurry of different emotions run through me. So many questions remained. I was angry, hurt, confused, and felt helpless, I wanted answers. I had no one to hold, no one I trusted to speak with, and no one else to help me make sense of what happened. Despite the emotions I was feeling, my main focus remained on my brother's medical condition.

All my life, I felt my brother's spirit and energy. Feeling him present even when I was far away allowed me to always connect with him when it was necessary.

I always felt that when he felt a trauma something came over me. Either on the day he was in crisis or the following day, I would feel something was wrong with him. Eventually, we would connect and I would learn of an incident where he was a victim or was in trouble.

On that early morning, I had not felt him. I felt horrible that he could be in so much pain and I was helpless to him.

While in my thoughts and reflections, I began to hear movement behind the door that remained locked to anyone in the hallway. I was hopeful this meant someone with good news would come from behind that door and tell me everything was going to be okay.

No one came out immediately. The silence returned. Once again, it was just me and this person. My thoughts were all over the place like a trapped animal trying everything it could to escape the trap. I was fighting to escape my pain and rage.

Had this person who shared this story been involved? Was he here to make sure the job was finished and report back to the others once it was confirmed that my brother was deceased? Would he be celebrating? Is he setting me up and giving accounts to where I was, who was with me, and could I be targeted? I am not familiar with this person, where he is from, or who he is associated with. I know that I am not interested in getting to know him at that moment and feel no trust in him.

I had all of this energy that I needed to gain some control over. I decided to get on the phone and call my wife. Finally, I began to cry as I felt that this was very wrong. I talked through my tears. "Hey, Smokey got shot, my brother got shot, my brother got shot," I cried into the phone.

As I gave her details on where to go and find me, I heard noise once again from behind that door. I ended the call and returned to placing my ear between the space on the door frame and the door latch.

I began to hear footsteps approaching. My heart began racing and I took a few steps back preparing myself for the door to open.

Suddenly at approximately 11:30 am the door was pushed open slowly and out came a male dressed in a medical professional's long white coat. He looked at me and asked, "Are you the family of Efrain Nazario?"

I replied a nervous, "Yes."

He asked, "Are you kin?"

I replied, "Yes, I am his brother."

His next words fractured my soul and have forever shattered pieces of my heart.

"I'm sorry. We did everything we could, but he didn't make it."

I felt as if I stumbled backward and fell into a tunnel, where the echo repeated every word he said in slow motion. I felt weak. I did not know how to respond.

He started walking back into the room where he'd come from and I asked, "Can I please see him?"

He replied, "Let me see what I can do." He closed that door again.

I felt as if I had left my body and needed someone to pull me back into existence. I could faintly hear the other person in the hallway screaming and crying as he was giving the news to someone over the phone.

I walked away in a daze doing my best to keep my mind focused on getting help to deal with this pain. I started calling anyone that I could to help me through this terrible moment.

I wanted to see my brother and confirm for myself that this doctor was telling me the truth. As the seconds and minutes passed by others began arriving and spilling into this hallway from the elevator. I could hear someone saying, "I think it's this way."

As others began to arrive. I realized a few of them were childhood friends turned brothers. They had come to my aid and to find out for themselves if the news was true. The news was out that my dear brother was dead.

I practically fell into their arms. I am not sure what I did next. I felt permission to feel what I had just been told.

We cried together.

After some time had passed the doctor came out and said that we could see him. With one friend under one arm and one under the other, I was escorted to the elevator that would lead me to the floor where my brother was. I felt as if I was gliding while at the same time, my feet were encased in cement.

As the elevator doors opened, there stood my seven-year-old son, my wife, and my daughter, their faces full of worry. I immediately said, "They killed Smokey." They all began to cry and rushed to hug me.

I remember my son being the calmest. Almost as if he heard what I said but wasn't completely sure what I had said or what it meant. I reached down to hug him and he said, "Papi, they shot Smokey."

I responded by saying, "Yes, I know Papi (the term of endearment meaning sweetheart)."

I explained through my tears that he was wiping away that Smokey was dead.

He hugged me tight and said, "It's okay Papi (dad). I will help you. It's going to be okay." Even in the midst of how I was feeling I was shocked.

My childhood friends explained they were taking me to see my brother and they stepped out of the elevator and just stared at me with concerned faces. The elevator doors closed. Someone pressed the call button for the floor we were headed to.

We arrived at the floor and exited the elevator. The doctor who had delivered the news was standing by a set of double doors leading into another hallway where either patients or victims were held.

As we were guided by the doctor to a hospital bed with the curtain drawn, someone else was there who drew the curtain open. It was there that I confirmed for myself that he was gone. I fell on top of him and cried for him to please wake up. My childhood friends were crying and still holding on to me.

Based on the cuts on him from the surgery I could tell that his injuries had been devastating. I could see his flesh open near his abdomen and could see portions of his insides through the gaping cut. I could see the bruises on his face from dragging himself on the sidewalk and from the initial fall after he was shot.

I can recall my half-brother sobbing near me and placing his hand on my shoulder.

I called out to him, and I said I was sorry. I wanted him to wake up and I asked if there was anything they could do to clean him up.

I was then lifted and pulled away from the curtain and the assistant pulled the curtain closed. It was the longest walk out of a room in my life. I looked back and cried.

We were once again back in a hallway with nowhere to turn and no more options for what we could do. I could hear a crowd in the hallway crying and consoling one another. I could also feel the anger and grief in the air.

The pain I felt is extremely difficult to describe. I slowly began to boil into an increased rage and the desire to confront who was responsible. I was not communicating this verbally to anyone. In my head, I was killing anyone and everyone responsible.

My mind and heart were filled with absolute disregard for anyone involved. My childhood friends began escorting me to the elevator so that we could leave this hallway and hospital floor. They wanted to take me somewhere to help me grieve or something.

While we were walking to the elevator, I heard a voice call out my name, "Iran."

I looked back and saw a Hartford police officer standing there. He asked if he could speak with me for a moment. I nodded yes. He said, "I am sorry for your loss" and asked if I wanted to speak with him and if I knew who was responsible for this.

I nodded yes, but I meant maybe another time. My childhood friends knew me well so one of them replied, "Not now, it's not a good time."

The officer handed one of them his business card. We continued towards the elevator.

Once we were on the ground level and the elevator doors opened, I could see a fairly large crowd outside in the hospital patient drop-off lot. I knew many had arrived thereafter receiving the news. I was not sure who everyone was but I remember that once I stepped outside all eyes were on me.

I was escorted to a waiting vehicle and taken away from the hospital.

While in the car I was asked where I needed to go. I desperately needed to see where this happened. *Where was it that he was shot? Where is this apartment? Who lives in it? Who else saw it happen? Is his spirit still there? Will I feel it?*

I said, "Take me to where it happened."

The ride to the location where my brother was shot was fairly quiet. As we arrived at the location there was a crowd gathered there with the all too familiar placement of candles and flowers near the spot where someone had died.

In my lifetime I have been witness to and participated in hundreds of vigils, candlelightings mourning the loss, and celebrations of life events. From the early age of nine or 10, I learned of the murder of a man by a field in the housing complex where I lived. He was beaten to death during a fight with another person. Although I did not know he was dead, it would later be communicated in the community that he had died.

As a young person growing up in the inner city of Hartford, I knew about conflict and death. Within the city, there were different neighborhoods, groups, and gangs that were constantly at odds or war with each other so death and violence were a normal occurrence. As I grew older, I joined street crews, posses, and gangs. That all came with the risk of violence or death. Unfortunately, the risks were high, death and violence were expected to happen with certainty.

Even though I had participated in vigils before, it didn't prepare me for how it would feel or determine how I would react to it being my brother's candlelight vigil and memorial space on the street.

I stepped out of the car and surveyed each person standing at the makeshift memorial for my brother. Confused and hoping to determine who was friend, foe, accomplice, or family.

In our community, violence would often take place at memorials for the dead. Memorials were filled with raw emotion, alcohol, and drugs. These would increase tensions and emotions that many times led to misunderstandings and eventually fists would start flying or weapons were used.

There were also instances where the persons committing the violence against the victim being memorialized seemed to continue the hurt and pain. They would show up and shoot at friends and those who are mourning the victim. It is a reality we all have had to deal with in Hartford.

Every person standing there had their reasons and I had to feel it out. I was greeted with hugs and sad faces. I make my way to the memorial site and break down crying upon seeing a trail of blood from the sidewalk onto the street. I understood that it was my brother's blood.

It broke my heart. I saw just how close this site was to my half-brother's apartment. I could imagine why he would want to go there for help. I imagined his desperation.

I looked around trying to imagine what happened and looked up at the apartment building where he was attending the party. It played like a movie in my imagination. It ended terribly.

I was offered a drink of Hennessy in honor of my brother. I was given some to spill on the memorial site, something that is all too familiar and ritualistic in my community.

After receiving dozens of people who stopped in to pay their respects I felt as if my heart and mind were convinced that my brother's killer would pay with his own life. If that meant anyone associated with him would be a victim also, so be it.

Every hug and handshake served as confirmation that I had the support to retaliate however I desired. Up until that point, my life lessons and experiences had taught me that death equals death or permanent major injury. It was how we found Peace and avenged those who hurt those we love.

I started walking away with my anger and rage in full-speed-ahead mode. I passed by several people standing around the memorial site. Once again, I could see the facial gestures that indicated *you have to do something about this.* I suddenly felt a pat on my shoulder, I turned to look. It was a member of a national gang who was a good friend of my brother and me.

This was meaningful because my brother and I were both members of a local gang. In Hartford, there were no greater rivals than a national gang and the local one. For over a decade war between these two gangs accounted for more than half of all homicides and violent crimes against persons in the city.

The war between these two gangs ballooned the murder numbers from 15 in 1992 to 30 in 1993 and 58 in 1994.

During these years assaults and shootings also were at an all-time high. People were murdered every single day in my community and I was losing friends left and right. In one year alone I attended 24 funerals for either people I knew well from my childhood or for members of the gang whom I had come to know.

These were men and women who in many instances were friends before the decision to join competing gangs escalated tensions between them and several instances led to murder.

There was no place to hide in the small city of Hartford.

Somehow, the murder of my brother had broken through the rivalry and many wanted to avenge him.

I turned and asked, "What's up?"

He pulled me close and whispered. "I've got a tool for you if you need it. I have a couple of hammers (big guns, high-powered guns) if that is what you need."

I paused and looked at him with genuine respect and appreciation that he would step out of his gang ties and offer to help me end the life of the person responsible for killing my brother.

3

—·—

INTERRUPTION

In 1973 a young Hungarian man began a career with the Department of Children and Families (DCF) in Hartford, Connecticut. DCF, which was originally named the Department of Children and Youth Services (DCYS), was created in May 1969. The same year as the birth of my brother.

DCF, which is now called the Department of Children and Families (DCF), was created to protect young people from abuse, neglect, and abandonment. Fewer than three years later his path would put him on a collision course with my mom. DCF deployed two street case workers under their preventive services department. The case workers had the responsibility of visiting clients who were receiving child welfare services to ensure that the clients were in compliance with the requirements for receiving their services.

Clients had to adequately provide safety and security, children, nourishment, and shelter for their children, and ensure they were receiving the support to thrive. Caseworkers also had to ensure that clients were in compliance with the agreement signed with DCF.

Clients were not allowed to have anyone reside in their homes that provided unreported income. In most cases, this meant any male who held on to a job and contributed to the income of the home but was not on the lease.

Caseworkers would conduct home or site visits and look out for any signs of a male resident in the home. Items they looked for were watches, men's shoes in the closet, men's shaving cream, and other items associated with a male at the time. Since Mom was receiving state benefits she was not allowed to have a male or anyone else in the home without disclosing that person's identity to DCF.

At 22, Mom was a single mom of four children. She was overwhelmed and had suffered a life of trauma. She spoke very little to no English and hadn't been in school since the age of 16.

During one of the site visits to our apartment in SANDS the case worker noticed marks on one of our bodies. The case worker asked Mom what happened. Mom stated that she had disciplined the child. The caseworker mentioned to Mom that she had the right to discipline her child but she could not leave marks or physically injure the child.

Mom used anything within her reach to strike the child she wanted to discipline. One of those items she frequently used was the electrical cord attached to the iron. The cord would leave swollen welts across our arms and bodies.

After repeated visits where bruises and marks were visible on our bodies the case worker advised Mom that he would need to take the necessary steps to remove us from her care if she did not use another form of discipline that would not cause us injury.

Mom was combative and defiant. She stated that we were her children and that she would do as she needed to ensure that we respected her rules and authority.

Beating your children with extension cords, sticks, umbrellas, or any other instrument was something she was subjected to growing up. It was what you were supposed to do.

The caseworker recorded in his journal all of the marks and bruises he observed and also the conversation he had with Mom. He began the process of putting together a case to defend his decision to request our removal due to child abuse and neglect.

The caseworker returned once again. This time he was more aware of what to look for and was prepared to take the necessary actions to remove us for our own well-being. During this visit, the case worker noticed what in his evaluation was a perfect triangle mark on my temple area. It appeared to be the markings of the heel of a shoe. It was deep and recognizable. I would come to learn that Mom would use a high-heeled shoe to strike me across the face when she was under the influence of a drug and go into a fit of rage. While in that state anything we as children would do was met with severe consequences.

Mom held a deep anger and resentment toward my dad. I suffered the consequences of that anger and resentment. Mom would hit me in the face and think of my dad because I looked most like him. At four years old with each strike of my mother's high-heeled shoe, I was learning the lesson: love equals pain and pain equals love.

The DCF worker confronted Mom with what he felt was this dangerous and abusive injury. In her desperation to reduce her risks, she angrily responded to the caseworker. She stated that if he was thinking of removing us from her custody she would do whatever it takes to make sure that did not happen. He requested to see all of the children to examine them for injuries and other signs of maltreatment.

He was devastated by what he found and immediately ordered that my siblings be taken to the hospital for observation. He filed an order within his department to have us removed for "failure to thrive, child abuse, and neglect."

Mom was furious and stated that if he returned to take us away she would kill us and then kill herself. As he was leaving to put in motion the removal, Mom yelled, "They are my children. I brought them into the world, I will take them out."

Upon hearing that threat, the case worker decided that time was not on our side and called to have us removed.

Sometime later, the case worker returned with six police officers to provide him with support to remove us. Due to the fact that there were four of us, he felt that it would be best to bring along reinforcements to help keep Mom at bay while they removed us.

The scene during our removal was chaotic. Mom was clutching onto one of us, screaming at the police and fighting with them. It was a traumatizing experience for all involved but it was for our own good.

This time would not be the last time the child welfare system or protective services had to become involved in removing me from the care of a parent due to child abuse.

At the time I was separated from my mom, I was also separated from my three other siblings. We were 2, 3, 4, and 5 years old. My brother Smokey and I were placed with a foster family until the courts decided the best next steps for us. My sister was adopted by a family and my youngest brother was handed over to my grandmother in Puerto Rico.

I remember how lost I felt after being removed from my mother's care. I remember the fear of the unknown and the sadness I felt for being removed from the only family I knew. I remember how strange it was to be traveling somewhere I did not know. It was by force, not by choice.

Although there was abuse and neglect inside the apartment we lived in with my mother, it was the only life I knew. It had become normal to me so I felt as if I belonged there.

I felt helpless and confused as to why this was happening. I remained quiet and suffered on the inside as I had done many times when I was faced with traumatic experiences.

After some time my father was found by DCF and summoned to appear in juvenile court in Hartford to take custody of my brother Smokey and me. We were in the custody of DCF until then. I had not remembered my dad at this point. I did not know what to expect. I knew that I knew the term dad or papi after hearing it from other kids or on the television.

I had come to believe that dads were these men who worked all day, came home and brought things with them such as groceries, cars, and other items needed in the house. I had come to learn by watching *Little House on the Prairie* that the role of a father is to be the provider and loving disciplinarian.

My imagined version of what a father would be was dramatically crushed once I met my father. Almost immediately I felt his dominant personality take over me. My father was raised to work hard, provide for his family, and to be a man's man. He would not allow his "soft" emotions to show. No crying, sympathy, or acceptance of those weaknesses. We had to do as he demanded, no matter how we felt or what we wanted to do. He required that we help around the house with anything that needed to be done, no questions asked. It was his way and no other.

He believed in paying the ultimate respect to everyone and anyone he brought to visit. He taught us to never *ever* address an adult without permission and he refused to allow us to behave like children and embarrass him in the presence of others. We were required to sit as boys should sit when company came over to the house. We had to sit with one leg crossed over the other in a triangle-shaped form. Violation of that rule would result in a beating and punishment once the guests left.

Another rule that could not be broken was to ask for more food than what we were served. Regardless of whether we were hungry or not, we had to remain quiet at the table. If there was anything left over after everyone ate, we may have had the opportunity to have some more.

During one family dinner, I made the mistake of asking for more food. I thought one of my brothers had received more than I so I decided to ask for more. My father became enraged. He asked everyone to leave the table.

He grabbed the entire steel pot filled with rice and slammed it on the table, demanding that I remain seated and eat all of the rice in the pot. If I failed to do so, he would beat me. I was forced to sit there and eat until my stomach could no longer fit any more rice.

He yelled at me while I was attempting to eat the rice. He stated that I was greedy and disrespectful.

I felt humiliated, hurt, and terrified by this experience.

That would not be the last time I felt my father's rage.

On one occasion I once again did something that my dad felt needed punishment. This time, he proceeded to punch me in the chest. I was injured, hurt, and could not breathe.

Before I could recover from my injuries he grabbed me by my shirt and quietly spoke into my face.

"If you tell anyone about this I will beat you again."

I went off to school with my injury the next morning. I stated to the teacher in class that day that I had fallen off my bike and had been hurt. I would not dare tell on my dad because I felt he was indestructible and would find out. I would then be broken by him for not adhering to his threat.

My father was a strong man. He was physically strong and had good fighting skills. He had learned these skills while growing up. He was a fan of boxing and often practiced his punches. When he punched me, it was extremely painful.

As the years went by I understood that my father ruled the home with an iron fist. Still, as an eight-year-old boy tends to do, I would forget some of his rules when I was all filled with energy or I was doing something fun with my brothers. This caused me to be punished many times.

I had felt the pain of abuse before at the hands of my mom so I had come to believe this was what I deserved and how I should be treated.

At some point, Mom became invested in seeing her two sons again and she decided to stop by my father's house unannounced. The door to the house in Brooklyn, New York where we were living remained closed most of the time. My mom was able to gain entry into the hallway and make her way to our apartment on the first floor. She made it into the apartment and demanded of my father's girlfriend that she be allowed to see us. According to a court order, she was not allowed to visit with us unless it was authorized and supervised.

My father's girlfriend refused to show her to her children. My mom became enraged and began searching the apartment for us. She entered the bathroom and to her shock found my brother and I locked in the bathroom.

We had been placed on our knees on top of a cheese grater. That was our punishment in that instance for a rule we broke. The cheese grater was made of metal and had serrated points. These points dug into our knees and caused us to bleed through our pants. It was extremely painful but it was not the first time we had been tortured that way.

My mom reacted with fury. She grabbed my brother and me by our shirts and demanded that she be allowed to take us away. My father's girlfriend attempted to stop her but my mom forced her way through and took us away.

My mom illegally took us from our home and an arrest warrant was issued for her arrest. We would once again be exposed to removal from our home.

An agreement was reached with the court to allow my mom to have visitation rights in the presence of my father. These visits resulted in my mother regaining permanent custody of us again.

4

SANDS

We spent several years living with our mother Isabel "Isa" in SANDS. It was a housing project in the North End of Hartford, Connecticut. As young Puerto Rican boys living in the North End of Hartford in the late 70s and early 80s, we stood out. We were around 10 and 11 years old.

During that era, there was a conflict between Latinos and African Americans. Fights would break out between them anywhere the two groups involved in the conflict saw one another. Even though most of the participants were adults, the conflict and negative feelings toward one another spread to the young people in the community.

My brother and I had returned to the SANDS community after having been removed from our mother's custody years earlier, but we were seen as newcomers. We were picked on simply because we were Latino. Together we would have to fight our way to and from school. We had to fight to get our respect and not become anyone's punching bag.

Sometimes we would be beaten by a group of young Black boys and other times we would be challenged to "fair ones" by someone who wanted to show the others that he was on their side. "Fair ones" to us meant that it was one person versus only one other person in a street fight and no one else could get involved in the fight. No one else could jump in and take a swing at either of the two people fighting. It did not matter how badly one person was being beaten, it was expected that no one would step in.

We lost more than we won against a group larger than two of us but we bled and fought together. Back-to-back, we gave it our all and survived.

Our first fight together against the boys from our housing complex did not happen by choice. My brother and I were taking our usual path back home from the elementary school, which was located within the housing complex. As we left the small building where our classes were held, we would walk between the gymnasium building and a high-rise unit in the complex.

The flat path became a steep hill leading to the center of the complex. The grass on the path had become dirt due to so many years of kids walking on it on their way to and from school. Once we climbed the hill, we would walk past several building units in the complex and the field where kids would hang out, play sports, or walk through to cut through the complex.

As we got closer to our apartment unit, we heard footsteps coming from a stairwell. We turned around and saw the boys who always teased and bothered us running down the stairs and headed towards us. The building units had three floors and these boys had been waiting on the second floor landing until we were in their sights.

My brother and I began to run towards our apartment door which was located on the first floor. That apartment location allowed us to simply walk out of the apartment into the complex without needing to go down any stairs. We could feel the boys getting closer and we ran as fast as we could.

Once we arrived at the door, we began to bang on it and call out for our mom. *"Mami, Mami, Mamiiiii, Abre la Puerta* (open the door), the boys are chasing us."

It seemed like forever until Mom opened the door. I felt a sense of relief. I thought I could go inside, avoid the fight and the beating.

My mom never stepped aside from the door's opening. Instead, she yelled out, "What is the problem? What is happening here?"

We both spoke at the same time, "These boys are chasing us! They are going to hit us!"

The boys arrived at our door and waited there. They looked at my mom and did not say much.

Suddenly Mom said, "*Basta ya!* (That's enough). Wait a minute!" She stepped outside the door, demanded our book bags and books, and told us to turn around to face the boys. I was totally confused and scared.

There we were facing the boys we had been running from.

Mom asks, "You boys want to fight? Well, fight." She shoved us towards the boys as we resisted stepping forward. She grabbed us both by the shirt and aggressively turned us around to face her. She pulled us close to her face by the collars of our shirts and said, "You either fight them now or I will whip you."

Fear gripped my soul. I did not want to get a beating from Mom. I knew that if she began to beat us the beating would last a long time and could become multiple beatings for not following her demands.

She then turned us both around and said, "Fight."

We lunged at the boys and started throwing fists wildly. Not knowing how to fight but throwing our limbs around as quickly as possible to make contact. The boys did the same. After several minutes I began to feel winded and tired.

It appeared as if we all did. There were some bloody noses, scratches, ripped shirts, and busted lips. The boys stepped back a little and we did the same. We remained standing there just looking at one another waiting to start fighting again.

Mom grabbed me by my ear and grabbed my brother by his shirt. She pulled us into the apartment and closed the door behind us. Once we were inside, she said, "The next time those boys bother you, break their faces. If you don't fight back, I will whip you."

My brother and I nodded our heads to indicate yes, we understood. It was clear that we would not let anyone bully us and that we would have to fight to make sure we saved ourselves from a whipping at home.

My mom had developed a tough exterior and refused to allow anyone to bully her or her children. Any outsider who challenged her would face certain physical harm. Mom was average in height standing about five foot, four inches. She kept her brown hair shoulder length. She had wonderful bronze-colored skin, high cheekbones, dark brown eyes, and a thin nose. All of the features she inherited from her Taíno ancestry.

Mom had come to New York City from Puerto Rico in pursuit of my father whom she had been separated from when he left to find work in New York. She was very bold and went after what she wanted. She was only a teenager when she left home. She had no high level of education and was raised in the old-fashioned way to serve her man or husband.

It was widely expected in the small village of Jobito in Puerto Rico that a woman must first always serve her male partner. It did not matter if the couple was married legally or not. If you were together as a couple in a long-term relationship it was considered the same. The man would tend to the farm or to the hard labor and the woman served as the homemaker and unwavering servant to him.

Talking back or not doing what one was told to do was met with anger, ridicule, embarrassment, and physical violence. No one would intervene regardless of how violent the relationship turned. Others outside the relationship would simply say, "Those are things that happen in a marriage, it is none of our business." Many times, the blame for the verbal and physical abuse would be attributed to the woman failing to do something. As outsiders would say, *"Bueno, algo tuvo que haber hecho para que le dieran."* (Well, she must have done something to be hit for.)

My father treated my mother very much like his property and demanded she comply with any and all requests without hesitation. He forced his will on her and turned any perceived disobedience into a lesson that included physical punishment, verbal threats, and abuse. Throughout my childhood and into my twenties I came to learn of the many times my mom suffered pain and torment at the words and hands of my father.

The most negative impact on my soul is the incident of domestic violence that led my mom to finally escape my father's torment.

According to my mom and aunts on this day my father had returned home intoxicated. He was known to enjoy his beer a little too much and it made him lash out in fits of anger against my mom for anything he determined was disrespectful or challenging to his authority.

Once he was in the apartment they shared in Brooklyn, New York he began to argue with her about their relationship and how he was not happy with her. Mom explained that she would leave and that led to him exploding into a fit.

While he was sitting quietly in his thoughts allowing the rage to build, Mom was putting things together to leave. She had no one to turn to but she was going to leave and face the world alone while caring for an almost one-year-old son and carrying me in her belly.

Suddenly my father rose up from his mental escape to engage my mom in an argument. At this point, she was in the bedroom of the third-floor apartment. She felt emboldened to stand her ground and finally leave.

Perhaps my father finally felt the tide turning and knew she would not back down. It was clear he had to depend on more aggressive efforts to ensure he dominated her and kept her in her place.

While she was gathering whatever things she could, he grabbed my brother from the bed he was lying on. He walked toward the window, opened it, and switched his grip from my brother's arms to his legs. He held him upside down and hung him near the window.

My mom and aunts have explained to me that she looked up in shock and dismay. She saw my brother hanging upside down as my father declared that if she left, he would drop their son out of the window. My father traumatized and terrorized her.

At this point in pure desperation to save my brother's life she screamed out, "Okay! Okay! I will stay, please put him down. I will do whatever you say and want."

She begged him over and over.

After several minutes he responded and placed my brother back on the bed. After gaining control over her again he decided that she deserved a beating for disrespecting him. He physically attacked her, punching her in the face and body while she was doing everything in her power to protect my brother and herself against this brutal assault.

With every blow, she suffered greater injury.

At the end of the beating, she was suffering from busted lips, swelling of one of her eyes, bruising, and pain to the side of her ribs and stomach. The beating was over and she had survived and managed to save my brother.

During the beating my mother was pregnant. I was the child waiting to be born.

Once the rage had subsided and the violence stopped my father fell asleep leaving my mom bruised and battered. This was it! She could no longer live this way. She had to get as far away from this dreadful situation.

She took advantage of his heavy sleep while being intoxicated and snuck out of the apartment. Somehow, she was able to make contact with her sisters in Connecticut and secured some help to leave Brooklyn, New York. She was finally able to escape and we made our way to Hartford.

Mom needed medical treatment and went to Saint Francis Hospital. Due to her injuries, it was advised that she be induced to deliver her baby. She was taken into surgery and doctors performed a cesarean section. I was born.

We arrived at SANDS in Hartford under a high level of stress, fear, and uncertainty, and having experienced years of trauma.

My mother's abuse and experiences turned her into someone who suffered depression, anxiety, self-doubt, and rage. This mixture of recovery from physical injuries, feelings, and experiences led her to reach for a substance to ease her suffering and also to develop a mindset that she would no longer be a victim. She would rather die than bend to the will of anyone.

She began to overuse her prescribed drugs and began spending time with the local gangs who supported her dependency on drugs. Members of the Ghetto Brothers gang would come by the house at different points of the day and night. She would welcome them in and they would party and I could hear everything that was going on. Loud talking, raspy and loud laughter, and banging sounds of furniture against walls. Loud foot stomping, music playing, and opening and slamming of the room door. I sometimes heard arguing or agitated screaming from my mom and others who were in the room.

I was very young but I remember their style of dress, attitudes, and appearance and they appeared to be large men. They wore leather jackets or vests labeled on the shoulders and around the back with their gang's name. Similar to a biker gang. Chains were clipped to their jacket or vest pockets that connected to their wallets. They also wore steel chains over their shoulders and belts around their waist that had sharpened steel spikes protruding from them. Most of the time they wore some type of steel toe boot on their feet. Their appearance was a little scroungy or looked scruffy and unkempt.

This was my first experience being around members of gangs. As I got a little older, I would come to know more about gangs and the places they hung out.

The members of the Ghetto Brothers never introduced physical violence into our home. They primarily used our small apartment as a hangout and gathering place where they could let loose, drink, and use drugs with my mom.

My introduction to the viciousness of violence in the community came from two strangers who I witnessed arguing near the highrise building in SANDS at the age of 10. I was playing near the football field side of the park inside of SANDS.

I was on the sidelines watching the older boys play football. The quarterback of one of the teams threw a high ball to a kid playing receiver but he was unable to reach the ball.

The ball rolled down the hill and onto the driveway right in front of the high rise. I ran down the hill to collect the ball and stumbled into a heated argument between two older men. Fights and conflict were frequent occurrences in the projects I grew up in and in the surrounding ones.

As I reached for the ball on the ground I saw the men begin to fight. Each one threw their fists quickly at each other while ducking for cover. One of the men knocked the other down and began to move closer to the man on the ground. Suddenly the man on the ground was able to jump up to his feet and escape the other man's grasp. Once he was up from the ground he reached for a metal pipe.

The other guy rushed towards him and without hesitation, the other man wound up and swung the pipe at the other man's head.

A cracking sound broke through the voices of people watching the fight and yelling at the fighters. The sound reminded me of the sound an egg makes when cracked on the side of a steel pan.

Immediately the man that was struck fell to the ground and became unconscious. Blood began to leak out of the side of his head and onto the asphalt.

I was in a daze and could faintly hear the *oohs* and *aahs* from those who were watching. The man who struck him dropped the pipe, said a few words to the unconscious man, and walked away.

I remained there stunned at the amount of blood streaming down the man's head and face. As I regained my place I could hear the boys behind me calling for me to return the ball as if nothing had happened. I ran up the hill with the ball in my hand and while shaking from what I just witnessed I fumbled it onto one of the guys.

Not one person cried for the injured man or stepped in to stop the fight. This conflict was a normal expectation and violence was the accepted form of conflict resolution. I had to live with and adopt that mindset if I was to engage in any conflict and come out victorious.

5

INDOCTRINATION

I was 11 years old when I ended up joining my first "crew" while living in SANDS. We went by the name of the "The GQ Crew." We named ourselves after the magazine *GQ*. The name was chosen by a childhood friend who was more like a cousin. He had a fascination with fashion and stylish dressing.

His mom was a very close friend of my mother. She was a nurse who befriended my mom and would come see my mom at SANDS. When those visits happened, she would bring her two sons along with her.

One of them was a very handsome, well-dressed, cool kid. He wore the latest fashion sneakers and clothes. His brother was younger but also pretty cool. I looked up to this fashionista. I wanted to wear clothes like his and have that kind of swag, too.

During one of their visits, we visited the bodega across the street from SANDS. We left our apartment, walked to the parking lot, and crossed Main Street. This street was heavily traveled and cut through our community, into the center of the city (or downtown), and eventually led to the of the city.

The bodega sold penny candies and my cousin would always bring money with him and take us to the store. We walked into the bodega and on the counter were these plastic bowls filled with all of our favorites like Chick-O-Sticks and Fireballs. A small newspaper rack near the counter held the most popular magazines. One of those magazines was *GQ* magazine.

My cousin grabbed the magazine and began opening the pages, flipping through the images and stories. He then said, "Here, take a look." He lowered the magazine towards me and asked me to look at the male model featured on one of the pages.

He said, "Yo, doesn't he look dope?"

I said, "Yo he does, he looks fly…"

My cousin looked at me with a smile. "We could be GQ. We can be the GQ crew."

I was super excited inside. I could be GQ! Wow, along with him. *I* was cool enough to be GQ.

He put the magazine back on the rack, paid for the candy and we walked out of the bodega and onto the sidewalk. I was walking on clouds. I was a member of the GQ crew.

From that day forward my cool cousin, his brother, and my oldest brother would refer to ourselves as the GQs. Little did we know the negative impact that decision would have on us.

Since I was so excited and proud to be considered a member and cool enough to be included, I began to openly tell anyone within earshot that I was a GQ.

That began to attract the attention of "real" street crews that had been formed in the neighboring housing complex, Bellevue Square. The Square, as it was referred to, was mostly minority families and the majority were African American. They had a real crew there called "BSN" or "B Square Nation." They had many members and unknown to me at the time had a very deep rivalry against any young people from my housing complex. BSN began to learn of GQ and eventually decided that they would look into who this crew was. I had no idea.

One afternoon I was on the main street outside of SANDS when I was approached by five guys. Three of them were older than I was and the other two were around my age. They asked me if I was down with the GQ crew. I responded yes. Immediately the tone and energy changed.

I was punched in the face by one of them. I had never felt a punch to the face like that. I had experienced many levels of pain at home but never on the street. Many of my blows were to the body. This punch was very different. It was delivered to break my face open.

I immediately fell to the floor and could not see them anymore. I was dizzy and unable to get my vision clear enough to see what was happening to me. They continued beating me with their hands and feet.

Every blow was similar to repeatedly falling face-first onto a cement floor. There were these sounds of knuckles smacking into facial bones and the thuds of feet kicking my back. At first, I felt the sting of the punches and almost immediately I felt the spots where I was hit go numb. I would lose feeling for a split second only to have the next blow increase the level of pain.

It happened very quickly. I was left bloodied and battered. I do not remember if they walked away or ran away. I eventually regained my ability to see around me and staggered home.

I didn't know why I was beaten. I would soon find out that it was because I was a member of the GQ crew and my openly sharing that was disrespecting them. I had to pay. Kids in our neighborhood talked about it. I had been introduced to the street crew battle and now had to be aware that I was a target.

This was not the only interaction that I had with members of the BSN. Not only was I Latino and living in SANDS I was also a known member of the GQ crew. This meant that any opportunity or chance encounter with members of the BSN meant certain conflicts and beatings.

I had to be on high alert any time I was close to their housing project or if they were in the area. On a nice weather day outside I engaged in a game of hide and go-seek with the few friends I had made in SANDS.

I chose to hide behind one of the school buildings near the Bellevue Square and SANDS line. While I was peeking out the side of the building, I heard voices nearby that I recognized. I turned to look and to my horror, it was members of the BSN.

I shook in place and started to think, how can I escape this situation without being seen? The only option I felt I had was to climb onto the roof of the school building. The climb was not a difficult one. The SANDS school units were about the size of a mid-level barn or oversized steel shed. This meant that it was not too high and the roof was peaked.

I managed to climb up and as I was sneaking from one side of the roof to the other, I was spotted by one of the members of BSN. I heard him say, "Yo there's that dude." I panicked. The other members looked up and began to run toward the building.

I jumped over the ridge on the roof and onto the side that faced SANDS. I sat on my rear end and scooted down the roof as quickly as I could. My heart was racing and I felt as if I had stopped hearing my breath or any other sounds.

As I made it to the bottom of the roof from the peak my feet hit the ledge and I lost control of my momentum.

I attempted to grab hold of anything I could but failed.

I began to fall off the roof.

I was facing the sky.

I closed my eyes and held my breath.

I slammed into the ground with my tailbone hitting the cement first. I gasped a little breath and immediately lost my ability to breathe. It was similar to being punched in the gut. I could not get up to run or move. I lay there in pain but could not cry because the wind was knocked right out of me. I did not even hear the boys from BSN round the corner and find me there. It was as if I had lost my hearing also.

When I finally was able to take a breath the pain on my tailbone was excruciating and paralyzing. No matter how badly I wanted to get up and run I could not.

The boys looked at me while I was on the floor trying all I could to move and began to make fun of me. They laughed a deep belly laugh and poked fun at me.

Once I started to move a little more, they kicked me a few times in the thighs and near my crotch area while I lay there with my arms folded trying to prevent them from kicking my ribs. I sunk my head into my hands to prevent them from kicking me in the face. They walked off leaving me in pain.

Once I was able to stand, the walk home was as painful a walk as I had ever experienced. Every step felt as if I was going to break into little pieces. I managed to make it to our apartment. It was one of the longest walks of my life at that point.

There was no turning back from having been humiliated and disrespected the way these boys had humiliated and disrespected me.

I either had to run, hide, and stop saying I was a GQ member or I had to fight back.

I chose revenge.

I arrived home after this beating and received no attention. There was no one at home to see my injuries or pain. I sat in my anguish and bruises. I thought of who these guys were and tried to remember their faces. After several hours I decided that each one of them would pay for hitting me.

I knew violence at a personal level and I was going to make sure they felt every single emotion in my being while I beat them. I believed that making them suffer would release my rage and make them respect me.

Earning respect from other boys in my neighborhood was paramount to survival. I could not allow anyone to make fun of me, bully, disrespect me, or challenge me. I had to fight against anything I felt was disrespectful. Even if it was a misunderstanding, I had to address it aggressively and make sure whoever I was standing in front of understood that I was no punk or sucker (as the kids would refer to someone weak).

The violence carried onto the baseball field. I played baseball in the park for a short period of time in SANDS. As a pre-teen, I managed to join a neighborhood baseball team. Many of the housing projects in the area had baseball teams that represented each neighborhood housing development. My team represented SANDS.

We played against teams from the Main Street area. These teams were mostly formed for recreational purposes and gave the kids a chance to be part of something fun. There were no long trips to other cities or championship games that I could remember. These games represented an opportunity for young boys to go beyond their city blocks or housing developments to other parts of the North End of Hartford.

This also meant that it exposed us to the negative experiences associated with the violent conflicts of the clashes between rival housing projects. During one game against the team representing the Stowe Village Housing Complex youth baseball team, I could see a large gathering of youth forming near one of the park bleacher areas.

These groups were part of the crew that called themselves "The Ville." They were there to get a look at the unwelcome visitors and to determine what action they should take against these trespassers in their claimed neighborhood.

While the balls and strikes continued to be called I could not pretend that I was not hearing the insults and threats coming from the group of youth who had now intensified their level of anger against us.

Anytime someone would be called out they would tease and cheer or say mean things. It was clear to me that they were hoping to get someone on our team to react so they could "rush" us. This meant they would all gang up on us and proceed to beat us until we were either bloodied, battered, fled, or remained lying on the field unconscious.

During one of the late innings the Ville crew began to inch closer to our end of the dugout. Our team understood this meant there would be a conflict. They were positioning themselves to make sure that we could not leave without having to engage with them.

Almost immediately after the last out was called the yelling and insults from the ville crew started towards us. We attempted to collect our baseball gear and belongings and began to scatter away from the field.

We were not successful.

Several of the Ville crew members caught up with some of our team members and began to "roll" on them. There were far more of them than there were of us since we were on their turf.

The fights began to spread throughout the field as players attempted to run or chose to stand their ground and fight back. This separated our team from one another as the coaching staff and very few adults attempted to stop the fights. In a desperate attempt to survive the onslaught, our team members began to use our equipment to strike the members of the Ville that were attacking us. We swang our helmets, gloves, and baseball bats.

Several members of our team were beaten bloody. As the chaos ensued it made it difficult for me as a young kid to know where to look, where to turn, who to focus on, who to hit, or where to run.

I stood in a guarded fighting position while facing a couple of Ville crew members. I had to survive and fight if I was going to make it out of there. I could not see that someone behind me was winding up and swinging a bat toward me.

The bat struck me in the face and I immediately felt pieces of my front teeth floating around in my mouth, my nose began to drip blood onto my lips and over my chin. My face went numb, and I raised my hands up to my head to protect myself from the next blow.

I crouched over while still protecting my head and began to run away. As I ran away I saw other members of my team that have gathered near the clubhouse bathroom facility. They were using the building as cover to protect them from being hit from behind.

I made it to the small building and was able to lean against the wall holding my nose and mouth. I could taste the blood and still feel the cuts from my teeth scraping against my tongue and cheeks. My front teeth would remain cracked into my early 20s.

The adults and team coaches were finally able to gain some control of the situation and the Ville crew members began taking off into the buildings that surrounded the field.

We made it back to SANDS. Many of us were bruised and beaten but we survived.

Just a couple of months before entering middle school I was learning how to survive the streets in our community. I had to be willing to fight, run, or choose a group of people that I could align with to crush those who were against us.

6

SMURF

I am not sure where I completed elementary school. It could have been in SANDS elementary school or at Public School 94 (PS94) in Brooklyn. My brother and I, along with many of the kids from SANDS and neighboring housing projects, attended Quirk Middle School. Any conflicts that happened in the neighborhood would also take place at the school.

At Quirk, I began to expand my connections with kids from other communities. It is also where I was given the nickname Smurf.

During my first year in middle school, I kept mostly to myself. My brother and I would walk to school from our apartment. We were poor and it was noticeable to the other students in my grade.

The grades were separated by "houses" that were corridors labeled by colors: blue house, green house, yellow house, etc. Several of the house colors were known to be assigned to students who were either unable to speak English or were unable to perform well academically.

During that first year, I was dealing with the trauma and turmoil of my home life. I was also not very fluent in English. My mom and almost anyone who visited us spoke Spanish.

I began to hear the whispers of other students in class, in the hallways, and in the cafeteria. I could see smiles and laughter at times when I would walk into a room or pass by a group of students from different grades. I was not sure what was happening but I knew it felt strange and I was becoming self-conscious. One day when I was walking toward class a group of boys began to chant the Smurf song.

"La la la-la la la. La la la-la la la."

The Smurfs were fictional small blue humanoid creatures that lived in mushrooms. At the time I was in middle school the cartoon version of the Smurfs aired on television and they were very popular.

I looked up and noticed some of the kids pointing at me. I felt shame run through me but was not sure how to handle it. I simply kept walking into the classroom. I felt sad because it appeared they were making fun of me.

I sat in class and thought about what happened and could barely focus on the lesson given by the teacher.

The class was over and I stepped towards the classroom door and walked into the hallway. Once again, a group of students sang the Smurf song. I looked up and searched through the sea of faces for anyone that I could recognize. I did not know any of the students who were singing the song. I continued walking away to the sounds of that song and their laughter. I was embarrassed and began to feel the level of anger in me rising.

The next few days I heard the song a couple of times and had decided that I was not going to allow them to continue to make fun of me. I'd had enough!

Later that week I encountered several of the students who were singing the songs and I asked, "Why are you singing that song when I walk by?" Some of them laughed and I grew very angry. I asked, "What is your problem with me?"

One of the boys who appeared to be leading the group chant responded, "It's that you think that you are a Smurf, always wearing blue stuff."

I paused for a second and realized that they were making fun of my pants and shirt. At that time I did not have many items of clothing due to limited resources at home. That meant that I wore the same clothes at least three times a week. My pants were blue jeans and my shirt was a light blue "Garanimal" name-brand shirt. The shirt had the image of a dinosaur on the left side of the chest.

I felt worthless and stupid. As they continued to laugh, I could feel my blood boiling. In a split second, I dropped whatever I had in my hands and began punching the kid who had answered me.

We crashed into the lockers along the wall and ended up falling together toward the floor. Once on the floor, I was able to get on top of him. I began to throw fists toward his face with as much force as I could.

After a couple of minutes, the school staff pulled us apart. I was blinded by my anger and could not remember how many times I had hit him.

I got in trouble and was suspended for three days. When I returned to my regular classes I did not hear the chants again. I was ready to beat anyone who made fun of me. No one did.

Word spread about the fight I had and I was receiving attention from other students from the different houses in the school. I was learning from students in my corridor that I was going to be challenged to a fight by those students.

I was not afraid. Instead, I felt as if I was important and cool. Those people were talking about me because I had fought and was going to fight again. I was not being made fun of because of my clothes. I was happy about that.

I didn't care about getting in trouble, I only cared about not feeling humiliated and worthless. After several weeks I began to be known as Smurf among the kids in the house where I attended classes. I now welcomed that name and felt proud about it. At the same time that I had been assigned the name, other students were also using nicknames that included the names of Smurf characters such as Jokey, Hefty, Papa Smurf, and others.

The following year when I returned to school I was no longer called by my name by other students. It was Smurf this and Smurf that. Other students with similar or the same nicknames fought one another for the right to keep the nickname. The loser had to stop using it.

I was challenged to fight for my nickname and gladly accepted. Most of the students in the school knew where to go to settle disputes without being caught by school staff. Once my challenger and I agreed to meet and fight for rights to the nickname a crowd of students met us at the location where the fight was going to take place.

The majority of fights took place at the lower level of the school near where the pool and locker rooms were. We took our places by the hallway and the punches began to fly. After the fight was over, I won. He had to stop using the nickname Smurf and everyone knew it. I was once again feeling accomplished and powerful.

Fighting and violence were my preferred methods of settling conflict and it was paying off. The rush of violent conflict made me feel something different than the shame and pain I felt inside due to my experiences at home.

7

THE ASYLUM

In 1982 Mom decided to make a move away from SANDS. At this point, she had been alone without a boyfriend for a little while. She began looking for a new start and place to live as my brother and I were completing middle school.

Mom found a second-floor apartment in a four-story building on Willard Street right off Asylum Avenue in Hartford. She also found herself a new boyfriend. The building we lived in and the building next to ours housed mostly Hispanic families. She established friendly relationships with most of our neighbors almost immediately.

Across the street from the apartment, there was a platform on the property of an office building where many in the community would congregate. It was an elevated platform that felt like a deck to us. We would set up chairs there or sit there and just hang out. Once one person made it onto it, others would start joining in everything fun that could happen there. We played games, shared jokes, and watched as people passed by. My mother had a direct view from the second-floor window and would know I could be found there if she needed me.

We were not the only ones who were aware that we could be found on that platform. Others from other communities who had traveled passed us on bikes or cars knew we were there too.

While hanging out one day with a few friends we were approached by a guy from a few blocks away. He had heard that we had disrespected his block or neighborhood by talking badly about them. He wanted to fight.

I gladly accepted his challenge. Fighting was my way of releasing frustration and rage. During the fight, we began to wrestle. Tugging and yanking on each other's shirts in an attempt to gain the upper hand over the other.

I was beginning to get him on the ground when he pulled a small knife from his pocket. I kept grabbing him and got him on the ground. We began rolling on the ground while he was holding the knife in his hands.

I felt the knife press against my arm and a burning pain rush through my forearm. He had sliced me. This infuriated me and I went into a blind rage. I wanted to hurt him badly. Until that point, it was a street fight, meant to beat someone up and win.

It was now a battle for my life. As I gained more control of him on the ground, I began to see more blood coming from different places on my body. I had been sliced on my upper arm and my chest.

I have to get that knife, I thought. I was able to get one arm free that was tangled up between our shirts and I began to viciously punch his head and face.

The more I connected the more he attempted to cover up. I finally got my hand around the wrist of the hand he was holding the knife in and turned it until he let go of the knife.

A crowd had gathered of my friends and people in my neighborhood. They noticed my blood and wanted to jump in. I remember saying no to one person who tried to kick the guy in the head.

Once I had the knife in my hand my goal was to bury it into him as many times as I could. He crawled back toward the wall on the platform and I got on my knees and began moving toward him to stab him.

Suddenly I felt someone grab me by my neck and place me in a chokehold. I looked back to see that it was my mother's boyfriend at the time. He was holding me down. He said, "*Tu mai* (your mom) told me to stop you." She had heard the commotion and looked out the window. Once she saw me fighting, she yelled to him to go downstairs and stop me.

The kid was able to stand up and he began to walk away backward. Some of my friends were following him and threatening to hit him. Once he was able to get further away, we all just let him go.

People were checking on me and asking me if I was okay. I felt the sting of the slices but responded that I was okay. I had won the fight and felt powerful even though I felt pain. I was congratulated by my friends and it made me feel powerful. I enjoyed violence and I embraced the expectation of responding to threats of violence with violence.

During this time, I was becoming more aware of the illegal drugs my mom was dealing and using. I started to notice that my mom and her boyfriend at the time would either be really hyper or very groggy and sluggish, almost unresponsive and falling asleep while standing up.

I never witnessed my mom snorting or injecting herself with cocaine or heroin. She would hide in her room, behind a closed door, or simply ask my brother and me to leave the room or the apartment so that she could use her drug of choice.

The evening hours in our apartment were very busy. Every few minutes there was a knock on the apartment door, someone would whistle from the sidewalk towards our apartment window to get Mom's attention, or there would be knocking on the back door of the apartment that faced the courtyard.

Mom would wake up or be up at all times of the night to open the door for anyone looking to purchase drugs from her. It did not matter the weather or the amount of time Mom took to respond to those looking for drugs, they would not go away until they were able to purchase what they came for.

Mom would use some of her own supply of drugs to get high. One afternoon there was no more hiding the impact of drugs on her. I was sitting on the bed in my room and staring out the window.

I heard a door slam and what appeared to be feet stomping on the floor. I faintly heard someone calling out my mother's name. Over and over I heard them repeating her name in a nervous heightened tone.

I became curious and left my room. I began to walk down the short hallway while looking to see what was happening. As I reached the bathroom door on my left, I realized the commotion was coming from the bathroom.

The door was slightly open and I was able to see inside. I witnessed two men leaning over the bathtub and could also see a pair of legs flopping over the edge of the tub.

As I looked closer, I realized it was my mom. She was almost motionless and the two men appeared to be shaking her violently.

I shook off my fear and shock and pushed the bathroom door open. I could see my mom's face. Her eyes appeared to be rolling into the back of her head and she had spit bubbles running down her face.

I was paralyzed. I wondered, *What the heck is going on?*

I began to ask, "What is the matter with Mami?" One of the men turned toward me and began to shove me out of the bathroom. Once he was able to remove me from the bathroom he closed the door in front of me.

I remained standing there shaking while I waited for anyone to come out and tell me what was going on.

Several minutes later my mom's boyfriend emerged from the bathroom. He looked at me and said, "Your mom has an evil spirit trying to take over her."

At that time I was aware that my mom and many members of my family believed in evil spirits possessing humans. Many times they would speak of Brujeria (Vudu) and the evil spells that people would cast on them when they hated them or were jealous of them.

I believed him and asked him if the spirit was gone. He responded, "Yes." I was terrified that the spirit would remain in the house and take possession of my spirit. I could not sleep much that night. I was fearful that if I fell asleep I would not be able to fight off the evil spirit.

I came to find out later on that Mom was actually experiencing an overdose. The image of her face in that state never left me.

I know from my involvement with the Department of Children and Families (DCF), conversations with those present during my childhood, and conversations with my mom that drugs were a part of my life from the time I was born.

My mom became addicted to drugs after her split with my father due to domestic abuse. She became addicted to pain medications. Eventually, she used cocaine and heroin as the addiction worsened.

One day, early in the morning, law enforcement kicked the door in looking to find the drugs my mother and her boyfriend were selling. They walked into my room with their guns drawn. I was not sure what was going on because I had just been awakened by the sound of the door being kicked in.

I was removed from the bed and taken out of the room. One of the officers proceeded to take me out of the apartment. He placed me by the stairs leading down to the first floor and demanded I tell him where the drugs were.

I had no idea, so I said nothing. He then grabbed me by the hair and said, "If you don't tell me I will throw you down these stairs."

I was terrified but I could not tell him because I did not know.

I was a quiet kid who kept to myself. I held the music inside me. There is a Spanish saying that means "he is one of the quiet but dangerous ones." I held all the emotions I felt within me. Like a furnace stores its energy.

After this experience, my image of the police changed and so did my interactions. I began to fear and resent the police due to the treatment I received that day. I no longer just saw them as people passing by in a car doing a job or going after bad guys like in cartoons. I saw them as bullies and people you stay away from.

My mom was placed in handcuffs. It was very chaotic, loud, and frightening. She was hauled off to jail.

Initially, my brother and I went to the apartment across the hall from where we lived with my mom and her boyfriend. We spent a few hours at the neighbor's apartment before I realized I could not stay there. The neighbor's daughter was a friend of my brother and mine. She was a closer friend to my brother than to me. A plan was discussed of moving to stay with their relatives in Ohio so we could have a fresh start.

I decided not to go, but my brother decided he needed to go. Just beginning my teenage years, I was once again losing all of my connections. This was an easier decision for my brother since he had been pursuing a romantic relationship with our young lady friend and her mother was approving of that. They eventually became a couple and had a daughter together in Ohio.

For the first time in my life, I was alone. I ran out to the street with nowhere to go. With Mom gone, I was no longer able to remain in the apartment.

At 13, this was not an experience I was prepared for. Although I had been removed from my home before, it had always been alongside my brother. I did not want to be placed with a foster family again while my fate was decided.

At first, it seemed as if it would all be okay because there were friends outside watching the police come in and out of our apartment building. Since there was something to talk about, I remained by the side of the apartment building talking with my friends about how the police kicked the door open with weapons drawn. I discussed how they forced us all either to the ground or out of the apartment. I shared everything that happened inside the apartment with my friends.

As the police began to conclude their search of the apartment, I left the side of the apartment building and hid in the hallway of the building next to ours. I am not sure if the police searched for me or not.

I spent many hours in that hallway. Different neighborhood kids that I knew lived there so I would talk to some as they entered and left their apartments. At one point a few friends stopped to spend some time with me and just chat. As nightfall came, I no longer felt the security and safety of the hallway. I was alone and had nowhere to go.

As the evening continued ticking away, I heard a voice call out to me while I was sitting on the stairs in the hallway. I knew the voice well. It was a dear friend of mine who was a few years younger than me. His father was the community mechanic and I would always see him outside working on cars with his dad. We also spent time behind the apartment buildings just hanging out or creating things to do.

He was a good kid and looked up to me.

He said, "Smurf come over here. My mom is home but you can sneak into my room."

I followed him into the room that he shared with his younger brother. We quietly hung out and talked so we would not alert his parents to me being in there. I hid in the small closet when she came in to check on them to make sure they were going to sleep and get rest for school the next day.

I remained in the closet for most of the night. Once they left for school with their mom or dad I snuck out in the mid-morning.

I was now back on the street with nowhere to go. I spent time between the hallway and the courtyard of the apartment building next door. I would nod in and out of sleep from time to time. Later that afternoon my friends began to arrive from school so I went outside to see them and talk with them. Once again, the day went by with nowhere to go.

During the day I had seen people come and go. Maintenance workers who managed the building where I had lived would go in and out of a utility/supply room on the basement level of the building. It was accessible from the sidewalk in front of the building. I thought several times that I could go in there and see what they did there and what they had in the building.

Once my mother was arrested, I not only could not go back to the apartment, but I could also no longer go back to school. Not only did returning to school expose me to being captured by police or DCF it exposed me to being taken away and placed in foster care.

I spent several weeks out on the street.

I was going from the hallway to the backyard to the street and into my friend's apartment when he was able to sneak me in again. I was unable to bathe or clean up and eventually, I began to smell and feel terrible.

I developed a fungus infection on my toenails that spread between my toes and on the bottom of my feet. I was feeling miserable but I had no other options at that time.

On one occasion, my friend snuck me back into his room while his mother was in her bedroom. I relaxed and took off my sneakers because my feet needed to breathe. I did not realize just how bad my feet smelled.

The odor was so strong that when my friend's mom came into the room to check on both of her sons. She asked, "What is that smell? It smells horrible." She began to search for the source and that led her to the closet where I was hiding. She found me.

Once she saw me, she said, "What are you doing here, eh-Smurfy?" She told me to step out. She realized the smell was coming from me. She looked at my feet and said, "Oh my goodness, your feet are rotten." She yelled at her sons for sneaking me into the closet. She asked me to leave.

Medical care for me during this time was not a priority nor was it accessible. I did not know how to access medical care and due to my lack of education, I also did not know how to speak up for myself. I cannot recall a moment when I visited a medical facility with my mom. It could be that those memories were wiped out due to trauma, a car accident, and an injury to my head in my early 20s. Or it could be that it simply did not happen.

I felt so dejected and sad. I was now back in the hallway where I spent the remainder of the night. Several days passed and I was once again between the hallway, the courtyard, and out on the streets. I would walk down Asylum Avenue to Farmington Avenue and back to Willard Street.

I decided to take the risk of being apprehended by police or to be placed in DCF custody and visited school sparingly. Hartford Public High School had been a place that I would go to for access to food and to remove myself from my reality at home. I had been suspended in my first year in high school and failed to complete the academic requirements to be promoted to the 10th grade.

When I returned to classes the following summer, I fared no better. I skipped classes and snuck into the cafeteria during different student lunch waves to socialize with anyone I knew or to simply fill my stomach with food. On many occasions, it was all I would eat for the day.

I was battling through homelessness the best way possible. What I would give to get back to hanging out with the Willard Street Boys. It was a small crew we had formed on that street. It was the crew that was responsible for fighting for the respect of our block, sneaking into the abandoned buildings and running through the halls of the different apartment buildings on Willard Street.

A few days later my friend who had let me sneak into his mother's apartment and his bedroom arrived home from school and called out to me. He mentioned that he could sneak me into his father's station wagon-style van if I could wait until later that day. I was so excited because I would be out of the hallways and off the streets.

He came down after it was dark and said, "I have the keys, I'll open the back door and you can go in. You have to be out before six in the morning because my father leaves for work."

I said, "Good looking out (thank you)," and stepped into the station wagon.

The night spent in that wagon was so uncomfortable. I could not find a comfortable position, the seats felt hard and I had no blanket so I felt exposed and unsafe. I also had to lay low so no one would see me and report me or tell his dad.

Every time I dozed off, I was awakened by a passing car or a sound from nearby. Once I was awake, I would feel the kink in my neck from having my head leaning in one direction while I slept. It felt like a long night of tossing and turning, dozing off, and being startled awake.

Once I saw a little light start coming through from the sun, I walked out of the back seat feeling achy and stiff from the cramped position I held for most of the night. Although I was thankful for his kindness I never wanted to sleep in there again and I didn't.

I wandered around again for a couple of days. It was difficult being hungry, tired, and dirty all day. I had no money and my source of food from time to time was something one of the guys I knew from the block would bring me from their house. I was grateful anytime they would split some of their rice, beans, and chicken dinner with me. In our Puerto Rican household that was a meal we ate often.

One day while walking up and down the block on Willard Street, I noticed the door to the utility/supply office was slightly open. I needed a place to go and this just might be my opportunity. I was surprised because it was later in the evening and no one from the maintenance crew was around.

I often noticed a dump truck was parked right outside that office and I associated it with an older white gentleman who worked on the maintenance crew. He was nowhere to be seen.

I slowly stepped in the direction of the door, thinking that at any moment someone would come out and ask me what I was doing there or someone would see me and call the police.

I gently pushed on the door and it swung open. The first thing I saw was a white-colored refrigerator with a single silver handle on the door and a separate freezer handle on the top. The refrigerator obstructed some of my views so I was not able to see what else (or who else) was down there.

I looked around the refrigerator and saw a long workbench made out of wood. It must have been approximately 10 feet in length. On top of this bench were tools, saws, spare plumbing pipes, a clamp, and many of the items you would see on a workbench.

I continued further into the basement office and realized that it stretched the length of the entire apartment building. It was a large space. There were spare stoves, carpets, paint cans, paint rollers, windows, and all of the equipment needed to maintain or repair an apartment.

I found a few long rolls of tan, fluffy carpet near the back of the basement. I stepped onto one of the rolls and made myself comfortable. Ah, finally, I was comfortable, safe, and able to sleep.

The morning came and I did not notice it. Since this space was in the basement there were no windows on that side of the basement for me to see the light of day. I had a nervous feeling in my stomach. I felt as if at any moment someone from the maintenance crew would come in and find me there. I was creating a plan in my head of where I would hide so I was not found. Perhaps I could roll myself up in these carpets or hide behind an old refrigerator that was most likely just used for parts.

As the day went on it remained dark inside there. No one came. I started to walk and feel my way around the space. As I got closer to the front door, I could finally see light peeking through the door frame and small windows on that side of the basement. The door was closed but unlocked.

At this point, I had no concept of what day it was, what time of day it was, and what the weather may be like outside. I peeked through the small basement window to see what was happening and who was outside. I noticed it was fairly quiet and there was little movement.

It suddenly dawned on me that the maintenance crew was not there because it was the weekend. That is why the people and car traffic were low. I felt relieved. I knew that the door to the basement was open and I had at least two nights where I had somewhere to go.

Monday morning came and I knew that the maintenance crew would return so I left the basement at dawn. I left the door closed but not locked and walked as far away as I could from that space so I would not be suspected of having been there.

That Monday evening, I roamed the block waiting for my opportunity to sneak back into the basement. Once I saw that the dump truck was gone, I made my move and headed toward the basement door. I was disappointed. The door was locked and I no longer had access to the basement. I was back to nowhere.

8

HOMELESS

Feeling as if I had run out of options on Willard Street and all of my resources and friends had become distant, I left that area more frequently in search of other places that I could find to survive. I walked to neighborhoods in the city that I was familiar with.

The days were busy with sitting at different parks and areas where I would watch people. I enjoyed watching people go about and I would always wonder what their lives were like.

During the spring, summer, and some fall evenings I would find cover where I could. Most of the time I would find myself at Bushnell Park in downtown Hartford. The back of the park was right alongside the local train tracks behind the Hartford State Armory Building.

That area was rarely ever frequented by people so it made it the best place to go unnoticed and to feel a little safer while I attempted to sleep. I would cover myself with cardboard or whatever I could find to serve as a blanket. As my joints and flesh settled into the ground I would begin to feel the crawling insects and flying ones crawl on my clothes and through gaps in my clothes to find their way onto my skin. I could also hear the sounds of buzzing in my ear from the flying insects. The biting from the bugs and the itchy welts that formed made it extremely uncomfortable to sleep.

I could hear other people either walking past the tracks or other homeless persons who would use the tracks through the night to cross into other sections of the city without being seen by the general population. A deep sleep could not happen. The risk to my personal safety was present.

During the cold weather, I managed to find a few places to stay. I bounced around from couch to couch. At different points during that time people I know would grant me access to their living rooms for a night of sleep or allow me to eat a meal outside of their apartments. My godfather, a good friend of my mom, a few friends of friends, and on many occasions, strangers I had met through others would give me a night or two wherever they lived.

One of those supports I sought out was my godfather. He was a person I had met at some point while I was with my mom. My recollection is that he visited with my mom when we lived on Willard Street. At some point, I must have visited his place or made contact with him over the phone to learn where he lived. I arrived at the front door of his apartment located in the Asylum Hill section of Hartford. I pressed the doorbell.

After several minutes he came to the door and called me by name. "Iran, how are you?"

I replied, "Okay, I need a place to stay."

He proceeded to pull the door open and I stepped by him and into the apartment. He asked me to have a seat on a circular-style swivel barrel chair. It required effort to sit straight up due to the sinking feeling from the cushions. I sat there and watched him walk away into the kitchen area. He returned with a cup of water for me.

We sat and talked about my life. He asked how I was managing out on the streets. He had known that Mom was not around. I guessed he knew that she had been arrested and that we had lost the apartment.

We spent some time just catching up. He had many artsy-style paintings on the walls and different statues of African figures on end tables. The apartment was very neat and felt warm and cozy.

I began to feel tired and he asked me to transfer to a couch that included a pull-out bed. Similar to a futon. I agreed and moved.

He sat next to me with his body slightly turned to the left so that he could face me. We continued to talk and he began to share how he thought that I was a good person.

I listened with no response. I was not used to hearing that about myself in that way. I mostly spent time in conversations that included hanging out on the street, girls, music, fighting, or food.

As I began to feel tired he asked me to relax and remove my sneakers. I was extremely tired from having spent all day roaming the streets just looking for something to do. I refused to remove my sneakers because I was self-conscious about my foot odor due to the foot fungus I had.

I decided to lay down and he sat up a little. He asked me if I knew how beautiful I was. I remained quiet and felt my forehead warm up. I did not know how to reply or how to accept what he was saying.

He stood up from the couch and retrieved a blanket that was draped on the armrest of another couch. He handed it to me and said good night.

I woke up very early after sleeping more than I had slept in days. It felt odd to wake up in such a quiet space. I had experienced so much noise and chaos while trying to find a place to rest.

I did not wait to see him and walked out of the apartment and hurried back into the streets.

I returned to his place several days later when I once again needed a place to sleep. He greeted me with a general hello and my visit was a repeat of a couple of days ago.

I once again began to feel tired and began to doze off while he talked. He called out to me and informed me that I was falling asleep. I sat up straight and focused on staying awake and keeping my eyes open while we talked.

He got up and poured himself a glass of wine. He then sat back down near me and asked me if I was interested in drinking something. I responded with, "No."

He decided to let me go to sleep and walked away into a nearby room.

I fell asleep.

At some point in the very early morning, I felt faint movement on the futon. I was a very light sleeper and since I was accustomed to sleeping on the streets and with no protection, I had to make sure to be aware of any movement near me to prevent someone from sneaking up on me while I was asleep or in a vulnerable position.

The movement I felt was light and in between sleep I was listening and feeling for any other movement. I slowly began to fall back into a deeper sleep.

I then felt a scratchy sensation similar to the rough end of a sponge on the back of my neck. I tensed up and in a fog wondered what was happening.

As I began to awaken further I realized it was a person laying behind me on the futon. I tensed up even further and felt as if I couldn't move. I felt frozen in place. My mind was racing. *What is happening? Who is doing this?*

I felt confused.

I realized it was my godfather behind me. He had spooned me and began to rub his face on the back of my neck. He kept telling me how beautiful I was and how special he felt I was.

I felt desperate to get out of the situation. I could not think of a way out. *Where will I go? Who will invite me in? How will he feel if I say something? Who will believe me if I tell? What should I do?*

He pressed his hand on my shoulder and began to slide his hand down my shoulder and onto my forearm.

He slowly moved to my hip and I could hear him breathing a little heavier and he began making light moaning sounds. As he continued to tell me how beautiful he thought I was I tensed up a little more.

He noticed that I was tense and asked me to relax and trust him. He said that he wanted me to let him bring me comfort. I was not sure how to fight him off without losing his support.

I felt as if I could beat him to death. I desperately needed his support so I kept tensing up and hoping that he would just stop.

He became more aggressive with his actions and attempted to reach toward my crotch from behind me. I pinned my legs together so that he could not gain access. I never opened my eyes. I did not want to see his face.

As he attempted to reach further into my crotch he began to get more excited. I began to feel myself becoming angry. I felt hurt that he had decided to touch me in this way.

He noticed that his attempts to fit his hand into my pants were not successful and he began to ask me to just let him touch my penis. He said that he would not do anything to it but just touch it.

Although I felt what he had been doing I had not directly known what he wanted. His voice confirmed that he wanted to feel my penis or to pleasure me by playing with my penis while he achieved his goal of pleasuring himself.

He continued to try different ways to convince me to let him have me but I simply did not respond to his requests. I simply remained in a tucked fetal position on my side and with that body language he eventually understood that I was not going to allow it.

He finally gave up, kissed me on the back of my neck, and walked away into the room he had appeared from.

I remained in the fetal position for the remainder of the night. I could no longer fall asleep or think of anything else.

As daylight broke through the curtains I opened my eyes and heightened my hearing to determine if he was moving around. I did not hear him so I quietly began to move my legs towards the edge of the futon and into a seated position.

I scanned the room quickly and sprang onto my feet. I wanted to quietly and quickly leave this nightmare behind. As I made my way to the door, I heard his voice call out to me from the room he had vanished into.

"Iran, you are leaving?" he asked.

I turned to him and nodded my head yes. He asked me if I could stay for some breakfast. I replied, "No thank you. I have to go."

He began to walk in my direction and I turned to walk away.

He asked, "Will I see you again later?"

I continued toward the door without responding, grabbed the door handle, unlocked the lock, swung the door open, and stepped out without ever looking back.

I felt pain in my heart and felt as if I had been destroyed by this person I trusted. I would never again allow anyone to violate me in this way. I would rather kill any other man who tried to touch me in this way again. I was furious and hated him for daring to break my trust and personal space.

Up until this point in my life, I had not known positive, nurturing, love from any adult male. This horrible experience further increased my desire to never connect with an adult male again.

9

— • —

BRITTLE

Willard Street was still that place where I felt a connection. I returned when I could reconnect with that block and whoever remained there that I knew.

During one of my visits to Willard Street, I noticed the maintenance crew member who drove the dump truck leaving from the basement and walking toward his truck. I was standing across the street on the same platform that I had spent time on many times before. He looked at me from over the hood of the truck and I nervously looked back at him. I was thinking that he had found out I had been in the basement or perhaps he was trying to determine what I was up to.

Suddenly he motioned toward me and said something that I could not make out. He motioned with his hand for me to come over to him. *Uh oh, I am caught,* I thought. I did not run, I figured I would just deny whatever he said I did. I pointed toward my chest and asked him, "Me?" He nodded his head and continued to wave me over to him.

I walked across the street still not sure what was about to take place and what he wanted with me. My heart was pounding and racing. I felt hot and a little shaky. I finally made it to where he was standing.

He gave me a quick look and said, "Hey, I see you roaming around here all of the time. I have seen you out here for a while now. Do you live here?"

"Yes." I pointed towards the second-floor apartment window where I lived with my mom, my brother, and her boyfriend before. By this time over two years had passed by since I had become displaced. It seemed as if it was yesterday.

He looked towards where I pointed with a puzzled look on his face. He looked back at me and said, "No, you don't live there." He stated that he had rented that apartment to a family with small kids and that he knew I did not live there. In my heart, I felt as if that was still my home.

It was the last place where there was a sense of normal even though there was drug use, drug dealing, and high tensions stemming from the uncertainty associated with illegal drugs.

He then asked, "Where do you live?"

"I don't live anywhere. I find wherever I can sleep at night and just hang around throughout the day."

He asked me, "Do you work or have a job?"

"No."

"I could give you some hours of work if you want to make some money."

I thought for a second. I have never had a real job. I had no training or any skills that I knew about to apply for a job. Before I had an opportunity to finish my thoughts, I heard my voice say, "Okay."

He said, "Well meet me here tomorrow and I will set you up with something."

I didn't know what to think or what to say. I just nodded my head in agreement and he got in the truck and drove away. I didn't look back at his truck.

I simply remained standing there for a few minutes thinking about what had just happened and what I would do next. What work would I do? Was he serious? Was he going to have the police waiting for me when I came in the morning? I also thought, how much money is he going to give me? When was he going to give it to me? I simply just got lost in those thoughts and questions.

I fought through all of my nerves and feelings of fear and uncertainty and arrived at the front of the apartment building in the morning per his request. When I arrived, he asked me to walk down into the basement. I knew the layout of the space since I had snuck in there before. I pretended it was all new to me.

He asked me to help clean the space and discard any garbage that was needing to be discarded in the dumpsters behind the apartment building. There were also old stoves and refrigerators that needed to be cleaned before they could be reused. I spent the day cleaning and throwing out trash.

At the end of the day, he gave me some cash and said, "See you tomorrow at the same time."

I was shocked, excited, overwhelmed with joy, and didn't know what to do next. I could finally buy myself something to eat or do whatever I wanted to do with the money. It felt great to have earned it.

This arrangement went on for some time. There were weeks where I would help him one day in the week and others where I would spend up to three days helping him. During that time, I was able to stay with different people across the city. Since I was able to give ten dollars here, and twenty dollars there, people were a little more willing to allow me to sleep on their couches or living room floors.

On one of the days, I received instructions to throw some old kitchen cabinets into the dumpster on the side of the apartment building. While throwing out the old cabinets I noticed my childhood friend leaning out of a hallway window just looking around at what was happening outside.

He called out to me when he saw me by the dumpster. "Yo Smurf. What's up?"

I looked up and acknowledged him with a "What's Up."

His call got the attention of a woman who lived above the hallway window he was calling out from. It was a woman I had not seen before and from where I was standing, she looked pretty to me. We locked eyes and I smiled and she responded with a smile. I was intrigued and wanted to know who she was.

On one occasion while I was outside, she appeared from the side of the building. I noticed her and immediately thought to say hello. I walked towards her and said, "*Hola.*"

She replied, "*Hola,*" and once again smiled. She walked off and headed to where she needed to go.

Every day I purposely placed myself in places where I thought I might see her. I was sure to speak a little louder when I was interacting with my childhood friend via the hallway window.

I was able to get her attention and we began a conversation from her window while I was on the sidewalk on the side of the building. We agreed to talk at another time.

After meeting her in the hallway of her fourth-floor apartment we began to get closer. She appeared to be older than me so I lied about my age to hopefully convince her that I was older and worth dating. We soon started a romantic relationship.

She allowed me to move in with her and that made it easier to show up for the job I had working with the maintenance crew. It afforded me shelter and the feeling of safety I was looking for. I was also off the streets and out of the public eye. This meant that I could avoid DCF and stay in the neighborhood.

Little did I know how unprepared emotionally, and psychologically I was for that relationship. Despite the newfound opportunity, I was still very much displaced and emotionally unstable. I felt hurt, abandoned, and angry.

All of this was within me boiling but was kept at bay by my need to find a place to stay and a way to survive the day-to-day struggle. Every minute of my day before having the opportunity to work I did my best to keep all of my rage and anger from coming to the surface and keep it from hurting myself or someone else.

I had suffered years of abuse, neglect, and trauma, and felt discarded onto the streets of Hartford with no support, or resolution for all of those feelings.

As perhaps it could have been predicted I ended up failing miserably in the relationship with this woman. I could not regulate my emotions, understand a healthy relationship with another person, or how to contribute to a home.

I only knew it felt good to have someone who cared about me and someone who could spend time with me. I did not want to lose that sense of stability or dependency on another person again.

Our relationship was not working. I turned to the learned behaviors I had stored in my subconscious from the unhealthy and violent relationships I had witnessed during my childhood. I turned my love for this woman into a desperate attempt to control her. Almost immediately after beginning our relationship, I began to use threats of violence to establish control over her.

What else does a man do to make sure a woman knows her place? There was nothing else I knew how to do. She reacted with fear and I felt as if I had set the tone for how the relationship would go. She was my property and I felt I should determine what she could do or not do.

My desperation to keep this woman by my side and salvage any form of relationship with her took me from head-over-heels love to pure self-destruction. The thought of being separated from another woman who was supposed to love me and nurture me drove me to take drastic measures to compel her to keep me as her boyfriend.

I could begin to feel she was starting to have second thoughts about having jumped into this relationship. I started to spiral into dark thoughts of ending my life to quiet the painful thoughts of being discarded again.

One late morning after yet another dispute over my jealous behaviors and controlling ways I broke. I quietly opened the door of the apartment leading into the hallway. I stepped out towards the hallway window and remained standing there for some time.

I thought, *How else can I go on without her? Where could I go from here? Would any woman ever really be able to love me? Was I so bad that I was not compatible with anyone? Was I meant to be alone forever?*

As I remained there in thought I felt my fingertips on the bottom of the window that was at the end of the hallway where I was standing. The tips of my fingers were firmly under the window frame and I was pulling the window open.

Once I had the window open I raised my left leg and stepped through the opening of the window. I hunched my body down and pulled my head and upper body through the opening of the window. I then raised my right leg and pulled it through the window opening while I held myself up by grabbing onto the window ledge. I was seated on the window frame with my legs dangling out the window and most of my body. It felt similar to being on a swing in a park.

My mind was made up. I was going to stop the chaos in my head. I was going to jump from this four-story building. Finally, I would have silence.

As I began to slowly scoot my butt further and further out on the ledge I could not hear anything else happening around me. Only the thoughts in my head were clear.

I need to end this.

I decided it was time to push off.

Here I go.

Suddenly I felt a strong pull on my waist near my butt and belt line. The tug pulled me back like a tow truck would pull a car being raised onto a flatbed.

I felt as if my stomach was being pressed against my back. I felt the pressure intensify as I was being pulled back into the window.

It felt as if it happened in seconds. I was on my back facing the hallway ceiling. I slammed onto the floor and when I attempted to stand up I saw several people standing over me. My neighbors had somehow seen me climbing out onto the window ledge and had taken action to pull me back in.

They saved my life. I was not sure how to feel. I was shocked to see them all there. A commotion formed in the hallway as more neighbors opened their doors to see what was happening in the hallway.

I could hear through all the voices, *"Que te pasa?"* (What is the matter with you?) *"Estas Loco?"* (Are You Crazy?)

I did not answer. I only remained on my back taking on all the comments from people who had realized what I was attempting to do. Most of what was being directed at me were comments about how stupid and crazy my actions were.

I did not succeed at killing myself. I got up. One of my neighbors who was very religious and prayed all of the time simply held me and said some prayers for me. After the adrenaline of the moment subsided, I walked away feeling defeated and sad.

I took a long walk around the community and returned later that day to ask this woman who I believed was going to end our relationship for forgiveness.

My heart felt as if I needed her. I had to get her to bring me back into our apartment and I needed to hear that she loved me. She allowed me back in and we quietly spent the rest of the day together. I had secured her presence in my life for at least a little bit longer.

By that evening we were fighting again. Someone overheard the fighting and called the police. When they arrived at the door, I was not expecting it so I opened the door and thought, *Who is here getting into our business?* I was surprised. After they spoke with her, I was arrested for threatening.

I was handcuffed, walked down three flights of stairs, escorted down the path by the side of our apartment building, and placed in the back of the police car.

I was then transported to jail. I remember looking back at the building as we drove away. I was feeling angry and lost again.

We arrived at the Morgan Street Detention Center in Hartford.

I was taken into the main lockup and placed in a cell. A short while later I was asked to step out for processing. I was asked to stand against the wall for a picture and then was taken to a nearby table for fingerprinting.

Once they are done with me, I am taken into an elevator in handcuffs and escorted into a room known as "the bullpen." The bullpen is where all the people that were being processed were taken after fingerprinting and photos. There were two bullpens side-by-side and you could see the other men being processed after being arrested in the bullpen through the bars. It was as if we were animals in cages or on exhibit at the zoo.

There were approximately 15 to 20 men combined between the two bullpens. I was a young kid. I was 17 and, in my mind, I was not sure why I was there. It was my first time being in that space. Everyone was there facing different charges. It could have been anything from larceny to murder and we were all together. It was the way it worked.

The bullpens were right next to the police officers' offices and you could see them working at their desks. You could also see law enforcement officers from different towns coming to either bring in someone who was arrested in their town or to pick up someone who needed to be processed in their town but had been arrested in Hartford. There was the constant calling of "officer, officer," or "CO" (corrections officer).

People were drunk on the floor, some people were mad, and some were quiet. Some people knew each other so they are talking to each other and were telling the story of why they got there.

I was just sitting there processing and absorbing it. I was not thinking much about my arrest.

As I was going through the process, I saw different detainees being called out of the bullpen by the officers, by a bondsman, or by an attorney. If you are not going to be issued a bond for release you sit in the cell and wait.

As the night went by, I kept seeing more and more people leaving and it came to a point where it was me and three other people in the bullpen. There were maybe about four or so guys in the other bullpen.

At the point where there were only a few men in the bullpen, I remember a man coming toward me and asking me where I was from and why I was there. He was looking at me very differently. I felt weird about it. He started coming toward me and I stepped towards the front of the bullpen where I could face the police officer or the corrections officers' offices.

I started calling out as others had been earlier. "Officer, officer, CO, CO."

I felt like he was going to try to harm me. He was a much older guy than I was and a bigger guy than I was. I was hoping someone would see something and say something to him. I needed the COs to come in and remove me from there.

Unfortunately, some prisoners called out to the COs so often that they were tired of it and would just sit there.

After a while without a response, I ended up having to fight the guy. He was trying to grab me in whatever way he could and pin me up against the cage.

I fought until the officers came and opened the door. I was moved to the wing unit inside the building where I met with an officer who interviewed me.

The officer asked, "Do you have a bond, anybody to get you out?"

I didn't have anything or anyone that could help me get out.

I noticed that the jail was old and dirty as we walked towards the unit in a very long hallway. As I walked down the hallway I was asked to turn right. I was hearing a series of sounds and then we arrived at a line of separate showers.

At those showers, I was asked to strip in front of the officers. I had never had to strip in front of a grown man before, especially in that position, and it was incredibly uncomfortable. It felt humiliating and I was so embarrassed, self-conscious, and apprehensive. It was one of the most vulnerable positions I had ever been in.

I asked myself, *Why is this necessary? Why does this person get to do this? What are his plans for me?* I was ready to fight with everything I could muster if he attempted to hurt me in any way.

My pride was hurt. My "manhood" was brought to shame. Although it did not last long, the impact of that experience lasted well into the night and into many years of my life.

I did not feel regret for the actions that brought me there. I did feel anger that I wasn't able to stop this search and humiliation from happening as I would have in other situations with violence to protect myself.

I eventually followed their commands. I was asked to step into the shower and was given a bar of soap and a bottle that contained a liquid to wash down with. It was explained to me that this would kill any potential lice or any kind of insects that could spread throughout the jail.

I was asked to step out of the shower to turn around.

I was then asked to bend over and spread my cheeks so they could look at my butt to check if I am hiding anything like drugs or any contraband.

I had never experienced anything like this. It was demoralizing to spread your cheeks open for someone to look between them. The palms of my hands were wet from the sweat and physically grabbing my butt cheeks to spread them felt like one of the most difficult commands to follow.

I was then asked to turn around and lift my testicles and cough. Once that was all completed I was taken to a holding cell. I believe that because I was 17, I was placed in a cell by myself.

I did not sleep all night long because I could hear loud noises coming from other cells. I now know that when people who are fighting addiction are locked up and are struggling because they do not have their drugs, they cry, whimper, and throw up.

The cell I was in had a window with bars and faced downtown Hartford. I could see the nightlife and people driving by and just moving about. I stared into that night sky most of the night. I felt dejected, soaking in all that had happened since I arrived at this place and thinking that when the police came I should have taken off running or jumped out a window and killed myself.

The following morning the door to my cell was opened and I was asked to step out. I was being transported to the courthouse. One by one at least ten of us were placed into a transport vehicle known as the "meat locker." It was similar to a mid-sized box truck outfitted for prisoner transport. The windows had metal grates covering them to prevent anyone from opening them from the inside or from the outside. The meat locker also had two long metal benches on two sides where we all sat cramped and handcuffed together.

They took me over to the courthouse which included prisoner-holding cells and bullpens in the basement. This bullpen was more of a den with a door with only a few steel bars. The white walls were solid concrete and you could not see the other men in the other rooms. There were offices and desks outside the rooms where the corrections officers were. These were called marshals. The bullpen held men from different towns across the state so they were different from the men at the Morgan Street jail which mostly had Black and Latino men from Hartford.

The walls had all kinds of graffiti messages from others who had traveled through. Some messages were made using matches or lighters. Before I was called up to the judge's court I was called out by name and inmate number.

Once they verified my identity, I was shackled to different people who were going to be seen by the judge and ushered to an elevator. The court is on the upper level of the building. Any time you were to move anywhere you had to be shackled on your ankles, waist, and wrists.

I was then placed in a different holding cell and processed again to make sure I was supposed to be there. I was moved to an isolated solitary room to wait to see the judge sooner or later.

While I waited for the judge, I was given a cold cheese sandwich, an apple, and milk for lunch. After lunch, I was taken out of that room and placed into another room to visit with a public defender.

I was asked by the public defender where I lived and all the different things that they ask of prisoners to get insight into who they are. It was apparent the public defender did not have a lot of time. The interview was super fast. I remember I said I wasn't really living anywhere because even though I had been arrested outside my girlfriend's house, it was not my house.

The public defender left and never came back. I was then taken to the courtroom. The public defender was very kind and proposed to the judge that I be considered a youthful offender and added to the youthful offender category. The court asked me several questions and I really do not remember everything. I was told that I would be released from there because they were going to refer me to a program or something. I was directed to the court office and ushered back downstairs to be processed for release.

After being processed for release, I was led to an open door near the garage entrance of the courthouse. The door led to the street. I was out. I stood behind the courthouse building wondering where to go next.

10

SECOND CHANCE

I returned to Willard Street. I decided that I needed to fight for what I thought was mine. I could not be discarded and displaced again. I was forgiven by my girlfriend and accepted back into the relationship. I was not emotionally ready for this. I had no time to work through my emotions and learn coping skills. I received no help.

I would end up being arrested two additional times within a five-month period for continued threats and assaults against my girlfriend. Each time I would spend a few days in jail and receive a suspended sentence as long as I agreed to the terms set by the court and I was back out on the streets.

Throughout this time, I was still "working" with the maintenance crew. Since the work was sporadic my arrests were not interfering with the times I was called to help.

My relationship was never able to be salvaged or it never became what I thought it would be. I became desperate again, I became a fuse to an emotional bomb that was set to explode. When I was told it was over, I exploded with rage and assaulted her. If I asserted my will with force she would stay and it would work out. I learned that would not be the case.

I was arrested for assault again and taken to the local jail on Morgan Street in Hartford to be held accountable for my crime. I spent the night in Morgan Street and once again was driven to the local courthouse in Hartford to have my case heard.

This time I would be asked to serve 90 to 180 days in jail. There was no more skating by and not being held accountable. The court had given me enough opportunities and I had squandered them.

I was now 17 years old and headed to prison. I hadn't learned my lesson and now I was going to be taught one. Once again, I was subjected to the humiliating process of processing before I was allowed into the prison.

This time I was at Hartford Correctional Institution also known as "the Meadows" prison in Hartford. I was cleared to be sent to a unit inside the prison. It was very clean with doors that locked electronically. I was able to look into the hallway through a hole in the door the size of the bottom of a soda can. On the side of the panel, there was a crack that let in a little more light. If I squished my face up against the panel and closed one eye for focus, I was able to see anyone coming towards or walking away from the cell.

The beds were made of metal with a small thin white or dirty white mattress with thin blue stripes, no pillows, and a metallic toilet. The toilet was very close to the window if you happened to have one. I did have a window unit in the first one so I was able to see outside from there. Each unit or wing held about 25 men in its individual cells.

After a couple of weeks, I was moved downstairs and across to another building where it was more like a dorm with probably 50 to 100 guys. In the middle of that dorm, there was this thing called a bubble. It was where the corrections officers sat so they could see in every direction of this dorm.

It was in a U shape so the bubble was in the middle. There were racks of bunk beds in each row or hall. The corrections officers would watch from cameras in the bubble or by looking through the glass. Sometimes they would bang on the glass to get the attention of passing inmates.

In the dorms, you can get to anybody you want to get to. There was nothing stopping you from moving where every other inmate was. Being in this dorm-style facility allowed me to start to socialize and start hearing and learning from other people what it was that they felt they were there for, what their stories were, and when they first thought their lives were out of control.

I learned that there were many fellow inmates who had experienced similar traumas as I had in my childhood. I learned they were constantly in survival mode as I was. They used every "lesson" or "skill" they were taught and had learned along the way to make the best life they could based on their perspective and lived experience. Even if those lessons meant they would be back in prison or jail for many more years to come.

I learned that many had addictions to substances such as drugs, alcohol, gambling, violence, sex, and the rush of the "fast" not so-fast life. I learned how many believed they had learned from their mistakes while committing a crime so they would not be caught next time.

On the opposite side of the spectrum, I learned that most had a partner, friend, child, or children, a community or social group they belonged to and cared about. I couldn't relate to this.

I learned about many of their dreams and plans. I unfortunately also learned that they were stuck in a revolving struggle to survive with limited abilities or capacity to challenge everything they learned. It was impossible to commit themselves to changing the learned habits and behaviors.

There were many internal battles taking place within them. Just like me.

I was released after serving almost 90 days of the sentence.

11

FARM

Once I was released, I did what I had always done when roaming the streets. I returned to Willard Street.

When I arrived at Willard Street the first person I saw was the maintenance worker who had given me some opportunities to work. He said, "Hey, I haven't seen you around for a little while." Before I could say anything, he said, "I heard you were arrested and were in jail. Is that true?"

I responded, "Yes."

He said, "That is not good and you cannot allow that to happen."

I explained to him that I lost control and he said, "Well... you need to keep cool. See you later, good luck, and don't get into any more trouble."

I was now somewhat of an outcast within my circle. People who were finding out what I had done were looking at me differently. Their looks were more like shame and concern. My friends from the block spoke to me and wanted to know what happened. When I shared the story, most responded with simply, "That's crazy, Smurf!" Some would say, "You need to chill."

I spent the day answering questions from friends and fending off looks from others who were concerned or disgusted by my actions. Once again, I felt alone.

That evening the maintenance worker saw me across the street from where he would park his truck. He called me over again. He said, "I have given this a lot of thought."

I was not sure what he was going to say. Maybe he was never going to let me help him again?

He then says, "I think you are a good kid and I wanted to help you so you don't spend your days doing nothing on the streets. Do you still want to help me or want to work?"

I responded, "Yes."

He responds with, "Well, that's good. If you want to keep working with me and want to stay off the streets, I will offer you an opportunity to do that. In order for me to help you and for you to continue working with me you have to leave this street and come stay with me. You will work for my other business in New Hartford and help me around my property."

I was numb, confused, scared, and speechless. There was so much to process. His look communicated that I did not have much time to make a decision. I was thinking, *Wait, I have to leave here?*

Before I could think anything else, he interrupted my thinking and said, "If you are going to come you have to hurry up and come now."

I shrugged my shoulders and spoke with uncertainty. "Okay."

I climbed into the dump truck I had seen parked out front of that apartment building for years and off we went. I was headed to where I had never been. I was headed away from home.

Regardless of all the suffering, uncertainty, and aimless wandering, it felt normal. Leaving my life behind as I had known it, was not. Was this my saving grace? Had I arrived at a turning point in my young life?

While living with and working for the maintenance crew worker in the town of New Hartford as a teen I came to know structure. I did not know at the time that waking up each day at 4:00 a.m. was the beginning of developing a sense of responsibility and accountability.

Each morning at four I was awakened and asked to help him feed the pigs, cows, and horses he owned. It was the first time that I had ever been around any pigs or farm animals. Making sure the farm animals were taken care of and that I helped around the farm was the arrangement I agreed to in order for me to live with him.

The maintenance crew worker was a fairly large, heavy-set, burly man. I can state with 100% certainty that he spent his entire life in heavy work, such as farming, construction, demolition, and landscaping.

He was super strong and you could feel his power even while sitting next to him in his truck. He had numerous missing teeth from an accident while at work. A tree fell on him and crushed him. He had long, dirty, entangled, messy brown/blond hair and extremely broken and rough hands.

One of the things he did every morning was stop at the local gas station and buy himself a room-temperature soda. Due to the loss of his teeth, cold soda was not a good idea. Many times, he would leave the soda in the truck all day in the sun and would drink it right out of the container.

The truck was your typical construction crew dump truck used for carrying sand, wood planks, steel posts, or anything needed for the job.

He played no games when it came to the jobs he was hired to complete and he expected 100% percent of your effort at all times. He didn't just sit there and bark out orders; he pushed himself beyond his breaking point and then found another level.

He never indicated being tired or in pain from all of the heavy work. I sure as heck felt every plank I carried, every concrete form I lifted and set, and every shovel we used to mix, pour, and level off the concrete poured into the foundations of homes.

At every site, we used shovels to dig the deep trenches alongside the foundations so that we could make sure the walls were even and measured evenly at each corner of the foundation.

I was taught how to carry concrete forms used to hold the concrete in place for the walls of the foundation. Each form weighed between 80 to 100 pounds. We had to carry one on each forearm and lean it towards our shoulders. All of this while walking on planks across the entire foundation.

Some of the planks would crack and creek under our feet. I would feel myself bounce with each step similar to a car when you are stuck in traffic on a bridge and you feel the soft movement of the bridge.

The weather we worked in was irrelevant. It did not matter if it was heat, rain, wind, cold, snow, or sleet. If a contract was secured, we had to meet the deadline.

I had never done that type of work. It beat me down every day. I had the best sleep I have ever had. I also had the most swollen hands and fingers ever. Luckily, I was young and eventually adapted to the work.

I was paid well for the work and it was the first time I felt as if I had money to purchase my own things. It felt good to do so. I felt an independence that was freeing and also satisfying. I had no knowledge of how to manage money. That was not a conversation I had ever had with anyone, so I burned right through every penny.

Every week we would go into Hartford from New Hartford to help manage the properties he had. After we were done at the properties I would get to go into the city and stop at local sneaker and clothing stores. I would proudly use the cash I earned from work to buy up all the trendy sneakers, clothes, etc.

I would then take a very familiar walk down Park Street or Willard Street and make sure to see as many people as possible. I was showing off and desired to be greeted with high regard. I wanted to belong and be popular.

Most of those who knew me remembered that I was homeless and unstable so I was made fun of many times and also excluded from being a passenger in a car or not allowed into some parties. This time around I was going to make sure that I was included and I was going to make sure that no one laughed at me.

I also had cash to spend so I could flaunt that as being cool. It worked and I was able to spend countless hours of my visit to Hartford just basking in my newfound "popularity."

Every weekend I would return with new clothes, sneakers, watches, hats, coats, and other items. During the week and on many Saturday mornings I was on the truck working my tail off. My goodness did I look forward to the weekend escapes.

I had grown pretty strong and muscular working in construction and caring for the farm. I also wanted to show that off. I was confident, cocky, and filled with pride.

During one of my walks on Park Street, I stopped off at a local barber shop and had the barber clean up my hairlines. I felt fresh and clean. After I exited the barber shop I scanned Park Street in each direction looking for some type of action.

While scanning I saw a girl who to me was very attractive. I immediately begin my act and my walk now has a little more swagger. I begin walking in her direction. While walking towards her I saw someone I knew riding a bike.

I asked the person if I could use their bike for a minute to talk with someone and I would pay them five dollars. The person said, "Cool," and off I went on the bike.

I was riding in her direction and as I got closer I said, "Hi, how are you?" I was doing my best to sound gentle and sexy.

She turned to me and said, "Hi, I am doing good."

Once I heard her response I felt as if I had to put on the charm even more. I even began peddling the bike in rhythm. One pedal, another pedal, swish, swish, swaying a little further left and a little further right.

Just as I reached her, I lost control of the bike. My right foot slipped off the pedal and I came crashing onto the bike frame. I fell onto the bike right by her feet.

I lay there. I could not believe this just happened. I could hear a gasp from her and then laughter from around me.

I was extremely embarrassed.

I could feel the scrapes on my elbow and some other parts of my body were throbbing. When I began to look up she was walking away and the bike owner was hurrying in my direction to collect his bike. I had failed miserably at being a Don Juan.

I thought that being popular and flaunting my newfound "success" was the fix to my other issues. That was moons away from being the truth.

12

Incident on Hudson Street

As the weeks and months passed by in New Hartford, I continued thinking about the guys who had jumped me in the past. Months turned into years of waiting for revenge.

I had re-engaged with the woman I had assaulted and entered into a long-distance relationship with her. Perhaps this dysfunctional situation was something that seemed familiar so she would let me hang around. It could also have been that she was terrified of me because I kept coming around and no matter what she did or what intervention she sought from the courts, I was not punished for long enough to allow her to move on.

During one of my trips to Hartford, she and I visited with her sister on Hudson Street. The apartment she rented was across the street from a housing complex known in the community as "the Hutt." I was leaning out the window of the apartment watching car traffic and people pass on by. I noticed someone walking towards the apartment building I was in. He seemed familiar to me for some reason.

As he got closer to the building, I immediately flashed back to the day I received my first beating by members of the BSN crew. To my surprise, it was one of the guys involved who was walking toward my apartment building.

I felt a rush go through my body. The feeling was similar to when a person gets into a very hot shower. I realized this was my opportunity to get revenge on this person and to release the anger I held on to for more than six years.

I immediately propped myself out of the window and ran towards the front door of the apartment. Before I pulled the door open, I grabbed a mini bat from next to the refrigerator. The mini bat was a smaller replica of a baseball bat with the Yankees logo on it.

I ran down the flight of stairs hoping that I would not miss my opportunity to make him pay. Once I arrived at the front door of the building, I pushed it open and looked to the left and right. I wanted to make visual contact with him.

I spotted him.

I felt my rage building. I walked toward him holding the mini bat on my right side.

I asked, "Do you remember me?"

He noticed my angry look and appeared to be surprised.

He responded, "No."

I immediately interrupted him and said, "You jumped me in SANDS."

Before he could respond again, I raised the bat and smacked him across the side of the face. He started to cover up and I continued beating him with the bat. I was unleashing all of the pain and rage I had felt when he and his crew beat me.

I felt excited, powerful, and happy.

As I continued beating him a crowd gathered. No one was intervening. They were just watching. Once he was on the ground bleeding and unable to defend himself, I started yelling at him. I made sure to let him know what I had been waiting for, which was to find him and get him back for what he had done to me.

Finally, after I had kicked him a few times someone stepped in and pulled me away. He was on the floor for a little while and eventually staggered onto his feet. I watched him as he stumbled away and thought, *That is what you get for hitting me.*

I did not go to jail or face any consequences for this incident. Despite the opportunity I was being given to work, earn money, sleep on a warm couch, and have a roof over my head I could not control my impulses for lashing out violently.

I vowed to get revenge on all of them. I was eventually able to find and fight with every one of those guys. Based on the lessons I had learned growing up I did what was supposed to be done. I had to maintain the only relevance I felt I had.

Most of the people in the audience who had watched me striking him were those in their late teens and early twenties who lived in The Hutt. They did not get involved because he was not from our neighborhood and was not Latino. The conflict that existed between our groups made it seem fair to beat each other if we were out of our neighborhood.

Anywhere these groups saw one another vicious fights broke out. People would use anything as a weapon. This included cars smashing into the vehicles of their enemies or the actual person. Not even city transit buses were safe. If you were seen on the bus in the enemy neighborhood you'd better jump out and take your chances at running. Most of the time they were able to stop the bus, jump in, and beat the person they wanted inside the bus. It made schools unsafe for anyone who was a target.

Many of these groups attended the same schools or competed against one another every year in sports. Any time the visiting team came in you'd be sure to see dozens of fights in the stands or outside by the buses. Schools had to increase police presence and sometimes lockdown games between neighborhood schools.

Being committed to these conflicts meant that I remained part of the crowd and was needed.

13
— • —

SQUANDERED

On a warm day in 1987, I made a call to Hartford. The call was to the home of the woman I had dated on Willard Street. During some of my visits to Hartford from New Hartford, I reconnected with her. She now lived at a different location and our "relationship" was rekindled.

It was clear to everyone looking in from the outside that our relationship was doomed to fail. My ego had now taken hold of me and I was more concerned with looking flashy and being relevant. I felt invincible and I was arrogant. She and I were constantly arguing in public and then making up. It was the type of chaos that I had been used to growing up. Conflict, aggression, and violence were expected and normal.

I could feel the destructive thoughts and behaviors from within me returning to the surface. I would not be in Hartford every day so at least Monday through Saturday afternoon I had to focus on work.

More and more frequently I would walk approximately five miles to find a pay phone at a local convenience store to call her. I would engage in all kinds of reasons to argue with her and question her love for me. I began to unravel. There was still something in me looking for belonging. That sense of belonging changed once I was removed from my community.

My work performance at the job sites declined and I was failing more and more on completing the requirements I agreed to at the house. At last, it all came crashing down.

I began to crack under my own pressure, thoughts, and unrelenting desires to be back in the community that I had known for most of my life at that point. I also wanted to have more control over my girlfriend at the time. Lastly, I had bought into the fake image I was creating as a way to show those who knew me for not having much of anything and being transient that I was a better version. All because I had a few means to buy the latest clothes and flash some cash.

In the meantime, I had not improved emotionally or psychologically. All of what helped create my mindset and the bad lessons life had taught me were still very active in my head.

I caved in. During one of those calls to my girlfriend, we got into an argument and she stated that she would no longer be in a relationship with me. She said it was over. My head felt like it could explode. After some angry words, I slammed the phone down and hung up the call.

I returned to the worksite with a recurring message in my head. *It's over.* I could not get it to stop. I was completely overcome by the desire to leave the site and get to her place. I was going to change her mind by any means necessary. I could not be dismissed again, discarded, and left alone. I felt as if my past experiences with abandonment and neglect were being repeated.

My boss at the job site noticed that I was not focused and that I appeared to be talking to myself. He yelled at me and pulled me aside. He asked me what I was doing and why I hadn't completed some of the work he assigned me. I replied, "Because I am mad and don't want to."

He became enraged and asked me to walk off the job site to get myself back on track. I stormed off the site and continued walking in an unknown direction in the hills of Canton, Connecticut.

I was wearing long jeans, a long-sleeved windbreaker-style jacket with a t-shirt underneath, and above-the-ankle work boots. I had learned from my boss that while working on-site it was important to wear clothing that covered my skin to prevent major sunburn, scrapes, cuts, and bug bites. I also had a bandana wrapped around my head in order to keep the heat of the sun from beating down on me.

While I was walking away from the site, I could feel my lack of control over my thoughts. I had decided that I was going to walk from Canton to Hartford and confront my girlfriend. I had decided to quit the job and give in to my desire to be back in Hartford.

I was not sure where to go while I was walking on the winding roads and hills in Canton but I was determined to find my way out of there. I just kept walking and looking for anything familiar or any roads that seemed like major connectors to a main road.

During my trips back and forth with my boss I remembered Route 44 being what we traveled. I kept my eyes open for a Route 44 sign. I finally saw it in the distance and knew I could get to Hartford from there.

I was 14 miles away from my target and nothing was going to stop me from reaching her. My fury would not be smothered by any other thoughts or words. I kept talking under my breath. "You are not going to leave me. Did you cheat on me? Who is with you in your house? Do you think that you can say that to me? Just wait until I see you." Over and over, I repeated these same things. I was a kid on a mission.

For more than five hours I walked in my work clothes and boots. I was burning up and sweating but I refused to give up. I had one goal and nothing would distract me from that.

I arrived in Hartford and finally began to feel the pain from hours of walking. I was passing by Elizabeth Park and decided to cut through a path in the park. I stopped for a minute.

I loosened my boot laces and gave my feet some air, pulled up my socks, re-tied the laces, and continued my walk.

I finally arrived at Washington Street in Hartford. I had achieved the goal of getting to where she was. Once I was able to gain entrance into the building she lived in I made my way up the flight of stairs up to the third floor.

I banged on the door and she replied, *"Quien es?"* (Who is it?)

I replied, "It's me." She knew my voice and I could tell (even through the door) that she took a deep breath of disbelief. She gently opened the door and there I was, face-to-face with my target.

She did not have many words to say. I quickly and loudly asked, "What did you say to me over the phone?" Before she could answer, I yelled out, "Say it again, I dare you."

Since we had many arguments in the past that turned physical with pushing and shoving, she responded with, "Enough! I said it is over, I can't be with you anymore!"

I grabbed her by her shirt, asking "What did you say? You are NOT leaving me."

We began to shove and pull each other. I was pulling her and she was shoving me to get me to release her.

We broke apart and she began to walk toward the living room and her bed-room. I headed into the kitchen and decided that I had to get more serious and stop her from leaving me, abandoning me, and discarding me. Not again.

I picked up a knife and headed toward the living room. I confronted her and she asked, "What are you doing? Stop and get out!"

I was blinded by rage, panic, and fear and could barely hear her over my own thoughts. I stepped closer to her. I wanted to make her stop talking and get control over the situation.

Suddenly, I snapped back to clarity and heard a yell coming from where she was standing. I saw blood coming from her shirt dripping onto the floor. When I continued to approach her, she continued to walk away and with her back to me, I had committed a serious crime. I had stabbed her multiple times.

It hit me immediately that I was in trouble. I had dealt with the police before for assaults I had committed and I knew this was even worse. I had to escape. I went down the stairs and out to the street.

I walked down Park Street not sure where to go. I just knew I had to get out of that area. Within a few minutes, I heard the police sirens and I saw police units racing toward the building where all of this had taken place.

It was not long before I was approached by a police officer while I was walking down Park Street. Suddenly there were two police cars on each side of me. The officers got out, approached me and asked my name. I responded, "Iran Nazario." They placed me in handcuffs and off to jail I went.

Many of the people I knew on the street were standing out there to see my arrest. I hadn't proven anything to anyone. They were right about me. I was a nobody with nothing. I was not worthy of saving. I had once again lost it all. Unhinged, with no structure and no direction I had become an abuser. I began to follow the cycle of the abused doing what I hate most. Abuse.

Only a few months earlier I had been standing in the same courthouse being read the same criminal charges. The prosecutor in the case stated that I continued to repeat the same behavior and I was escalating the level of violence. I had pled guilty on three other occasions to assault and other charges. I failed to complete any required steps implemented by the court. I had violated probation, violated protective orders, continued to get into fights, and did not secure employment that was on the books.

It was recommended that I serve jail time and complete any portion of suspended sentences from previous arrests.

The judge agreed and sentenced me to three years in prison. I remained standing there and had no reaction. I don't think I could understand what that much time meant. I was escorted back to the basement cells and it was explained that I was going to wait for transport to Manson Youth Correctional Institution.

14

PRISON

I arrived at the gate of Manson Youth Institution (MYI), a prison in Cheshire, Connecticut for teens and "adults" in their early twenties. I was taken to the processing unit. On my way to the processing unit, I saw people playing basketball outside and walking between buildings and recreation areas.

I was handed standard prison wear and kept whatever I was wearing on my feet. I was provided the standard underwear from the prison. I was taken into the unit and asked a number of questions. I was then isolated by myself in a cell in the processing and orientation unit for approximately two weeks while I completed all of the steps to enter the general population.

During my time in that isolated unit I reflected on much of life, the actions that brought me there, and pondered what would happen next. I thought of who was at this institution that would challenge me or that I had been in conflict with on the streets.

I paced back and forth in the room, I punched the walls believing that it would make my knuckles harder and help me inflict greater pain on anyone I fought. Every sound or voice that came from outside the cell required me to head to the door for a look. Now that I had no place to go and no distractions, I was forced to face all of the chaos and inner turmoil in my head.

I felt as if I was losing my sanity. I was becoming more and more aggravated. I had to escape the silence and get back to the masquerade that was my life.

Once I was cleared to leave the processing and orientation unit I was escorted to a unit that seemed very far away from the processing building. The path to the unit was long and windy. The sky was clear of clouds and I felt as if I could see for miles in each direction.

Buildings housing many teenage boys were spread out on these grounds. I felt as if we walked for twenty minutes.

I was placed in a cell with somebody I'd never met. A general rule was that the person who comes in second to the unit gets the top bunk because it's harder to get up and get down.

I remember having to use the bathroom for the first time. My roommate was on the bottom bunk and it was my first time having to use the bathroom in front of another person. Having to go number two or number one with somebody's bed literally right next to the toilet was humiliating. It was the same thing when they went to the toilet. The way to offer some privacy was to put up a towel on the bar that you have on your bunk bed or to turn your body away from the person who wants to use the bathroom and face the wall.

I would stand a little to the side when I had to pee so that he did not have to see my penis or so that I would not splash urine on his mattress. There is a sense of shame. With every trickle of pee hitting the bowl you hope it's not too loud or that you're not splashing onto the floor. You barely take a breath and you absolutely don't make a sound or say a word. Number two heightens the level of shame 100 times. You are seated there and can see this person. As the normal bodily functions happen you pass gas, there's a splashing sound, it smells and you flush to hopefully keep the noise from the entire process from being heard too much. There is nothing else that can be done. I would try to hurry up and end the shame. After a while, I found I could schedule it around when I knew he was going to be out of the room.

The Meadows and Morgan Street were both in Hartford so 95% of the people you saw in those jails were people from Hartford or from the surrounding towns. The number of people I knew made a difference because it meant I felt a little bit more connected to the community. If someone shared stories of things that happened in my neighborhood I would remember or know the people involved.

At MYI they were pretty much strangers. They were from across the state. I felt isolated because MYI was so removed from my community.

This institution forced enemies from Hartford to come together in order to fend off attacks from other prisoners who were from different parts of the state. Since I was from Hartford, that meant that I had rivals from Waterbury, New Britain, New Haven, Bridgeport, and other areas across Connecticut and Massachusetts. Even if you had never crossed anyone it was understood that being from different communities meant you could not associate with one another.

Those of us from Hartford had to stay together to survive.

I began lifting weights and doing what I could to become stronger. I needed to be ready for a fight. I had to develop hatred for people I had never met or had a conversation with.

It never became a space where I could focus on my internal struggles. Counseling, mental health, anger management, or anything like that did not matter. It became a space that allowed me to eat food high in starch like potatoes and other fatty foods to help bulk me up. All I cared about was how to get bigger and stronger and louder and more respected and more knowledgeable than anybody else.

I was focused on external things. Showing toughness, control, and fearlessness would keep you from becoming everyone's target or victim. It sent the message that you were willing to fight to defend yourself and that you were physically able to.

Becoming a target or being known as the unit victim would mean that anyone and everyone could have all of your possessions, take anything from you, remove you from game tables, hang up your calls, or deny you your time entirely. It meant they would skip you at chow hall or that you could become their servant and do as they demanded. Once that happened a group mentality would kick in and others would take advantage of your perceived "weakness." Rarely did you see anyone quiet receiving the kind of attention and respect as those who were loud. It was about fitting in and not standing out. It is about masking your true self in order to survive and be visible.

I was not much of a basketball player so when I was let out into the compound or into open areas, I hung out and did other things. I was able to walk the compound. I could not visit other units or buildings but I could go to the basketball courts and recreation areas. That is when I started to see different towns and cities fighting each other.

Youth from New Haven and Hartford hated each other. I didn't know why but I had to be involved and defend the youth from Hartford even if it meant my life.

Violence was a common occurrence on the compound and in our unit. I remember a young man came in and the second night he was there a couple of guys ran into the room and appeared to be raping him for a long time. I don't know exactly what he was incarcerated for but the rumor was that he had molested a kid or something like that and people took it out on him that way. Everyone could hear this young man screaming and yelling and there was no intervention. Everyone kept quiet, nobody said anything. I don't know for sure if anybody was held responsible for that or not but I know that I never saw anything happen to anybody. It was just one of those experiences that was expected.

His screams reminded me of the internal screams I wanted to desperately let out when I was abused, neglected, or traumatized as a child. I learned how to express myself with destructive behavior, self-defeating actions, and violence.

During the time that I was incarcerated at MYI, no family or friends visited me. I received a visit from a priest from Hartford. He was always involved with visiting people in prison. Not receiving visits from anyone else was very lonely. Not having positive influences advising me against violence allowed me to form different thinking of what a man or young man is supposed to be.

I had learned that a young man is supposed to be loyal to his friends, violent, and aggressive. No positive goals, no plans for the future, no need for education, and to never ever say you are sorry.

These lessons trace back as far as I can remember.

The relationship my mother and father had was one filled with conflict, verbal and physical violence, disregard, and disrespect on my father's part towards my mother. Beatings, mental torture, and complete isolation from loved ones helped control her, including the threat of hurting my oldest brother. All of those clashes had a direct impact on me from inside my mother's womb. Once my mother decided she'd had enough and moved from New York to Connecticut the exposure to a life of drug addiction, depression, violence, neglect, abuse, and lack of care became my reality.

When a caregiver's sole focus becomes the next fix, there is little else that matters.

Beatings with power cords, closed-fisted punches to the chest and back, beatings with shoes, isolation after beatings so you could process why you deserved to be beaten, mental torture via threats of more and greater physical violence, abandonment or depriving of food, water or sleep for hours.

My lesson was this is how you gain control; this is where your feelings, thoughts, and emotions belong (in the dark, inside of you) and nothing is more important than what you want.

This was my school. Where I learned how to love, behave, speak, believe, and think.

I practically became my situation and created my coping skills and response to life challenges from there. I chose aggression, suppression of feelings, and taking control of others through acting out and violence.

This included destroying everything that was good in support of this distorted way of thinking and believing.

All else would be punished for my comfort or to keep my control.

This prison experience continued to make those thoughts seem more reasonable and more acceptable in my head.

I finally completed my sentence and it was time to leave MYI. I did not have a place to go. I had lost my job years prior and no one was coming to get me.

I entered MYI weighing approximately 154 pounds and left weighing almost 215 pounds. I was still full of rage and resentment. Now I was bigger, stronger, better trained at negative thinking, and had no direction.

Outside the gate of MYI, I waited for a van to transport me back to Hartford. I got in the van and off we went. In 30 minutes, I was back in the city where I learned to survive. I was ready to survive by any means necessary.

15

— • —

THE ORIGIN

In 1989, at the "street mature" age of 19, I was released from Manson Youth Institution (MYI).

By 19 my rage was on full display. I was using physical aggression and violence to resolve my conflicts. I would threaten violence almost immediately after feeling annoyed or frustrated. I would punch myself in the face when angry. I sought to place fear in the heart and mind of anyone who I felt deserved it.

I had not received any type of rehabilitative services. There was no counseling, mentoring, mental health support, or contact from any services that could help stabilize me and help me begin to identify a path to a positive purpose.

I was released to a halfway house in Hartford. Several weeks after I arrived at the halfway house, I was able to secure a job at Futuramik Industries, Inc. They specialized in plastic processing. I worked on an assembly line that produced plastic parts by the thousands and my job was to separate the plastic pieces from any unit that had become stuck together during the melting and design process.

This was not the job that I chose. In order to remain at the halfway house, every former inmate was required to have a job or else face the consequence of a return to prison. It was a requirement to earn freedoms such as furloughs for the day.

Those furloughs would allow us to spend time outside the halfway house with anyone we had added to a list of contacts that was approved by the halfway house staff. Since I had no one on the list I could not go anywhere for a furlough. Whenever I earned time out of the halfway house, I would use it to go shopping for clothes or sneak off to see friends on the street. I would make up a location and have someone sign off that I was there and this allowed me some freedom from time to time.

I completed my time in the halfway house and was set free to find my way. I left there carrying a black plastic bag full of my belongings. I headed towards the South End of Hartford with no real plan. I was just happy to be out of the halfway house but needed a place to put my stuff down so I could go to the streets.

After some time of going from street to street, I ended up on Asylum Avenue at my childhood friend's house. He had helped me when I was displaced and homeless on Willard Street. He still lived with his mom but now on a different street.

He opened his door as he would always do, offering me some food and a safe place to stay. His mom yelled out, *"Ah, mira it's Eh-Smurfy!"* (Ah look, it Eh-Smurfy). I recalled my younger days when she first began saying my nickname that way.

My time working at the factory did not last long. There was no mandate to work there, and having no supervision gave me the freedom to leave. Once again, I looked to the streets for my survival. It was a place I knew well and had become comfortable living in. As uncertain as it was, it was my normal.

I had thought about many things during my time at MYI, especially my family in Brooklyn, New York. I had lost touch with my dad and my brothers and sisters for a number of years since I returned to Connecticut to live with my mom.

As the days passed by, I thought more and more about leaving Hartford. I continued my daily routine of finding any place where I could sleep and spending the rest of my time walking the streets. I traveled to every corner of the city. By this point, I had lost track of all of my clothes and belongings that I had from the halfway house.

One day I decided to leave Hartford. I chose to head to Brooklyn, New York to once again connect with my father, father's girlfriend, brothers, and sister. I arrived outside a three-story red brick building on 6th Avenue in Brooklyn. I visited this home at different times during my childhood. No matter where life had taken me, I never forgot how to get back to this place.

I knocked on the window closest to the stairs. I remembered that is where my father and stepmother slept so I knew that eventually someone would come to the window and see me. I leaned over the railing again and knocked on the window. No one answered.

It was during the day so I thought my father may have been at work and my stepmother was in the kitchen area at the back of the house. It was impossible to hear someone knocking on the window from there, especially if the television or radio were on.

I looked over the railing and remembered that there were stairs leading to the basement access door. I walked down the stairs towards the door and remembered that as a child I would often spend time in that basement with my brothers. We played, laughed, slept, fought, dreamt, and talked about everything under the sun.

I banged on the door and finally, someone heard me. I heard a voice coming from the window above me. It was the voice of my father's girlfriend. I began to walk back up the stairs that were to the side of the main stairs but a portion of the stairs and landing was covered by the first floor of the house. It was like entering a castle door made out of bricks.

Once I came up the stairs my father's girlfriend saw me and said, "*Oh es Iran*" (oh, it's Iran). She walked away from the window and soon thereafter she unlocked and opened the door.

I stepped inside with uncertainty, nervous excitement, and happiness at the thought of seeing my brothers and sister. Perhaps this was a fresh start?

I was very much aware that my father would have expectations of me. He would be expecting that at this age I would be in school or have a job. I knew I had to share with them where I had been, what I was doing, and what I had done during the years I had not seen them.

He was very old-fashioned, strict, and demanded respect. It was expected that I ask for permission to speak. If I were in his presence, I could be seen but not heard. If adults were speaking it was expected that I would leave the room and I would always have to ask permission to do anything. There were no questions asked about anything he demanded or said. If you looked directly into his face, it was a sign of challenge, but if you didn't it was a sign of disrespect.

His pride and reputation in the community were more important than the truth. If you were accused of doing something wrong by anyone it meant a beating even if you said it was not true. Physical discipline was his first action. It was no one's business outside of the home. It did not matter how severe the beatings were. You must have deserved it.

I was allowed to stay with my dad, his girlfriend, and my siblings as long as I found a job or went to school.

I managed to land an overnight shift job at Century 21 Department Stores in Brooklyn. I was hired to work in the women's department on the overnight shift. Due to my lack of a high school diploma and criminal record, I was unable to get a job anywhere else.

I was just going through the motions in order to survive. Eventually, I lost my job due to not coming to work on time. I pretended for about a month I was at work so that I could be allowed to have a place to stay. I still left the house as if I was going to work. Late at night, I would walk out of the basement door that automatically locked behind me. Someone inside had to let me back in when I returned at five or six a.m.

I was not allowed to have a key. I was never told why. I believe that it was a message to me that this was a favor and that as soon as I was able to afford my own place or that I could leave, I should. I felt like an outsider. Once again, I felt ostracized. This continued to fuel my depression, anger, and desperation.

As I left each night, I wandered the streets, and I hung out at train stations and platforms to keep warm. Sometimes I would stay with people I had met while spending time in my neighborhood. They were mostly women I had managed to charm and use for the purpose of having a place to crash when I could.

While the train station platforms in the subways offered some reprieve from the streets it also exposed me to the dangers that existed in that underground world. Crews and individuals roamed the trains looking for potential targets to rob or to engage in conflict with people that were from different boroughs in Brooklyn.

When I slept on the trains I had to make sure it was not a deep sleep. Being able to feel and hear someone or others getting close to me was a matter of safety. At each stop the train made I would have to sit up and scan the faces and read the body language of anyone who entered the train.

During one of my trips underground to catch the D train to Coney Island I was suddenly summoned by a voice I did not recognize. I was filled with curiosity as I stepped down each stair on the path of the station's platform.

As I reached the bottom of the stairs I hunched over a little to get a better view of an upper stairwell wall that blocked my view of the full platform. I was able to find where the voice was coming from and immediately recognized my brother.

He says, "Smurf, we got beef!"

I began to run in his direction and never asked a question. I grew up being told that when someone who was family said they had beef or a problem with someone else I was not to ask questions. I simply was to back them up no matter what was happening.

I reached my brother who had one foot inside the train and one foot outside the train. He was pointing at a man I did not know and asking him, "What's up now?" He still wanted the conflict to happen because the tables had turned.

I made eye contact with the man and scanned the rest of him quickly to assess how I could engage him. I noticed that he was holding on to a thick steel chain that included a heavy steel lock at the end of it. It appeared as if he was using it to secure a bike onto a bike rack.

I stepped onto the train while my brother remained in between the train and the platform. By remaining there my brother ensured that the train doors could not close and therefore the train could not leave that station. I approached the man and put my hands up into a fighting position. I had no idea what was happening but I knew I had to protect my brother and teach this person a lesson.

He took a step back and began to swing the chain wildly toward me. I was able to avoid the chain and I timed one of his swings perfectly. I stepped in during his backswing and grabbed the chain with my left hand.

I pulled on the chain and this brought him closer to me. I began to beat his face with my right fist. One blow after the other. Finally, he released the chain. I was then able to step under him, pick him up, and guide him outside of the train doors. We both came crashing onto the platform. I mounted him, wrapped the bike chain with the lock around my right hand, and used it to land blows to his head and face.

I was releasing deep rage on this man's head. I wanted to crush his skull. The more I struck him the more enraged I became. He needed to suffer. It did not matter why. I was expected to protect my brother and I was doing so.

After some time I began to hear passengers yell at me to stop and my brother asking us to leave the station before the police arrived.

I slowly released my grip on this man and made my way onto my feet. I quickly glanced down at the man and noticed that he was in a fetal position and there were visible streaks of blood around his head. I stepped back, turned around, and ran towards the stairs leading to the street-level train station entrance. I made it outside still holding the bike chain and lock that was wrapped around my right hand. I stepped away in a different direction from my brother and never looked back.

I had fed the beast inside me. I had nurtured the addiction to violence and trauma I felt was my only way of being relevant, accepted, and loved. The feelings of loss, disappointment, uncertainty, fear, and depression were once again quieted for the moment.

This immediate relief did not solve any of my problems. I continued roaming the streets.

One night while I was just walking from one train station to the other, I ran into two guys that I knew from the neighborhood. One of them was from the Coney Island area of New York. Like me, they were just hanging around the train station. They invited me to join them on the train ride to Coney Island and to hang out.

I had a few dollars from the last check I cashed while working at the department store.

I decided to join them. What else did I have to do?

For a few weeks, our trio visited many of the boroughs and neighborhoods around New York. Although they lived with their families as I did, they preferred to be out all night hanging out around the city and then spend the days at home.

This worked for me because it would keep me busy at night while my family thought I was at work. I could be at home all day and no one would know I was not working.

It also worked for me because it gave me something to do. I was once again roaming the streets at night as I had done when I was homeless. This was something I could do without any hesitation. It felt familiar.

During the times that I would meet up with the guys, I was open to whatever they wanted to do. They knew the city well. We took many risks together to enjoy our time.

They introduced me to train hopping and surfing. We would get on a train, slip to the platform between train cars, climb up on top of the train when it reached a stop, and stay there while the train moved to the next stop. It was a thrill. It was dangerous and it made me feel free.

I did not have to focus on my troubles. I only focused on the adrenaline I felt, on keeping my balance, and on laughing with joy.

Spending time with them filled a void in my life. I felt as if they were becoming family. They desired my presence and appeared to truly care for me.

I needed that.

Eventually, my lies and propensity to find trouble caught up to me. By this point, the department store had sent a letter with a final check inside. The letter detailed my last day of work which had been weeks ago. The letter included other information that I could use for tax purposes now that I was no longer employed with the company.

I was caught.

I was scolded and given an ultimatum. Either find another job or leave. Go elsewhere.

I half listened. Having had experience roaming the streets, I felt that I could survive if I was asked to leave.

With free time on my hands and no options for employment available at that moment, I began to explore the streets around the Bay Ridge Brooklyn community where I was staying.

Around the corner from our house, there was a schoolyard where many of the local handball (or wallball) players hung out and competed in heated battles for the prize of a reputation as the baddest handball player in the neighborhood.

I would stop by from time to time and play a few games, and catch up with the guys who were waiting their turn or were simply there to take in the experience.

My interests went beyond the schoolyard. I wanted to see more. I wanted to learn about each block and check out who hung out on them. I was especially interested in the ladies who called those blocks home.

As my travels continued through the different blocks I noticed a young lady leaving her apartment building. I hurried to catch up to her before she made it down the flight of stairs of the building.

I said, "Hello," and introduced myself as Sepster, the street nickname my two friends I rode the train with named me. I realized that when I said that name she had a curious reaction.

I then said, "My name is Iran. How are you today?"

She responded that she was fine and that she was headed to 5th Avenue to buy something. I asked if I could walk with her and she responded, "Sure."

After walking to and from the store, I asked for her number and she handed me a piece of paper with her number written on it.

For the next month, we would talk over the phone and meet up outside of her building. On many occasions, we walked to Sunset Park, a local park in the middle of our community. I enjoyed spending time with her and felt as if I could get lost in our conversations and many times I forgot about the troubles I was having at home because I was not working or contributing anything financially at the house.

One evening I was escorting her home and we decided that we wanted to spend a little more time together. We turned down the block before hers and agreed to walk around the block and back up to hers.

Halfway down the block, our conversation was interrupted by some shouting and catcalling. I turned and looked to my left and noticed several guys standing outside and leaning on a car. They were making hand gestures and raising their arms up to their sides. I was not sure what they were shouting. We continued on our walk and eventually their voices faded away.

The following day I was walking towards her block and quickly glanced down the block where the guys had been standing outside the car. A few of the guys were there. I made a mental note of the group's tendency to hang out in that area. Once I met her outside the apartment building I mentioned that I saw some of the same guys from the previous day outside and we both agreed to avoid that area.

Less than a week later she and I were returning from having some dinner and were walking on 6th Avenue in Bay Ridge. A vehicle pulled up close to us and someone lowered the passenger window. He began to compliment the girl I was with and the other passengers in the car begin to chuckle and point towards me.

I watched them intensely and could feel my temperature rise. I felt disrespected. I started to tighten up all over my body and wanted to lash out with insults and caution them against disrespecting me.

The girl I was with was holding on to my arm and began to pull me away from the curb and asked me to walk away. She repeated, "Let's go, let's go." She yanked me harder and once again said, "Let's go." The driver parked the car and opened the driver-side door. He began asking me if I wanted to have a problem or if I had something I needed to say.

I held my tongue and followed my friend's lead. We walked away.

I realized at that moment that I had become a target of the group and that the attention they were giving my girlfriend was intended to anger and challenge me. I began asking around the community about the group of guys that hung out between 6th and 5th Avenue.

I learned that they were involved in high-level drug sales and distribution. The driver who had exited the vehicle and challenged me was the leader of the group. I was very familiar with individuals who were involved in that lifestyle based on my lived experiences in Hartford.

My mindset had to change from simply existing and enjoying my relationship with this girl to being on high alert and prepared to fight for my respect.

I refused to appear weak or be bullied by anyone. I did not care about their group's size, status, or reputation in the community.

I knew that inevitably our paths were sure to bring us face to face again.

My premonition was realized. As my girlfriend and I walked back to her apartment building via a completely different route, we were approached by two of the guys who had been standing at the corner of her block. We had not seen them there before. One of the guys moved closer to me and began to say that I owed them an apology for disrespecting them before.

I smiled and told him that I would not apologize. My girlfriend once again pulled me by my arm and asked that we leave.

As we began walking away the guys said, "Well, see you around soon."

I felt that threat pierce my skin. I wanted to turn around and engage them in a back-and-forth but I also thought that my girlfriend would be in danger.

I left her outside her apartment and began my walk back to my father's house. I flipped a switch in my head that allowed me to access the darkest parts of my being. I relied on that darkness to face any threat with absolute fearlessness and rage. I would not back down once I believed I was at risk of being hurt.

I was only able to make it two blocks before I noticed the car belonging to the group's leader parked alongside the street. I had to walk past the car in order to reach my father's home. As I got closer the car doors swung open and four men stepped out of the car. They began walking towards me aggressively asking me to apologize.

I did not respond and hoped to quickly walk past them. I was not successful.

The leader of the group extended his arm to grab me and I instantly responded by slamming my closed fist into his face. I quickly followed the first blow with a second blow. I felt his lips smack against my knuckles and against his nose. Blood gushed onto my arm and he began falling towards the ground. As he was falling I stepped through the gap created by him falling and began to run.

The other guys seemed shocked and stuck in place. They extended their arms to grab and lift up their leader off the floor.

I continued running until I arrived at my father's house. I remained in the house for a couple of days to avoid running into the group again. Remaining in seclusion did not work out well.

One afternoon my family approached me and asked me to sit down. They wanted to share something very important with me. I was informed that a few guys had come to the house looking for me and threatened to return with more guys if I did not come out of the house and pay the price for having punched their leader and disrespecting them.

My heart sank as I thought about the problem I had caused for the others in the family living in the house.

I shared the story of the girl, the encounters, and the fights. They expressed disappointment in me for not sharing the incidents before and for getting involved with that group.

I had to make the decision to leave the house. I snuck out one night and roamed the streets until I found a place to rest for one night. I managed to secure the necessary funds for a bus ticket.

Goodbye, Brooklyn.

16

RETREAT

I returned to the streets of Hartford that I called home. While walking up Oak Street on another dark and quiet night with nowhere to go I decided that I would check in with a guy I knew from the street. I was hoping that he would let me stay with him for the night.

There was no one else walking on Oak Street at the time except this woman who was on the same side of the street as me. As I got closer to her, I could see her veering a little towards me. I looked up to keep an eye on her. I had no idea who she was or why she was out on the street.

For one instant I thought she might be a street worker. The closer I got to her the more I realized she was just someone heading to a destination. She did not appear to be a threat to me.

As I was about to pass her, she said in Spanish, *"Con permiso, solamente te quiero decir que Dios me ha dicho que te pasara este mensaje. Tu tienes un llamado de Dios."* (Excuse me. I just wanted to tell you that God spoke to me and asked me to share a message with you. You have a calling from God.)

The homelessness and displacement continued for several weeks after this encounter. I continued surviving the best way that I knew how. I took on under-the-table jobs as a bouncer at local nightclubs, stripped for pay at bachelorette parties, helped people who needed to move furniture, and helped clean backyards.

This was not the first time I had turned to the streets and other activities to earn money. At the age of 13, I would join breakdancing crews and we would dance for money on the streets outside of the old G. Fox building in downtown Hartford. It was something I did along with some friends to make a few dollars. On some days it meant that was the only money I had to grab something to eat.

All of it allowed me to earn a little money without having to resort to selling drugs or other substances. I refused to allow myself to do that. Drug use hit close to home.

During this time of simply existing I did my best to blend in with the crowds of people from the community engaging in different activities. This included going to festivals in the community, parades through the neighborhood, and concerts at different venues. One way or another I even found my way to events in other cities.

My brother Smokey and I ended up at a concert that included the likes of Big Daddy Kane, Run DMC, and other legends of hip hop. This concert came to New Haven. We hitched a ride with a few of the guys from Hartford.

I believe that every person from Hartford headed to New Haven for the concert understood there was a possibility of a fight breaking out between the groups representing the two cities. The tension in the air felt as thick as a dense morning fog. The concession stands, the bathrooms, the hallways, the stairwells, and the foyer were packed with people from all over the state. The crews from Hartford and New Haven remained close to their members and were on the lookout for one another.

The music was blaring and the sound of people singing along to the music was deafening. I could barely hear the guys I had come with and the lights were dark enough that it was difficult to see where anyone else was. Only the people within a few seats from me were visible.

As the concert continued a shift in the energy and positions of the New Haven crew changed. It appeared they had collectively made a decision to surround our crew. We could see dozens of bodies making their way to us and climbing over the chairs of the concert venue. In seconds, they were directly in front of us. I could faintly make out several guys making hand gestures to each other in the crowd.

As the song being performed came to an end, the lights came on for a moment and in an instant, the fights began to fly.

A huge melee broke out.

Bodies were entangled in almost every row of the section we were in. We were surrounded and heavily outnumbered but we stuck together in a tight circle and fought them off as best we could. After several minutes of brawling, we began to feel the momentum turn in their favor. We began to lose the fight and started jumping over seats looking for a way to exit the venue's seating area and head towards the hallways.

As our group broke apart from each other, the New Haven crew began to smother and relentlessly kick and punch anyone they believed to be with our crew. I continued fighting alongside my brother and a couple of the guys who had given us a ride to the concert.

As we went to climb over another seat we saw that numerous members of the New Haven crew had made their way behind us. Some of them had broken off the armrests of the seats and were swinging them at us. I did my best to stand by my brother but I lost track of him.

I was able to locate him for a split second and noticed that he was wrestling with someone. The person managed to pick my brother up and slam him face-first into a guard rail. I noticed my brother's body wobble and I was filled with instant panic. I felt a rush of desperation through me. I was able to break away from the group that was surrounding us.

I made it to where my brother was. He was on one knee and holding on to the guard rail with one hand. I managed to pull him. I yelled at him that it was time to go. We began to run.

Several of the members of the New Haven crew chased after us.

We were able to push a door open and make it outside.

We have no idea where to go. We took off running on the street just looking for something familiar. There was nothing.

We continued heading toward where we saw a large gathering of cars at a traffic light. The concertgoers were leaving the area and there was a traffic jam heading towards the onramp to the highway.

My brother had his hand over his mouth and under his chin.

As we slowed our pace I asked him while trying to take a deep breath, "You alright Smoke?"

He removed his hands away from his mouth and tried to speak. He was not able to close his mouth shut.

He was in agony.

I asked, "Yo Smoke, is your tooth broken?" He could not respond with words. He grabbed his mouth again, held it tight, and grunted.

We continued walking for several blocks. We looked closely at every car that passed us by.

We were not sure if the people inside the car were from the New Haven crew, some other place, or from our home city of Hartford. At any moment we could be discovered by the crew from New Haven and we would most certainly sustain a serious beating.

As we arrived closer to the highway onramp we noticed a vehicle slow down as it moved toward us. The window of the car rolled down and to our fortune, the guys were from the Hartford area. They asked us if we were going to Hartford and we said yes.

We got into the car and off we went. The next day I discovered that Smokey had a fractured jaw.

The crew from New Haven had won the fight against us that night.

17

PEAS IN A POD

Between 1991 and 1992 I spent a lot more time in the same spaces as my brother. We were both wandering the streets of Hartford, mostly around the Frog Hollow section.

During a visit to Pope Park North aka Baby Pope Park in the South End of Hartford my brother was challenged to a fight by a couple of brothers who were members of the Devil's Disciples. This was a junior gang whose members were mostly young men ages 15 to early 20s. They were the youth faction of the Savage Nomads.

The Savage Nomads were an older, more well-established gang that primarily called the Frog Hollow section of Hartford home. Their gang color was red and they wore red bandanas either on their heads or they would hang them from their back pockets.

We were at the park to play handball. We had learned how to play the game at some point when we spent time in Brooklyn with our brothers.

One-wall handball, also known as 1-wall, wallball, or international fronton is an indirect style where the player hits a small rubber ball with their hand against a wall. The goal of the game is to score more points than the opponent. The player then hits the ball, and the ball bounces off the wall and the floor within court lines. If the opponent fails to return the ball, the player scores a point.

Since the park did not have a wall we were using the fence that wrapped around a tennis court in the park as our wall.

While we were playing with several other boys we noticed two guys walking towards the park. They were wearing red and black short-sleeved vests. On the front of the vests, we could see the letters DD embedded into the left front chest area of the vest. We knew what they represented from seeing other members of the Devil's Disciples in the community.

As they approached the fence to the tennis court one of the brothers called out Smokey's name. He said that Smokey was disrespecting them with some actions he had taken at another time that week.

We stopped the game.

Smokey said, "I did not disrespect you."

They thought differently.

They decided to come around the fence and onto the tennis court. They told Smokey that he would have to be dealt with. The energy turned from curiosity and conversation to threats against my brother.

I was not going to stand by quietly and allow them to hurt my brother. I began to feel anger and rage take me over.

Smokey was also responding with anger and rage. He decided that we would challenge them to hit him. He asked in an angry tone, "So what do you want to do? I knew that meant that he had reached the point of inflicting violence on them if they did not back down.

I jumped to my brother's side and we were now shoulder to shoulder. I could see that the two DDs were a little surprised that I would step in. It was not common for anyone to step in between them and their business.

One of the guys charged at my brother and the fight began. The other guy started to jump into the fight against my brother and I began to beat him with blows to the head and face. All four of us began fighting. Some of the other boys watched and some walked away for fear of being associated with having disrespected the Devil's Disciples.

We all ended up on the ground wrestling and dragging each other across the cement. We continued fighting until they felt they were no longer able to win or they felt defeated. We all had scratches and scrapes and were dirty and disheveled from rolling around on the floor.

We stood facing each other waiting for the next punch to be thrown. They started stepping back to walk away. As they were stepping back they said, "We are going to get you." They threatened us with retaliation.

My brother and I did not back down and responded that we would be around.

We never encountered them again.

After many months of bouncing between places to stay, I finally found a space with a family friend who my mom asked me to address as Padrino.

He offered me a place to stay in New Britain, Connecticut as long as I helped with chores around the house. I found myself moving around with him everywhere he went. I was happy to be in a somewhat stable setting.

One evening Padrino asked me to join him on a trip to John F. Kennedy Airport in New York to pick up some people who needed a ride from the airport to Connecticut. I agreed to go.

The trip to the airport was uneventful. We arrived and took our place in the very long line to the terminals. Once we arrived at our destination, we exited the car and went into the airport. This was pre-9/11. We had the ability to go right up to the gate for the airline and see the passengers of the flight as they exited through the tunnel at the gate.

Padrino greeted the family. I did not know them. We walked back to the car and everyone got in. I was still in the front passenger seat. The family of four sat in the back seat. There were three small children and a woman.

We exited the airport and made our way down Interstate 95 North headed toward Connecticut. The drive was full of conversation between Padrino and the woman in the back seat. They spoke in our native Spanish language and I sat there half listening since I did not know her and the conversation was not directed at me. I dozed off to sleep as they talked.

Suddenly I was in a fog. I felt somewhat awake but closer to sleep. I was no longer in the vehicle. I felt the ground under me and through a haze I saw what appeared to be lights flashing in the distance.

I heard a muffled voice near me and felt someone holding me. I felt hands on the top of my head but I was not sure if this was real or not. I was dazed and unable to gather myself. I passed out.

I am not sure how long it was before I woke up. I slowly come back to consciousness as my eyes adjusted. I realized I was in a hospital. By my side was a girl I had been dating and she was crying on my chest. She rested her head on me and sobbed.

I had no idea why I was there. *How did I get here? How did she get here? Why was she here? Am I dreaming?* As I slowly came to, I took a deep breath and felt the most severe stabbing pain I had ever experienced. My entire body felt as if I had been sliced with a razor and someone poured alcohol on each open wound.

I let out a grunt and she looked up from my chest. I do not remember her first words. I was still processing the pain that I was feeling. It was excruciating. I soon came to learn from her that I had been in a car accident. I learned that on our way back from the airport our vehicle had veered off the road, flipped over a guard rail, and fallen several feet down an embankment.

A nurse came into the room soon after I woke up and began to explain to me that I had been hurt in an accident. She asked me if I knew my name, birthdate, and what state I lived in. I responded correctly.

She then began checking my head and I realized that I was injured there. Slowly she began to unwrap a bandage that had been placed on my head. I was in great pain, still unable to breathe without feeling as if I was breaking into pieces.

Once she completely removed the bandage the girl I was dating gasped. Most of my head felt cold. This was strange to me because at the time I had a full head of long curly hair. She began to touch around and I could feel her fingers on my scalp. *What is going on here?* I thought.

The nurse grabbed a pan filled with a liquid and a rag. She begins to pat my head with the rag. When she pulled her hand back towards the pan to soak it, I saw the unmistakable color of blood.

I felt a sense of confusion and asked, "What happened?"

The nurse replied, "You have staples on your head that are helping to seal a wound you suffered during your accident."

I was in shock.

The nurse finished cleaning my head and face and said she would call the doctor to come in and speak with me.

As she walked out of the room, I looked into the eyes of the girl I was dating. She had tears flowing down her face. I asked her what was wrong. She said, "You have a lot of staples on your head and your head is shaved. Your hair is gone."

I felt devastated. I was hurt and extremely sad.

The doctor came in and explained all of the injuries I sustained in the accident. I had suffered a partial fracture of my skull, a torn left ear, a wound to my forehead, a broken collarbone, a slight fracture of the sternum, two broken upper ribs on my left side, and a sprained wrist.

This accident had been serious.

I asked about my friend and about the others in the car. The doctor explained that my friend had been released and that all of the others had been released too. Some had suffered serious injuries but had survived. I was the only victim of the accident still in the hospital.

The doctor explained that I would need rehabilitation in order to recover from the injuries to my chest, ribs, and shoulder areas. He also explained that the injury to my head was most likely to affect my ability to recall information in the short term. I had also suffered a concussion. This would mean days of headaches, blurry vision, and dizziness.

It would be a long road to recovery. My injuries made it hard for me to take a deep breath, carry anything, get out of the house, or do much of anything. I felt useless.

Eventually, my inability to help pay for bills where I was living or to offer any assistance with chores made it difficult for Padrino to let me stay. The time came when I was confronted with my lack of contribution around the house. I had no answer because I had not yet fully recovered from my injuries.

My brother Smokey also lived with us while he was working to save enough money to find a place of his own. He had managed to secure a job with a moving company and spent most of the day outside of the house helping to move homeowners to new locations all over the state.

It was decided that I needed to be with family members who would not mind giving me time to heal completely from my injuries. With nowhere else to go in Connecticut I ended up leaving the state and headed to Puerto Rico to live with my grandmother. Smokey provided me with the funds to purchase a one-way ticket to Puerto Rico.

Being in Puerto Rico for an unknown time was not what I ever imagined. Not having been there in a while I really had no clue how to navigate being there, what the expectations from my family would be, or what direction my life would take.

Jobito, the community in Villalba, Puerto Rico, was the polar opposite of the concrete and brick buildings that make up the city blocks of Hartford. Leading to Jobito are a series of winding, turning, elevating, and dropping roads hugging the green mountainsides where horses, cattle, chickens, and other farm animals would graze.

My grandmother's house was placed at a higher elevation. From her home, we could see the entire central part of the island. Looking at the mountains I felt as if they had no end.

It took me a while to acclimate myself to the surroundings. My style of dress, slang talk, and way of thinking seemed very strange to those in my family. I received many stares and looks whenever I walked out of my grandmother's house. I was a stranger who had grown up on the mainland and was not necessarily seen as one of the true, genuine Puerto Ricans.

Several weeks passed and I began to settle in and become familiar with the ways of the community. Most of the children and adults in the community were up very early and found ways to stay busy doing just about anything, from walking into town to purchase food or home goods, running and playing around the property, or working on cars to make sure they were in top shape.

By being in the calm and nurturing home of my grandmother for a few weeks I healed from my injuries.

I began to venture out to the center of town in the hopes of finding entertainment and other activities. Day in and day out I would head out and find myself befriending anyone that was willing to speak with me. I felt lonely without my community back in Hartford, even if that community was filled with uncertainty. It was normal to me.

In town, I found a small martial arts school that was actively recruiting students. I spoke Spanish well enough to stop in and ask questions about how I could become a member. I was allowed to join.

Every day I would head out and immerse myself in the martial arts training. The sensei began to ask that I improve my endurance and asked me to increase my cardio work. He suggested that I use the walk to and from the school as my opportunity to jog or run the entire time. I followed his advice and began to run to the school and back daily.

Unbeknownst to me, the locals had taken notice and assigned me a nickname, *"El karateca"* (the karate guy.)

One day while at my grandmother's house, I was informed that my brother Smokey was headed to Puerto Rico to spend some time visiting. I was super excited.I believed he would add some normalcy to my time in Puerto Rico.

My brother and I began to frequent the center of town. If there was activity happening of any kind, you would find us nearby.

While I was alone and simply keeping myself busy with martial arts and other isolated activities I found no trouble. Once I began spending time with my brother, my time at the dojo decreased and my time hanging out in different spaces in the center of town increased.

A space we frequented was the local high school. My brother and I had become the interest of several of the high school-aged girls and some of their older friends who would also stop by the school after classes let out.

The frequency of our visits to the outskirts of the school began to get us noticed by some of the local groups of boys and men who wondered who we were and what our story was. My brother and I were having too much fun to notice any threats coming our way.

During one of our many visits to the school, I found myself removed from my brother's side while I hung out with a few girls I had met and some of their friends. We had gathered at a local food stop that primarily served toasted ham and cheese sandwiches on sweet loaf bread, slushies filled with fruit juices, chips, and other snacks. The food stop played music and had only a few tables for customers to sit at. Most of the visitors ate their treats while standing outside the stop.

While engaged in conversation a bad feeling came over me. I felt a chill rush through me. The chill made me uneasy so I looked up from where I was seated and away from the girl I was talking to.

What I saw launched me to my feet. I did not see faces or hear any voice from where I was standing. I saw a large commotion and a tuft of hair swaying in the middle of the gathered crowd.

Immediately I knew it was my brother. Something was happening to him and I had to get to him. I began a desperate sprint toward the commotion.

Like the Flash, I raced past everyone on the path to my brother. They were blurry images of shadows.

As I began to get closer I could now see a path open up and I could hear, *"Mira, por ahi viene el karateca!"* (Hey look, here comes the karate man!)

Whoever was saying it understood that I had trained in martial arts and they were either warning those in the circle or simply announcing my arrival.

Once I was able to see into the circle I saw my brother in the middle of the circle engaged in a violent fight with two other people. His face was bloodied and he was trying to pull one of the guys off of him while the other person was throwing punches at him from behind.

There was no talking or second-guessing what I had to do. I was going to break these guys into pieces for hitting on my brother. I engaged the guy who was swinging wildly at my brother from behind and he immediately began to back up. I was able to land a couple of punches before he disappeared into the crowd that had gathered to watch the fight.

I then turned back toward where my brother was and noticed that he began to gain the upper hand after the other guy was no longer taking cheap shots.

His advantage did not last long.

I saw the crowd begin to move aside and noticed two other guys headed into the fight. I realized that reinforcements for the two guys fighting with us had arrived.

I thought quickly. I had to get Smokey out of there and get us to a safe space. He was beaten along the face and blood was still dripping down his face and onto his shirt.

I reached for him, grabbed him by his shirt, and yelled, "Come on, we have to go."

He followed my voice and I led him out of the circle. We ran down the street to the food stop where I had been before I noticed the commotion.

It was the only real place that I felt I could turn to. As the crowd that was standing outside of the food stop noticed we were headed toward them they scattered. The person working behind the register began to frantically wave us back.

I could hear him saying, *"Aqui no. Aqui no"* (Not here, not here.) He did not want us to bring trouble to the shop.

Before he could lock us out I was able to make it inside. He stepped in front of us and began to force the canopy-style cover down. He yelled at the guys chasing us that they could not come in. I could see over the employee's shoulder and noticed that one of the guys chasing us was carrying a knife. They were intent on winning against us and were determined to win by any means necessary.

We sheltered there for some time until other adults began to arrive and the group of guys left the area. I thought they did not want to be seen by anyone who would call the police on them.

I tended to my brother's injuries, thanked the person who sheltered us, and we carefully stepped out of the food stop.

We arrived at my grandmother's house and everyone visiting with her had already heard from others in the neighborhood that we had been involved in a fight near the school. She was furious.

She told us that we had started a fight with a group of brothers who had a reputation for fighting and other criminal behavior. She was concerned they would come to Jobito and cause trouble for the family.

We both apologized to my grandma and attempted to tell our side of the story. She wanted no part of that. She reprimanded us and warned us that if we started more trouble we would have to leave her house.

Our experience with these types of situations meant that we were most likely going to find trouble again. We had our first fight and word had spread that we were trouble markers. It would not be the last time we were involved in a fight together. That was eventually what led to us being asked to leave my grandmother's house.

My brother returned to Connecticut a few weeks after another violent altercation and I moved in with my uncle in a different community hoping to escape from the reputation we had developed.

A few months passed with no issues and I eventually saved up the resources to purchase a ticket back to Hartford. I was headed to that wild place I called home.

18

THE NEST

While I was in Puerto Rico my aunts connected me with my mom by phone and I was able to learn where she was living. My return to Hartford brought me back to living with her.

She secured an apartment on Lenox Street in the North End section of the city. At this point, my time spent with Mom was more based on need than on choice. I have to admit that she was doing her best to be a doting mom but we had not talked about my childhood. I was not focused on having that conversation and she appeared to be content with simply having a role in my life for however long it would last.

I wanted to head out to a familiar place to catch up with old acquaintances. The trek to Park Street from Lennox Street was a dangerous one, due to the conflict that existed between members of the Avenue crew or "the Ave" and those that represented the Park Street Posse. Although I was not a member of the Park Street Posse I spent time in their claimed neighborhood so it made me a member by association. I had no permission to be in the Albany Avenue section of Hartford. The fact that I was Puerto Rican made me a target anytime I stepped out of the house. Regardless of the risk of injury or death, I would still walk to the South End of Hartford on a daily basis. At the end of the day or late into the night, I would create ways to sneak back onto Albany Avenue and cross onto Lenox Street.

One night my luck ran out. I was confronted by several men who wanted to know what community I was from. My experiences had taught me that if I allowed them to get up close I would be assaulted before I could answer any questions they had. It was the way conflicts unfolded. It was a rule of the streets that many who were participants in the conflicts understood. I began to run toward the apartment building I shared with my mom.

I made it into the hallway and began calling for Mom to open the door. As she opened the door slightly a couple of the guys who had asked me questions pulled the entry door to the building open and began to walk toward me.

Mom pulled the door completely open and yelled at the guys. She was holding a kitchen knife in her hand. I was confident that she would not hesitate to use it.

The guys backed up a little and she slammed the door shut. She immediately began to ask me what the problem was with those guys. I explained that they did not like me because I was Puerto Rican and hung out on Park Street.

Mom asked me to stop testing my fate and to stop hanging out on Park Street. I was not ready to listen and shortly after the encounter with the guys on Lenox Street I took whatever I could carry and left that apartment with no real plan or place to go.

I wandered the streets and as the days and weeks passed I had less and less to carry. I would leave items at each place I was allowed to spend the night.

One evening I was desperate to find a place to rest and simply take care of my personal hygiene. I had a little change in my pocket to use a pay phone to call a friend I hung out with in Hartford but who lived in Meriden.

It was after midnight when I called. After several rings, he answered the phone. I told him that I needed a place to stay. He said that he would allow me to stay with him but that I had to find a way to get to his house.

I knew that at that time of the night, I would not find someone to drive me from Hartford to Meriden. I said, "Thank you. I'll be there in a little while." I hung up the phone and began the six-hour walk to Meriden. I made it there as the sun was coming up.

I knocked on the door, he let me in and I slept most of the day.

The South End of Hartford afforded me the most opportunity to run into many of the people I knew so I made sure to remain in that general area.

I made my way to the South Green section of the city. I found myself walking down Webster Street with no purpose.

At the corner of Queen Street and Webster Street, I saw a young boy standing by the entrance to a parking lot. I did not recognize him at first glance. I lowered my head and continued walking past this young boy.

As I continued on my walk with no destination I heard, "Smurf, hey Smurf. What's up?"

I turned and looked for where this voice was coming from. I noticed it was the young boy I had passed on my way down Webster Street. He said, "It's me, June June."

As soon as he said his nickname I remembered him. He was the son of a friend of my mom. I walked back towards him and said, "What's up June June? What are you doing here?"

He answered me while simultaneously pointing toward the building at the end of the parking lot.

"I live there," he says. "Me, Dad, my sister, and my dad's friend."

I knew his father as Padrino. His dad was one of the individuals that had been in the vehicle when we were involved in the accident. He asked me to come upstairs and say hello to his dad. I followed him into the parking lot and we made our way up the rear stairwell of the building. We arrived at the second floor and he opened the door. As we walked in he said, "Dad, look who is here."

His dad asked, "Who is here?

As I turn the corner from the kitchen area into the living room his dad says, "Oh hey Smurf, *como estas mijo?*" (How are you?)

I answer, "I am okay." He asks me to have a seat.

He asked, "What are you up to around this neighborhood?"

I shared that I was looking for a place to stay.

His eyes opened wide and he declared with a loud voice, "Well, *mijo* (a combination of *mi hijo*, which translates to my son) you can stay here with us. If you don't mind sleeping on the couch."

I was filled with joy.

I had no job and no prospects for finding employment so I spent the days and nights walking the streets and hanging out in different parts of the city. On one occasion I was roaming the streets I passed by a library on the corner of Campfield Avenue. As I passed the entrance I saw a familiar face exiting the library. It was my former girlfriend. The same girlfriend who I had been dating during the time I was involved in the car accident.

I said, "Hello, how are you?"

"I am good." She responded. "How long since you came back from Puerto Rico?"

"It's only been a little while."

We spent a few minutes catching up. I asked for her telephone number. She gave me her number and asked me to only call her during the middle of the day. After several conversations over the phone, we began dating again.

As with most relationships, we started off happy and in romantic bliss. We were not able to sustain that blissful relationship. I began to destroy that feeling and our relationship.

I had nothing going for me. She on the other hand was going to school and had a job.

My insecurity and lack of motivation allowed jealousy to creep into my thinking. I began to accuse her of cheating on me at school or at work. If I was unable to reach her at home or if she did not answer the phone I would explode with anger.

I felt as if I was once again losing control. She began to pull further and further away from me. I became consumed with making her respond favorably to me.

I proceeded to call her from different phones or from blocked numbers. I was obsessed with having control over her.

I refused to allow her to leave me.

Every minute I was not sleeping I spent it thinking of how I could charm or force her into wanting to be with me.

One evening I placed a call from a blocked number and she answered the phone. I had not heard her voice in more than a week. The tone of her voice was sweet and kind.

Initially, I was excited and my heart was pounding. I asked, "Hey, why haven't you been answering my calls?"

She calmly replied, "You are not being very good to me and I don't want to be with you anymore."

She confirmed my worst thoughts. I had spent over a week dreading the breakup and now I had lost her.

My body began to shake with fury. I began to yell at her. "You will not leave me. I will find you someday outside of your house and you will regret this."

She replied, "Don't do that. Do not come around my house anymore. My family is aware of what is happening and they will get involved if you come here."

I yelled, "I do not care. If they try to get in my way I will beat them up. I promise."

She replied, "You can try that but I just want you to leave me alone."

I punched the wall near where I was standing and yelled, "I am on my way, let's see if they can stop me."

I walked several blocks and arrived outside her family's house. With each step, I convinced myself that violence would have to be the answer to the situation. I was hoping to encounter someone who would allow me the opportunity to engage in a fight.

I welcomed violence. I would be able to lean on the one skill that I felt confident about.

I walked up the stairs to the front door of her family home. It was early in the evening and the sun was no longer shining.

I began to bang on the door. I was confident that I have the upper hand once I was able to gain access to the inside of the house.

I continuously pounded my fists against the door. At one point I listened for any sounds coming from the inside.

I began to hear the lock on the door click as if someone was switching the lock into the open position.

I prepared myself for a physical encounter with whoever was on the other side of the door.

The door swung open. No one was standing there.

I was blinded by rage and did not process the fact that no one greeted me. I stepped inside.

I was blinded by a bright light aimed at my face. A series of very loud voices pierced the silence. I was confused and unsure of what was happening.

I felt as if someone was pulling on me from different directions. I began to resist whoever was pulling me.

The voices became a little louder and clear. "Hartford Police!!!"

"Get on the ground!!! Get on the ground!!!"

The light was no longer blinding and I could see several officers grabbing me and attempting to wrestle me to the ground.

Another officer approached me from behind and pulled me down to the ground.

I had been set up.

My ignorance, arrogance, and blinding rage did not allow me to think of any resistance that could stop me. Even if someone was waiting for me with a weapon, I did not care. I was prepared to die if it meant that I would get my way.

I was rushed outside of the home and pushed up against a waiting police car.

My adrenaline began to slow and I was now able to realize what had happened. I felt stupid. My pride was injured.

An officer began to search me for weapons, anything I had on my person that could injure them, and anything illegal that could lead to additional charges.

While the officer searched me another officer exited the house and hastily made his way toward me.

He walked right up to my face and asked me, "You think you are a tough guy? Picking on a woman! Pick on me! C'mon, tough guy!"

I began to smile.

He asked, "What the hell is so funny? You think this is funny?"

I said nothing. I only smiled. My silence and continued smiling enraged the officer.

I often smiled when I was threatened or triggered by a violent response. It was automatic for me. I was not afraid.

Suffering a beating or being threatened was something that I was accustomed to. The officer fed into the darkest parts of my soul.

I didn't have to focus on what I had done wrong when my mind was focused on a response to his threats.

As the officer became increasingly angry, he looked away toward other officers. He then turned his attention back to me. He stepped directly in front of me and leaned closer to my face.

He says, "Okay tough guy. Would you be so tough if I took you to the Connecticut River and threw you in?" I still refused to respond with words. I simply looked him directly in the face.

He then grabbed my shirt in a rough manner, opened the door to the police car, and shoved me into the back seat.

As I sat waiting to be driven to either the river or to the police station for booking I began to cry quietly.

I was handcuffed and had no way of controlling what happened next. I had calmed down and realized that this separation from this girl was real. I had lost again and I was responsible.

19

THE GANG

I was back at the Meadows, a jail I had been held at before. This time I was considered a man. I was no longer a teenager needing support or considered troubled. There were no "youth at risk" labels or youthful offender programs for me. I would not be afforded any of those considerations. I was like any other inmate or criminal who had committed a crime and had to be held accountable.

I was quickly processed and escorted to the dorms. I was familiar with what to expect. I assumed the role. I scoped out each bunk I passed on my way to where I would spend my time until my case was resolved by the court.

While I had been roaming the streets I would hear conversations regarding neighborhood conflicts between street crews. I learned that national gangs had started to claim city blocks in Hartford as their turf. I was not very involved in the conflicts at that time but I did pay attention to what was happening.

It was a matter of survival to know.

As the days blended into each other inside the Meadows I noticed that in the dorms I was in, large groups of men were congregating daily at specific bunks. These men spent the day together talking. They would walk in line together for breakfast, lunch, dinner, and recreation time. I noticed that one person, in particular, was always leading the group and appeared to have all of the influence over the group.

One morning I was sitting on the top bunk that was assigned to me and was approached by one of the men from the group I had seen regularly together. I had not had any visits. I had no money for the commissary, the internal store where inmates could purchase items not provided by the Department of Corrections, so I had no extra items for personal hygiene.

The group or someone in the group was paying attention to my daily activities.

The person who approached me asked, "Where are you from?"

I responded, "Hartford."

He nodded his head in recognition of my answer.

He then asked, "Do you need anything such as slippers, shaving cream, snacks, or clothes?"

I responded, "It would be cool to have those things."

"Wait right there. I'll be back." He stepped away.

At this point, I hadn't talked much to anyone. I kept to myself.

He returned with shower slippers, face towels, and a towel stuffed with assorted snacks. I hopped off the top bunk and said, "Thank you."

As he walked away he said, "Let me know if you need anything else."

I was grateful to have something else to eat and other items to make the time I was spending there a little easier.

A couple of days later the man returned to speak with me. He asked me, "Do you have family out there?" He was referring to the outside, beyond the jail walls.

I said, "Yes, but they are not around here."

He said, "I noticed you have not had a visitor."

I replied, "No, I do not have anyone who would take the time to visit me."

He said, "We have a family here that can offer you some support."

I listened with interest. Having an adult male mention that he was willing to care for me and offer me a family support system was way out of the ordinary for me.

I longed for belonging. I longed for love. I longed for relevance. I longed for togetherness. I longed for purpose. I longed for partnership. I longed to exist for others and to feel safe.

I thought maybe this could provide me with these things.

After speaking with me for several minutes he asked me to take a walk with him to the bunk where the other men were.

I learned after meeting the others that they were all members of an inner-city gang. I spent some time with them and learned where they were all from and what they were in jail for. They mentioned that I could chill with them by the bunk when I saw them there.

I went back to my bunk and waited for time to tick by. I could not see the outside from the dorm. It was hard to keep track of the time of the day.

As I was lying in bed staring into the space above me I felt a tap at the foot of the mattress. It was one of the guys from the group. He said they needed to speak with me. I jumped off the bunk and followed him to where the group was gathered.

Upon my arrival, the members of the group turned toward me and greeted me. The tone quickly changed from simple greetings to a serious tone that I knew from having lived a life surrounded by and involved in conflict.

I was pulled aside by two of the members of the group. They mentioned that they believe in respect and protecting that respect. Having anyone violate their group, disrespect their group, or dishonor their group meant immediate consequences.

The two men explained that someone in the dorm had violated one of their members by disrespecting them while they were waiting to eat in the lunch line. They explained that I could be in their favor if I disciplined the individual who had disrespected them.

I felt as if I wanted to ask many questions to understand better but I knew that asking many questions could be seen as fear or disrespect. We were not taught to ask questions, we were taught to believe the disrespect happened and to immediately turn to violence as the solution. On the streets, we fought and many died protecting what they felt was a direct threat to how respected they were by others.

They stated that I was chosen to handle the situation.

In my head, I thought, *What? Why me? How am I going to do this and not get caught by the corrections officers monitoring us? If I refuse, does this guarantee that I will become a target?*

Since they had shared their plans with me, I was sure that there was also a plan to deal with me if I refused.

I felt as if I needed to be a part of something to have a support network. Using my violent tendencies to gain entry into a group that I could call brothers appealed to me.

Shortly after speaking with them, I nodded my head yes. They explained where I could find the person and that I should discipline him after the evening count.

Every day at different times of the day the corrections officers would have to count the number of prisoners to ensure that no one was missing and to also take a quick look at each prisoner to determine if they were well or if they noticed anything in where prisoners were that was a violation of jail rules.

I was provided the weapon that I would use to punish the person who had disrespected the group. The weapon was made of two socks stuffed into each other with several very hard bars of soap inside the socks. The socks were wrapped tight. They felt as if I was holding a rope instead of a pair of socks.

After the count, I took a look over at the bunk where the men would congregate and received a nod from the leader of the group. That was my cue to complete the mission.

I stepped out of my bunk area and headed straight to the bunk where the person who had violated the group's rule was. He was on the top bunk.

He did not see me approaching. I grabbed him by the sweater he was wearing, pulled him off the bunk, and slammed him onto the hard concrete floor. I began pummeling him on his face with the weapon.

I used the other hand to punch him and to keep him on the ground. I beat him until he was bloodied.

Once I felt he had been punished severely enough I stepped out onto the path that led back to my bunk, tossed the bloody sock under another bunk as I was instructed to do, and returned to my bunk.

My heart was beating so hard I felt it was going to split my chest open and fall out of me. I was sweating and sore from punching this man. I had also missed a few punches to his face and struck the cement floor. I was lying on the bunk thinking, *Someone saw me and was going to tell on me. Someone is coming to get me for that. I was going to be taken to solitary confinement for violating the rules. What now?*

After what seemed like forever one of the guys from the group came over to me and said, "You are all set. It's done."

I was surprised that there was no other action towards me. In jail, there are many instances when assaults happen to prisoners and are never reported.

The final count of the evening was completed and I never heard anything else about this assault. There were no consequences for me.

I did not sleep much that night wondering about what was going to happen next.

During the morning walk to breakfast, I walked alongside one of the group members and there was no mention of what happened the night before. It felt as if nothing ever happened.

There was no embracing me, congratulating me, or any type of celebration of it. I was still the same jailed man.

There was no change in influence, title, or status. Nothing.

Several days later while on my way to the bathroom, I was approached by another member of the group. He stated that I needed to see a guy named "T." T needed to speak with me and would be waiting by the usual place where they met.

After finishing up in the bathroom I headed to see T.

This person was very muscular. He resembled Iron Mike Tyson. Almost identical in build and size.

He knew who I was but I had never met him. T began to tell me a little more about the group he was a member of. He mentioned that they were looking to increase their membership and wanted to know if I was interested in becoming an official member of the group.

I responded that I was interested. I had spent time with members of the group during my time inside the dorms so I felt as if I knew a couple of them well enough to join them.

He mentioned that I would have to meet them at a specific time in one of the bathrooms and be bounced in.

A bounce is a beating handed out to incoming members by two or more current members. The beating is administered for a predetermined period of time by the person in charge of the group.

The members to participate are chosen based on a comparison of the person being bounced in. If that person is five feet 10 inches tall and weighs 190 pounds the members who will inflict the beating will be approximately the same size, weight, and build as the person being bounced.

He explained that after the bounce it would be determined if I could be a member or earn my colors. That is another term for being given the right to wear the colors members of the group wore as a sign of membership. These colors were red and blue.

I met several of the members in the bathrooms nearest our side of the dorms. Correction officers were not allowed to view the bathroom through cameras. As long as they were seated in their offices and watching from there, most anything could happen in the bathrooms.

One of the members turned his back to face the opening that led into the bathroom. His role was to watch for the corrections officers or anyone else who might enter the bathroom. Two other members were standing across from one another looking at me. T was standing nearest to the member guarding the entry to the bathroom.

T requested that I stand in between the two other members. I followed his request.

I was then told by T that I would receive a three-minute bounce to become a temporary member. This was similar to an apprentice who would need to prove himself in order to become a full-fledged member.

I was not sure what to expect but my desire to be considered part of this group and exist to someone was great.

T said, "Go."

Immediately the two men began to drill me with punches to my back, arms, ribs, stomach, thighs, butt, chest, and everywhere they could with the exception of my face, throat, and crotch.

Initially, the first blow surprised me and I had an automatic response. I stepped to the side as if I was standing in a fighting position to defend myself. I could tell by their looks that this was not acceptable.

I had to remain there for three minutes and receive blows without responding with punches of my own.

It felt much like when I was little and was beaten by my parents. It was expected that you would receive the blows without retaliating or covering up.

After several blows my feelings went from surprise to thinking about how best to move to avoid as many of their blows from landing squarely on my ribs or stomach.

The pain began to worsen. With each blow, I could feel as if my muscles were softening and their knuckles dug deeper into my bones. The punches to the stomach region felt the worst.

I felt as if I wanted to vomit and several times I felt as if my ability to breathe was being limited. I became lightheaded and dizzy but I refused to fall. I began to push out as much air as I could when I felt a deep blow, hoping that by breathing out I could reduce the pain.

Punch after punch I was hoping it would end soon. One of the members began to focus his blows on my thighs and my legs began to buckle. My arms began to fall away from my body as I looked to place them near my thighs to perhaps absorb some of the blows on my forearms.

Suddenly I felt a devastating blow to my lower back near my kidney area. I felt as if it lifted me up and backward.

T had joined the bounce and I was now being beaten by three members. Each time T would hit me I felt his power. I was convinced he was breaking bones and that I would be bleeding internally.

Several more blows and suddenly it was over. I was still bracing for more blows when everyone stepped back. I felt as if my entire body was swollen and battered.

The two men who had been beating me the longest were asked to stand aside and T addressed me as I remained standing there with tears rolling down my face.

I was crying tears of pain and anger. After I was able to defend myself, I made a promise that I would never allow anyone to abuse me physically or sexually again.

I had failed. I desired a family so much that I allowed myself to be tortured to belong to one.

T said, "Okay brother, you are now a temporary member." He reached out his hands and gave the group a salute of two fists banging over each other with the left over the right.

The other guys gave me the salute and left the bathroom along with the lookout.

T said, "See you later brother," and walked away.

I remained there for several more minutes unable to move my legs due to the pain I was feeling on my thighs.

My entire body was in pain.

I managed to walk to my bunk but could not climb up to the top bunk. I managed to get myself onto the floor and remained there for a while.

When the count was announced I had to stand and I felt as if I was moving in slow motion. My bones and muscles felt as if they were going to rip off. I managed to get up. The corrections officer completed his count. I remained standing.

Some minutes later the CO returned to my bunk area and requested that I head over to his station.

I followed him there and he asked me to see the other officer at the office window. I announced myself to the other officer and he handed me a pass to see a counselor.

Right at that moment I remember thinking, *What is going on? What do they know?* As I made my way to the counselor's office I continued to feel the debilitating pain from the bounce.

The session with the counselor was not associated with the bounce or anything related to the group. They wanted to see me to discuss my needs, court date, and other personal information.

I used the opportunity to request pain medication and the counselor requested that I be sent to the medics office. I was allowed to visit with the medic where I complained about leg pain. I was given two Tylenol and sent back to the dorms.

When I returned to the unit I noticed several members staring at me. I walked past them and they asked if I was okay. They were not concerned about my injuries. They were asking if I had said anything about the beating.

I said, "No."

They responded with, "That's good."

I spent the next few weeks with the group and simply carried on with the daily routine of being in jail. Meal times, watching TV, playing cards, having conversations, laying in bed listening to others talk on other bunks, or getting lost in thought while staring at the ceiling.

Finally, my day arrived for my release. The brothers gave me hugs and asked me to check in with the other brothers on the street.

I replied, "Okay, I will."

20

Apprentice

I was escorted to processing and set free through the side entrance of the jail. It let out onto Meadows Street. I was out again. My return to the streets from jail felt different this time. I was a member of a gang that I considered a family. I had promised to check in with the leadership outside of the jail. I was expected to report to them and declare my membership.

If I failed to report I would be considered a deserter and would suffer the ultimate punishment which could include a severe beating that could lead to death.

Regardless of the violence that had been unleashed on me to join and what could happen to me if I were to ever be accused of disrespect towards the gang I wanted this family. I needed this family.

Once again I returned to stay where I was staying prior to my arrest. The apartment building was located between Campfield Avenue and Webster Street.

This community was claimed by the national gang as their turf. I was a member of a different gang. At this time there was no war or major conflict between the two gangs so living there was not a problem. I was not in any danger.

I did not check in right away. I was doing my best to settle in after being in jail for several months.

I went out into different communities across the South End of the city to hang out.

While spending time throughout different communities in Hartford I ran into a lady friend I had known for a little while. We spent some weeks together and I ended up getting her pregnant. I would eventually marry her in a ceremony that included a celebration with hundreds of members of the gang I joined.

There was a different energy in each neighborhood I visited. The communities felt fragmented and divided. As I walked north on Webster Street towards New Britain Avenue I could not avoid seeing the groups of men at almost every block wearing black and yellow or gold-colored beaded necklaces. I also saw them on men who drove by me in cars or motorcycles or even peddled by me on bicycles.

Everyone saluted one another with a hand sign from a distance or with a physical handshake that was specific to the group. In my head, I compared it to a major community block party where everyone was celebrating a culture or pride for a specific race or nationality. Everyone wore the same colors.

As I made my way to the Frog Hollow section of the city colors went from black and yellow to red and blue.

I stopped at the corner of Washington Street and Park Street. While I was at that corner I felt the same energy I had just felt in the South End. The only difference was the colors I was seeing.

Red and blue everywhere.

It was clear that I had arrived at the local gang's claimed turf.

As I remained on the corner simply taking in all the sights and sounds I noticed that I knew many of the individuals riding or walking by who were wearing the red and blue beads or clothing.

I had never seen the city like this. Everyone was representing one of the two groups.

Prior to this, every block in the neighborhood had a crew that mostly covered or claimed that block.

These groups seemed much larger and more organized.

I spent the next two weeks roaming the streets and returning to the apartment late in the day. With each passing day, I was learning what was happening in the community and exactly what areas were claimed by each gang. I decided that I needed to go check in.

I learned through members of the local gang that I knew as friends prior to their becoming members that the gang frequently congregated outside an apartment building on the corner of Park and Zion Streets.

That apartment building was known as the headquarters of the main chapter of the local gang. I was to arrive at that building and report to the members there.

I arrived outside of the building and was immediately met by a member wearing red and blue beads.

He asked me, "What do you need bro?"

I responded that I was reporting in and that I had received my colors while at the Meadows.

He asked me who approved my joining and I responded with, "T."

He guided me into the apartment building hallway and instructed me on the next steps I had to follow in order to be considered an official member. He said that on the weekend they would be meeting at a local park and that I was expected to attend the meeting to be welcomed in.

I responded that I would be there. He then gave me the group salute and I walked out of the building and back onto the street.

That weekend I attended the meeting at the park. I was shocked by the amount of men that were gathered at the park for the meeting. I had never witnessed anything like this.

There appeared to be close to two thousand people. I could only compare it to when a high school let out at the end of the day and students spilled onto the streets.

The group was called to attention by a member who everyone immediately responded to. They formed a huge circle while standing shoulder to shoulder two to three rows deep.

I was asked to stand at the front of the first row of the circles. I was absorbing the experience and simply following the steps of other members I saw. I had no idea what was expected of me or what I was supposed to do.

The meeting was called to order by several of the members who were inside the circle. These members walked within the circle and observed the group. Once everyone was accounted for and the men in the middle of the circle had everyone's attention they asked everyone to bow their heads and repeat after them.

They recited a prayer and similar to a church service everyone repeated the prayer. Once the prayer was completed the meeting began.

The first order of business was new membership. I was not the only person reporting in. There were other new members who had been in other prisons or jails across the state and were reporting in. There were also new members that were being presented for consideration by current members out on the street.

It was my turn to be presented to the group. The member who had met me at headquarters spoke on my behalf. He shared with the full group that I had been granted my colors while at the Meadows.

I remained silent.

I was curious as to what would happen next.

The member who presented me to the group began to ask the larger group if they had any objections to having me become a member or if anyone had any reason to remove me from consideration.

I was shocked.

I was not aware that this was part of the process and that the risk of being dismissed existed. I had taken the beating and had also completed all of the asks from the group at the Meadows.

No one objected and I breathed a sigh of relief. I was starting to shake nervously wondering if attending this meeting would lead to a severe beating and dismissal from the group due to the acceptance of an objection.

The likelihood of being permanently disfigured or killed was high. With so many members present the beating would include as many as the leadership appointed to hand it out.

The question, "Does anyone object to having this person become a member?" was asked again.

I once again took a deep breath. My heart felt as if it was skipping beats with each second of silence.

No one objected.

I was glad it was over.

I started to feel better when suddenly a second question was asked of the group.

"Does anyone have any beef with this person and would like to express that at this time?"

Once again my heart rate shot up.

I scanned the portion of the circle so that I could see any faces that I was familiar with. Was there someone in that circle that I had a confrontation with before that was not settled or they felt they needed to mention?

The member presenting me for consideration to the group placed his arm around my shoulder and began to turn me around.

He was making sure that the entire group had an opportunity to see my face and determine if I was someone they needed to resolve a beef with.

I waited with bated breath as the seconds crawled by.

I'd been involved in many conflicts and fights in all of the communities in the city and with so many members in the circle I was sure someone present would raise their hand to claim they had an unresolved beef with me.

As I completed the turn someone called out, "I do."

I heard the voice but it was not familiar to me. The person stepped out from the second row and to the front of the circle.

I now recognized the person.

Over a year before I had been working for a drug dealer as his hired security and bodyguard. I was hired because I had proven myself to this person as a friend in the past when he was faced with a threat and I intervened to stop the threat. I informed the person threatening him that I would hurt them if they attempted to challenge or do anything to him. I had a reputation in some circles for not backing down and being willing to take on anyone.

This person had stepped out of the circle to confront me about our conflict.

I remembered when, where, and why we had come to engage in a violent confrontation.

One evening during a regular trip to the trap house (drug house) where the drugs and money were stashed I was in the passenger seat with the dealer. He pulled the car right up to the apartment door.

He walked into the apartment to retrieve what he had stopped in for. I was scanning the parking lot to make sure that there was no one hiding or waiting in a vehicle to ambush us or rob us.

The dealer stepped out of the apartment. I noticed a vehicle behind us parked on the side of the road suddenly turn into the driveway of the apartment building. It was dark out and the vehicle's headlights were not turned on.

It was a hit or robbery.

I opened the passenger car door and stepped out as the vehicle was speeding towards us.

I retrieved the firearm I had on me from my waist and yelled at the dealer that someone was coming for us. He ducked back into the hallway of the apartment building.

The vehicle accelerated and began to veer toward the car we were in.

I aimed.

Pow Pow Pow Pow!

I squeezed the trigger, over and over. The vehicle continued barrelling towards me. After the fifth round was fired the vehicle began to swerve and lose control.

The driver ducked.

I could no longer see much of the person in the car.

I then recognized the vehicle. It belonged to someone in the neighborhood we were from in Hartford.

The vehicle regained control as it accelerated again and continued at a high rate of speed out of the exit driveway of the apartment complex.

The smoke from the gunfire was still lingering in the air around the car we were in.

The dealer ran out to check on me and to make sure to get the hell out of the driveway and away from the apartment building.

We were sure the police would be on their way and if we were located there, they would most likely find the gun I had and that would lead to the discovery of the stash in the apartment, and we would spend many years in prison.

It was time to go.

We left the area and made sure no one was following us. The stash house had been discovered.

This member mentioned that I had fired upon him during an incident and that he wanted to know if I still harbored anger toward him. He was asked to directly address me.

He asked, "Smurf, we still have beef?"

I responded that I did not have beef with him.

He responded, "Then I don't have beef with you."

I made it past the questioning period.

I believed that I was in the clear.

The leadership gathered together. When they emerged from their private conversation they requested that I be bounced in again.

My heart felt as if it shattered into a million pieces. All of this time I believed I had a new family. I was secure and a part of something. I learned right there, live and in person, that was not the case.

My heartache turned into deep anxiety and anger over the fact that I had to once again be subjected to a beating to earn the right to be a member.

As it happened when I was in the Meadows, two members of the group matching my height, weight, and build were selected from the circle and asked to step into the middle of the circle.

One of the members in the circle held a watch in his hand. The leadership mentioned that we had three minutes for the bounce.

This time I could fight back. I was allowed to defend myself. I did not feel any better hearing that.

I felt as if I had been through it before and did not deserve to go through this again.

The member with the watch said go.

We all began to throw blows at each other with the intensity of someone fighting for their life.

We were all trying our best to win. We had to be willing to inflict as much pain on one another as possible to make it to the three-minute mark and still be standing.

Anything less than that meant that we would be punished further by the leadership. We would be bounced separately again if we lost.

Blow after blow, blood dripping from my nose and from having my lips busted open from several blows to my face.

There was no time to worry about any of that. Survival was the goal. Time was called.

I survived.

The two members gave me the group's handshake, a hug, and the circle erupted in a chant welcoming me into the gang. Beaten and bruised, the chant and acceptance felt like a temporary numbing agent.

I could not feel it. I was filled with pride and a feeling of achievement. More than that I now felt as if I had a family. I mattered.

From this point on I could wear the group's colors openly as an indication and statement that I was a full-fledged member to anyone outside of the gang or in other gangs.

After joining the gang I returned to my apartment. I was pretty bruised up and immediately caught the attention of my mother's friend who I was living with.

He asked me, "What happened to you?"

I shared with him that I had joined a local gang.

He took a deep breath and asked, "Why did you do that?"

I explained to him that I had joined while in jail and that today by going to the meeting I had made it official.

He advised me to be careful.

21

— . —

WAR

The relationship between the national gang and the local one was friendly at first. There were no major conflicts or misunderstandings. It was common to find members of each group at the same parties, clubs, stores, restaurants, community events, and city blocks.

The Peace among the groups would not last.

In 1993 after several years of being able to live and play within the neighborhoods war was declared between the two major city gangs. From that time on the violence in the capital city increased substantially and no one was immune to it.

As the violence intensified I continued living at the apartment building on Webster Street and Campfield Avenue. That area was declared the national gang's territory but was not a hangout for many of their members. I was able to get in and out of that area without detection easily.

That all changed when a salon next to the apartment building changed ownership and became a barbershop. As members of the national gang began stopping in to receive haircuts I could see from the apartment window that the volume of visitors increased.

This began to compromise my safety and the safety of those who shared the apartment with me.

On several occasions, the members of the national gang caught a glimpse of me headed out of the apartment and into a waiting car. They would immediately start moving quickly towards the vehicle making comments and displaying their gang's hand signs.

My mother's friend was paying attention to all of the chaos happening in the city and eventually asked me to leave. He had two young children in the apartment and did not want anything to happen to them.

I managed to get out without being seen and once again began searching for somewhere to live.

Now that I was wearing the colors of the gang every minute of the day and night, it became more and more difficult to find anyone who would let me stay with them. No one wanted to risk their lives or the lives of those who lived with them to allow me a place to stay.

I bounced from place to place once again leaving belongings scattered at different locations.

I found another friend of a friend who gave me a place to stay. He mentioned it would only be temporary until I found something else. This reprieve allowed me to develop a plan for what I was going to do next.

This block of the city where I was staying was pretty neutral. It was composed of working families and schools. The apartment I lived in was nearest to the local gang's turf. The block was mostly made up of school-aged children and working parents. There was not much to do there or many people congregated on the block. I was relatively safe there in that quiet building.

For several days I remained in the house. I assisted with taking out the trash to the rear of the building and with chores inside the house. I slept on the couch in the living room and had a dedicated closet for my belongings.

The renter of the apartment asked me to begin a job search so that I could help with the bills around the house. I was able to secure a job working for an apartment maintenance company on Washington Street in Hartford. The apartment building was in the middle of two adjoining blocks that were evenly claimed by both gangs. I was able to earn some money and help out around the apartment. Everything was going well.

The streets on the other hand had erupted in violence. At any time of the day, the firing of gunshots was heard.

Those shots were closely followed by police, medical, and fire responding to either investigate, help the injured, declare the deceased, or clean up the blood left behind.

The police had their hands full as they did what they could to reduce the incidents of violence and crime that were taking place.

The City of Hartford leadership identified and formed a task force to investigate, arrest and deter members of the gang from engaging in acts of violence.

This task force was allowed to use any and all tactics to bring the gang violence and chaos to an end.

After joining the local gang I began to frequent the Park Street area. On one occasion while I was walking near the corner of Park Street and Putnam Street an unmarked police car crossed from the opposite lane of traffic from where I was walking, jumped the curb, and opened its doors.

Out of that vehicle stepped several members of the task force. They immediately surrounded me and began to ask me for my name and to search my pockets.

One of the task force members says out loud, "We've never seen you before. Where are you from? What is your name?"

I responded, "I am from Hartford and my name is Smurf."

He responds back, "Oh, okay. I've not seen you around here."

As they continued checking my pockets and clothing for what I may have on my person they began to say that I was going to be seeing them a lot.

I remained quiet. When they were done searching me, they asked me to remain still. One of them pulled out a Polaroid instant camera and snapped a photo of me. They all turned around and headed toward their vehicle. Before they sped off one of them yelled, "Thank you for the information Smurf."

This was their way of falsely sharing with other members of the local gang watching that I was snitching or providing information to them about the gang.

If the members believed them it could lead to my termination or death. Luckily for me, they did not and they brushed it off as a known tactic the task force would use to break the loyalty code and trust between members of the gang.

When I was at the apartment I often thought about the war happening outside. I remembered how many of the members from each gang had friendly relationships that in some instances dated back to elementary school.

There were members of the same family that ended up choosing different sides and now had to fight against one another or take the ultimate action and kill a member of their own family.

This war escalated quickly across the entire state.

To make matters worse, a second and third conflict began between the four major gangs in the city. There were no longer any parts of the city that were considered safe spots or neutral territory.

The chaos became uncontrolled.

Meetings, gatherings, and social events had to be moved regularly as a precaution to gunfire erupting due to the ongoing war.

In one instance a gang meeting was called inside a local gambling hall. The place was small. It was about a 1,000-square-foot box.

As the conversations were happening between members of the gang, gunfire erupted outside. Tires screech and a car comes to a full stop outside the pool hall doors.

Bang, bang, bang, bang, bang. Round after round was being fired into the door.

Bullets began whizzing past the heads of those inside. Everyone scrambled to cover under tables and chairs, others ran towards the back exit and towards the bathrooms. When the gunfire stopped the car revved up and sped away.

Miraculously no one was shot. The fear inside the pool hall turned into anger and immediate retaliation was called for.

Shootings took place inside pool halls, outside of barber shops, inside the foyer of the local jail, and outside the courthouse as members of each gang were reporting to the court to be arraigned on different gang-related criminal charges.

Each day and night was a miracle for anyone that survived. Childhood friends, former pee wee league teammates, dance team members, football team members, and family members were openly hunting each other.

Violence, pain, despair, uncertainty, fear, sorrow, heartbreak, loneliness, incarceration, and death were the main course again. Many of us had been prepared by
our life experiences for this very moment. I knew no other existence.

My involvement in the gang, regardless of the reasons, led to federal racketeering charges. I was back in cuffs, back in a cell, back in the meat wagon, back in
court, and back to serving time. 18 Months.

22

RIVALS TURNED ADVOCATES

My indictment and sentencing all took place several years after I had begun to work as a youth violence prevention and youth engagement specialist. The war between gangs from across several neighborhoods had devastated the city.

Despite the trauma inflicted, blood spilled, tears shed, and hatred between the groups there were moments when hope of Peace was offered as an option. Moments when the possibility of ending the suffering was within reach and members of each group took positive steps to work for a purpose greater than the groups they belonged to.

As I sat in federal prison I reflected back to that time of Peace when I received my first-ever recognition.

I was subcontracted to work at the University of Connecticut Institute for Violence Reduction under the leadership of my mentor Professor Michael "Mike" Borrero. I was charged with the mission of assisting Mike in making connections with members of the gangs within the Hartford CT community and also leading discussions and violence prevention sessions with middle school students within Hartford Public Schools.

The Hartford Advocate "Good Egg" Award was issued by *The Hartford Advocate* in January 1997. It was awarded to a collection of men and women who serve their communities well.

The recognition was presented as a news article. On the front page of the newspaper in large bold letters, Hartford's "Good Egg." The cover photo featured three young men holding hands while displaying gang signs.

It was me, a member of the national gang and I believe another member of the local gang. Under the headline in smaller print were the words, "Bracing for a long hot summer." It appeared that the article was celebrating the possible success of the work being done by the Institute for Violence Reduction of bringing rival gangs together to end the conflicts and actually commit to serving the community in a positive way.

The cover page also in part hinted at the possibility that these relationships being formed between the members of different gangs would deteriorate and eventually revert back to conflict and war.

The opportunity to have members of the gangs featured on the cover came from a unified effort between the gangs to force Saint Francis Hospital in Hartford to hire more people of color during an expansion of the hospital.

It was a massive project with the addition of a new building and we were picketing and protesting so that the people from our community would be afforded opportunities to work on the project. There were dozens of cement mixing trucks, men with hard hats, cranes lifting metals up to different levels of the new building structure, and lots of hospital staff foot traffic.

We walked in a circle as coordinated as possible while holding up signs that read, "We want work!" We chanted as loud as possible, "We want work, we want work, we want work!" The local gang, national gang, and two other major gangs all together united for the purpose of sending a message that we were worthy of the jobs created by the project.

This effort all began with one call. I was contacted by Dana Wright. He was the owner of a small minority-owned construction company in Hartford that afforded opportunities to men in Hartford to work on projects he secured in the construction field throughout the city.

He had been involved in discussions with the hospital about hiring Hartford residents for the project. Apparently, he felt as if the hiring practices excluded those who lived in the community where the hospital's addition was being constructed.

I received a call from a community organizer who had learned of my role at the Institute for Violence Reduction and thought that I could help. Since the local gang was a major gang in the city with thousands of members, the community organizer felt that I could mobilize a large group of people to protest at the hospital.

I was asked to attend a meeting at a local entertainment and event venue in Hartford's North End to discuss the strategy for the day we would march on the hospital to demand work.

I walked into the venue wearing my gang colors and making sure to be aware of any traps set by anyone in or outside of the venue. Although I was working at the Institute, I was still an active member of the gang, and that came with the understanding that war could break out at any minute and that you could be a target at any time.

Once inside I met a few community organizers, most of the African American community. I served as the voice for the gang and the voice for the institute. That is where I connected with a young attorney by the name of Joe Muniz.

He was well-known in the community for having worked on cases related to police brutality and discrimination against the African-American community. He was a tall man who originated from the Cape Verdean Islands.

He spoke of our rights to protest, our rights as citizens to be treated fairly, and about employer laws that required fair and equal hiring practices. He explained that he needed help bringing people together for the purpose of confronting the hospital and ensuring they understood that the community would not stand for the unfair exclusion of its members from working on the hospital expansion project.

Each time he made a strong point in the room you could hear cheers and grunts from those in the audience. All were in agreement with his description of the problem and with the actions he felt we had to take.

The room was mostly filled with members of the African-American community. There were only two of us from the Latino community. I was then introduced to the group and asked to help with recruiting Latinos from the South End of Hartford to participate in the demonstrations.

At that time Hartford was very divided between the North and South end of the city. It was divided between Latinos and African Americans. The challenge was that they had not been able to bring them both to the table in a united effort. I was selected to be the person who could make that happen.

I felt powerful at that moment. I felt like I was a necessary piece of the puzzle to make this happen. I felt as if I had some control and an important role in the decisions and actions of the group. I felt as if I mattered in a major way.

At that time, I had some experience bringing groups together for projects at the Institute and at my previous work site, the Hartford Housing Authority, where I worked as an outreach worker within the public housing communities across the city.

I left that meeting with a sense of purpose. I had a mission to accomplish and I was not going to fail.

I had begun my work at the Institute for Violence Reduction in part because I wanted to help my fellow gang members find opportunities for work and ways of supporting themselves that led to living more productive lives.

I had been given an opportunity to work and because I was extremely loyal to those who I made friends with I could not allow myself to be the only one profiting from the opportunities I had been given.

I felt as if it was all about taking care of my family. I always wanted a family unit that sacrificed everything to make sure everyone in that family was well. I was going to show that I was the person to make that possible. I was going to make their lives better and by doing that I was going to show them that I loved them.

I embarked on my mission of recruiting as many of the brothers and sisters in the gang to help with the demonstration at the hospital. I did not have a strategy or a plan for how I was going to accomplish the mission but I felt that if I was passionate about the reason why it had to happen that I could convince the leadership to send some members to the hospital with me on the day of the rally.

I attended the next meeting where all of the members of the gang were present. I was allowed to address the entire group. I remembered what I had heard from the different community organizers at the meeting and repeated everything I remembered. I was animated and excited, making sure to drive the point home that this was a matter of survival for us and that we desperately needed to participate.

After I was done, the crowd went quiet. I stood there waiting for a decision to be made by the higher-ranked members. No one would speak out of turn because that would mean an automatic punishment. It would mean discipline in the form of a "bounce."

At last, one of the ranking members asked the larger group, "Who wants to join in on this?" One by one hands began to rise up and by the end of the meeting, I had several dozen members who had agreed to join me. I felt accomplished. I felt proud of them for wanting to participate and for choosing to explore something different. It was brave.

Interestingly enough that was the easy part. I now had to separately convince the leadership of the gang to allow me to invite members of other gangs in the South End of the city to participate. This would mean that our members would be marching alongside members of rival gangs.

I was determined to prove my point and to make good on my promise to those who chose me to lead this effort at the community organizing meeting.

At first, I was asked in the most serious tone possible, "Are you crazy or stupid? We are beefing with those dudes."

Feeling as if I was going to be denied I made the most insane statement in my entire life at the time.

"I'll go by myself and talk to their leadership. If they kill me, then so be it."

I am not sure exactly what went through their minds but a few of them murmured a few words I couldn't make out. After a few minutes of discussion among the leadership one said, "Go ahead bro, if you get popped (shot) that's on you."

I nodded my head to declare that I understood and went on my way. I was not sure how I was going to do this. I walked home after that and thought about what had just happened and what I had convinced the leadership that I would do. Now what?

A couple of days later I reported back to Mike Borrero at the Institute that the leadership had agreed to let members participate in the demonstration and that they had given me the go-ahead to engage the members of the other gangs to determine if they were interested.

Mike stated that he would help in any way he could and that we were welcome to use the University as a neutral space to hold a conversation.

I still was not certain how I would engage the leaders of the other gangs. I knew many of them from the community we all grew up in. Some of the members were really good friends or associates who had joined other gangs for different reasons known to them.

I began to think that I could get to them despite the tensions between our groups. A couple of days later I said to myself, *What the hell, I'll just go for it. I'll just reach out or show up to their area and tell them what we want to do.*

Once I made that decision, I contacted one of the community leaders and gave him an update on the progress made to recruit others to support the demonstration. He stated that he was thankful and excited. He also gave me an update on where the next community organizing meeting was going to be held. It was scheduled at an old warehouse building located approximately four blocks from the hospital. The factory had long closed down but the structure was sound enough to be used for a meeting.

I explained to him what I still needed to do and he went quiet. Once he broke his silence he said, "I'll go with you. I'll drive you." I had no car at that time. We agreed on a meeting point, time, and day.

The day had arrived when I was going to show up to the areas where the leaders of the other gangs were known to hang out. I was calm and pensive. I was thinking about all of the possible scenarios and how I would communicate my request to them.

In between the time that I was planning my visit with them, I had made some calls to people I knew in the other gangs to determine what their reactions were to what I was going to propose. Most of them took my call and the majority just stated in a surprised tone, "Really? You for real?"

Once I said yes, the response by each one was the same. "Yo, Smurf be careful."

I met the community organizer near Hartford Hospital. That was a pretty neutral area at the time so the likelihood of a conflict was low.

Once he arrived, he had this nervous look on his face and his voice also appeared to be shaky. He was determined to help me. I jumped into his minivan and off we went. The ride consisted mostly of questions. "Are you sure Smurf? What do you want me to do? Where should I wait?"

He was trying to make sure that he had all of the scenarios covered and how he could make sure that I was safe. I explained that I wasn't sure how it was going to go but that I did not want him to wait too close by, in case something went wrong. I did not want him to become a victim.

We arrived on Franklin Avenue and I explained to him that he could leave me at one of the corner streets. I would walk the rest of the way. Franklin Avenue was known as the territory of the national gang.

He pulled over and once again asked, "Smurf, are you sure?"

I turned to him and said, "Yes."

I opened the door to his minivan and started to walk towards one of the buildings on Franklin Avenue where the national gang members would congregate.

My head felt as if it were on a swivel. Side to side and front to back I turned my head. Knowing that at some point I would be recognized or that the gang colors I was wearing would be noticed. A gunshot could come from anywhere at that time. Guns were available in abundance and members of the city gangs were using them at a high rate to cause the most harm to their enemies.

I walked a little slower than normal toward this building as I continued looking in all directions. My gaze was like a laser beam focused on the front door entrance. *Who is going to come out of there? Is someone going to come out shooting? Have they noticed me yet?* My thoughts are all consumed by what would happen next.

I took a few more steps towards this building and noticed a few guys standing outside a business two buildings to the right of where I was headed. They turned to me and began walking my way at a hurried pace. I could now hear words coming from them but I was not sure they were directed at me.

Their faces looked angry. I heard them call out to the building where I was headed. I had been spotted and these guys were coming for me.

I slowed my walk to give me an opportunity to look at their hands to see if they were holding a gun or any weapons. I saw none. Suddenly the front door to the building opened and out came a few more guys. There was no mistaking who they were representing. They wore the trademark black and yellow beaded necklaces I had come to know as the national gang colors.

Now I knew for sure that I had a problem but there was no turning back. If I turned to run, I might get shot in the back or chased down and stabbed. There were many scenarios of violence that could have played out if I ran.

My steps were now slowed to a snail's pace. I came to a stop and yelled out. "Yo, I am here to talk about some jobs! Can I speak to H?" That was their known superior leader for that neighborhood. My call was ignored. They appeared blinded by anger and curiosity.

Their faces appeared to ask, "What the hell are you doing here? How dare you come to our neighborhood? How dare you wear your colors on our turf?" I could also feel their intentions. They were going to beat me or hurt me as badly as possible for being there.

I am sure they also wondered what my plan was. I was after all in their territory with no visible weapon and by myself. Was I there with a set-up? Was someone parked watching from somewhere and would begin shooting once they were closer to me? That was the mindset we all needed to have as members of the gangs in the city. We never knew when death or serious injury would happen.

I put my hands out in front of me and once again said, "I want to speak with H about some work for all of us." Not one of them responded to my request. I could hear their voices all at once but I could not make out much of what was being said.

Suddenly I was slapped in the face and the punches began to fly. I was punched over and over. I covered up as best I could but the punches continued to my head, back, and body. They grabbed me by my hair and pulled my head back trying to expose my face and release my arms so that the punches could land on my face.

As they were holding me and tossing me around, I heard a voice yelling. They continued punching and kicking me. The voice got closer and closer. It got louder and louder. The punches lightened up and they began to separate from me. I looked up as I raised my head up from being tucked to avoid blows to my face. I peeked through my arms. The voice yelling out was H. He had told them to chill, stop, and back up.

He appeared to not know what was going on but had most likely either heard a commotion or was told something was happening outside. Once he saw me, he asked with a surprised look on his face, "Smurf? Yo, what are you doing here?"

I explained that I was there to recruit a few of his brothers and sisters to help us walk the demonstration line outside of the hospital because we were not being offered jobs and they should benefit from those jobs also.

His head tilted to the side in a similar way a dog's head may tip to the side when it hears a loud whistle and is trying to make sense of it. I realized by the look on his face that he was completely shocked. It communicated a sense of confusion. He said, "Bro, you came here to tell us that? Are you crazy or something?"

I responded back that I was serious. I used all of the selling points I had learned at the first community organizing meeting. After a while of back and forth talking he agreed to send a few of his brothers and sisters. He shook my hand and asked me to leave.

I began to walk away feeling I had accomplished my goal. I had added his number to my list and I would be reaching out. I walked a few blocks to where the community organizer had been waiting. I hopped in the minivan and he immediately asked me, "Man, are you okay?"

"Yes." I was sore around my head, ears, neck, back, and legs from the punches and kicks.

He asked me if I needed to go to the hospital, and I told him, "No. Let's get out of here before they realize you are here or other members see us."

We began to drive away and I told him, "They agreed to come. They gave me their word."

He said, "That's good Smurf."

It felt painful but he was right, it was good.

A few weeks later, we were all together as one people demanding opportunities to be considered for work. No screaming at one another, no fighting, no guns, no war. Just our voices in concert, "We want work, we want work, we want work!"

The hospital was surrounded by hundreds of police vehicles from not only our city but from neighboring towns. There were also parole officers, drug enforcement agents, and state police cruisers. All watching us and waiting for something negative to take place.

We had no knowledge of the rules related to a demonstration of this type. We were told that we could not impede motor vehicle traffic, people traffic, or emergency services traffic. We were told we were to remain on the sidewalk and off the street. We followed the rules and it was going well.

Suddenly I saw a commotion at one end of the circle. It appeared an officer and one of the demonstrators were engaged in a verbal discussion. I looked to see and noticed the officer reaching for the demonstrator. Like a detonating cord on dynamite, the fuse had been lit and the explosion was quick and powerful. The circle broke up and people from within the group of demonstrators began to physically clash with the police. It was no longer a unified calm. It was chaos.

Sirens were blaring, lights flashing, people yelling, and car tires screeching. The event had come to a halt and the focus now was on getting out of there before it turned even more violent or perhaps deadly.

Police were yelling at us to disperse or face arrest. I remained by the side entrance to the hospital with a few other guys who participated in the demonstration. We looked over at the entrance to the job site which was now blocked off by police.

We were approached by several officers and asked to turn around. We were informed that we were now under arrest for breach of Peace. All we were fighting for was the right to be considered for a job. Now we were in handcuffs.

While we were being escorted to a waiting vehicle the chaos continued around the job site. Pepper spray had been deployed to disperse the crowd and the battle between the demonstrators and law enforcement continued raging on.

I recalled the officers escorting us asking what car they could place us in. It was so hectic that the officers were losing track of their cruisers.

I sat in the back of a police car choking on mace because a police officer sprayed pepper spray inside the car, closed the doors and windows, and left. It was a very hot day and I sat next to a member of the national gang in handcuffs. I remember the national gang member saying he couldn't breathe.

He asked me if he could lay on top of me so he could kick the police cruiser's windows out so that we could get some fresh air. We managed to get him to lay across my lap, putting his head against the other side of the car. He started kicking on the window to break it so the officer could see that we needed to breathe. It worked!

The officer opened the door, yelled at us a little bit, and rolled the windows open leaving a crack so we could breathe.

After we got our breath back, we both looked at each other and we forgot about our colors. I think for both of us, it was the first time we were doing something that was bigger than the gang.

We were then taken to the local police station and processed. The charges of breach of Peace were explained and we were asked to sign a promise to appear at a court date. There were dozens of guys being processed who were at the demonstration. The "bullpen" was full.

I could feel the stares from many of the other men who were in the bullpen after the demonstration. As I was escorted past the first few cells, I looked their way. I could see they were frustrated with me and with what had happened. Some of them walked around in circles.

I then heard, "Smurf, you said we were going to get us work and here we are in jail!" They were half serious and half smirking. Breach of Peace was not a serious charge but they were just not happy to be in the bullpen with so many others and having to go through processing.

After a few hours, I was released.

I felt that despite being arrested we had accomplished something and that it made a difference. We got something done. I never got a job at the hospital and I don't know if anybody else did either but we did get the attention of the hospital.

There was a sit down with construction workers in Hartford and they negotiated an agreement that residents of the city would be considered for the available jobs.

Some of the guys involved in the demonstrations went on to continue their advocacy efforts and eventually obtained employment. That was the beginning of their journey to success even though sitting in the bullpen it did not feel that way at the time.

23

— . —

AFTER THE FORT

Party Like It's 1999. The song was released and performed by Prince in 1982. I remember not being able to see that far into the future. How could someone who was abused, neglected, discarded, illiterate, unskilled, and angry even believe in getting to the next century or see a future? All that was on my mind at 12 years old was survival.

Yet, there I was in 1999 at the age of 29, getting ready to be released from a physical prison. For me, there would be no party.

Instead, there was a metal-colored bench, white solid brick walls, cold steel bars, and the consistent sounds of echoing keys rattling as each federal correction officer moved. Each step and sway of the hips allowed for the many keys on their belts to clank together.

The ceiling was clean inside this prerelease cell. I lay on a bench staring into space and catching myself wandering in my head. I wondered about so many things while in my thoughts. I've always had many fantasies play out in my head. I would conjure up some pretty fascinating stories. I once wandered into a daydream where I could fly. It felt so real that if you asked me to this day, I would with most confidence say that I levitated once.

I thought about reaching out to my contacts when I arrived home so that I could get a job and make some money. I believed a job would get me back on track and could keep me from returning to places such as these.

Each time I returned from a trip inside my mind and thoughts I saw the ceiling again in a different way, still surprised at how clean it was. I could make out the ridges between each cinder block used to create the walls. No one had burned their name or written it in, which was surprising with the total number of men that had traveled through that space.

In my teens and early twenties, I had been arrested and incarcerated in other institutions in Connecticut for domestic violence crimes, violent assaults, and gang involvement. The state prison system experience was very different from the federal prison system. Those experiences were even more different than at what is known as "holding" in the prison system. This is usually called a city jail and is where persons accused of crimes are held until their case is resolved.

In the state and city facilities, you would see more writing on the walls and other images carved in using illegal sharp objects or belt buckles, written in with pencils or markers, and in some cases burned in with smuggled lighters. These messages could be gang communication, love stories, or identifying those who were suspected or known to be informants (snitches).

To me, it felt as if there was less noise in the federal system than in the other facilities I had spent time in. There seemed to be more aggression, more despair, and less tolerance between people.

The cells or rooms felt smaller and less forgiving. While at Fort Dix I was in a dorm-style room with 11 other inmates. In the holding facility and state prison, there were more two-man cells or rooms. For a short period, I was at the dorms in the holding facilities that held approximately 60 individuals who were waiting to have their cases heard, be bailed out, or receive sentencing.

At Fort Dix, it was expected that all inmates keep their attire neat and shirts tucked into their pants. In the other facilities, they may have issued prison suits but there was no real emphasis on how you would dress or how to wear what you had.

The black and white wall clock with large hands appeared to click in slow motion. I was still dressed in khaki pants, a khaki polo-style button-down shirt with a white t-shirt under it, and tennis shoes that were issued by the facility for every inmate.

I waited for the moment when a bag with a different set of clothes would make its way to me so that I could feel one step closer to leaving the room.

I took a few moments, rolled off my back from the bench, got to the floor, and started doing pushups. I don't want to get too sweaty because I would not have a way to clean or dry up. I just needed to keep busy. Time waits for no one but it sure felt as if it was pausing itself for moments at a time. Soon I'd be free.

Fort Dix Federal Correctional Facility in New Jersey was my home for just a few more long hours. I was headed to Hartford, the city I'd called home for most of my life, the place where I would once again freely roam, the place that would test my freedom. All was on hold until I was allowed to leave that space where everything echoes.

As loud as the echoes were, I was certain I could hear my heartbeat. I was convinced that the federal guards could hear my thoughts. I felt as if I was being loud, that I was unable to control the crowd in my head. All of these plans I had, all of these conversations I was envisioning, and all of the fears I had of how I would be received. *Oh, how I have missed my family. My daughter, my wife.*

Eighteen months of my life to reflect. Eighteen months of my life to experience. Eighteen months of my life to think about the next steps. Eighteen months of my life to miss the things that I took for granted. Eighteen months to feel the lost potential gains I had made.

Tik, tik, tik. The clock continued to slowly remind me that I was not in control of anything but myself. I felt relief that I was able to be in the position I was in but I also felt tired. I came to understand the repetition of each day in this place. I developed a hate for it. I'd heard hundreds of stories from other inmates, some of them more times than I'd like to.

It was Groundhog Day, déjà vu, and every other term for rinse and repeat. Before arriving here, I had gained a sense of what I wanted to dedicate myself to. I wanted to help guide, steer, and direct young brothers and sisters in my community toward a life of non-violence and the pursuit of positive goals.

I'd learned that I needed to take different actions, be around different thinkers, and needed to assign importance to the things that I needed to do for a different path to be set in my life. I honestly did not have an idea of how to break habits and patterns in thought to ensure I remained free.

Heavy footsteps in the distance let me know that someone was making their way towards me. Finally, my time had arrived.

"Inmate Nazario," his voice says. At that time, I was the only person headed home.

"Yes," I said.

He opened the door to the bullpen-type enclosure where I had been sitting, pacing, thinking, dreaming, and anxiously waiting to be set free.

I was handed a brown paper bag with my belongings in it. Inside this brown bag were any items that I was holding on to while incarcerated. Items that were of value to me. They included letters from loved ones, photos of loved ones, any paperwork related to my case, and school papers from the different classes I participated in while at Fort Dix. All of the courses were basic education courses such as reading, and math, with a few small business concepts courses, sprinkled in.

Mercer County Community College in Trenton, New Jersey offered classes to federal inmates. The classes were not mandatory. It afforded those held in prison the opportunity to leave their rooms, pursue college credits, or build on their education in the hopes of returning to their outside lives with something to show prospective employers. A degree or perhaps a business plan could help launch the transition back to society on a positive note.

My GPA was 3.0 during the time I attended with the pre-tests showing that I was strongest in English and struggled the most in reading. I had never been an avid reader and most of the language I had learned was from listening to others speak and using words they used in conversation.

I had chosen to enroll in business classes in part because I had witnessed my role models leading their respective businesses. There were business skills that I felt I could learn to improve my chances of leading my own business someday.

The bag was given to me before my release and included the clothes that I was going to change into for my trip to Hartford.

I was asked to step out and head to an office where they were going to process me to make sure that I was the right person they were releasing. I sat down. I was asked for my prison ID, inmate number, birth date, Social Security number, the reason I was there (what I was convicted of), and how long I was there.

Misprision of a Felony is the deliberate concealment of one's knowledge of a treasonable act or a felony. This is the charge that I pled guilty to that determined this stint in federal prison. Between 1995 and 1997 I was a defendant in a federal indictment charging members of a Hartford gang with several crimes under the Racketeer Influenced and Corrupt Organizations Act (RICO). This law was designed to combat organized crime in the United States. It allows the prosecution to charge groups for criminal activity and assess civil penalties for racketeering activity performed as part of an ongoing criminal enterprise.

These indictments led to the arrest and conviction of thousands of men and women members of that gang. Due to my role as a leader in the gang at the time I received a higher level of scrutiny which made my case a high-profile case.

Tap, tap, tap, tap on the computer keyboard. *What does he see?* Thoughts raced through my mind as I recalled when other guys who were excited to be going home were returned to the unit with new charges, warrants, or holds due to paperwork not being filed correctly.

When you are in jail there is no way to know what is happening in the courts, offices, or anywhere else that will lead to keeping you locked away. Especially when you are not in your city or state.

Everything comes back all clear. No holds, warrants, or incorrectly filed documents. Yes, it is me who is up for release. Whew, what a relief.

I was escorted out of the building and onto the sidewalk outside of the prison. There was a van on the other side of the prison fence waiting to drive me to the bus station to begin my journey home. I was on the outside of the fence! What a feeling.

I turned my head back toward the fence and saw it behind me. There was still a little sense of nervousness that someone would say, "Hey, officer so and so, return the prisoner to processing and booking."

I took a few steps towards the van and suddenly in the distance, I heard a voice from inside the fence I had called home for almost two years. A voice shouted, "Hey Nazario."

I immediately thought, *Oh what is it now?* It was the federal officer who led the landscaping crew where I worked while I was incarcerated here.

All prisoners during processing and booking were asked questions about employment experience and other work skills. These interviews many times determine the work site you will be assigned to once you are cleared to work.

I had described on the intake form that I had experience working in the construction and maintenance fields.

Perhaps that is why I was placed in the landscaping detail. I turned towards the federal officer also known as the landscaping foreman and I smiled. He was very honest, genuine, compassionate, tough, and kind of relaxed. He was a kind soul.

He believed that we were all adults and that once he gave instructions on the tasks for the day our actions would determine how he would have to handle us. He said, "Take good care of yourself."

"Thank you," I said. I got in the van, and off I went.

I do not remember the trip to Fort Dix, how interesting that this place was so close to a suburban neighborhood, with pretty homes with lawns that looked as neat as the field during a championship game of an outdoor sport on TV.

A few times while traveling on this van to the bus station I saw the shapes of the men working and noticed the trademark khakis I wore and the ever so visible bright orange cotton skully hats we were required to wear.

Those were the guys who had received clearance to work outside of the fence. They were more likely to have low-level/nonviolent offenses such as white-collar crimes.

I remember seeing them from the inside of the fence mowing the lawn on the outside of the fence. When they made their way back into the prison from their shift, I thought about how lucky they were. They were able to spend eight hours outside of the fence. Each day they got to feel some freedom only to be returned to where they did not want to be. I wasn't going back. I was way beyond the prison gates and could no longer see it behind me.

I had no idea where I was headed, nothing looked familiar except some of the people on the streets who appeared to be Latino or African American. There wasn't much traffic in the area but every once in a while, there were small groups of people walking somewhere.

I wondered who they were and what their lives were like. We finally arrived at the bus station and the driver said, "Okay man, you are here. Take care, have a safe trip, and report to your parole/probation officer or you're required halfway house."

I said thank you and asked, "Where do I go to get my ticket?"

He pointed me in the direction of a small window attached to a mid-sized concrete rest stop-style building and I nodded my head.

I purchased the ticket using the money I had earned while working for the landscaping crew. The weekly pay, although not much, along with my wife's financial support, helped carry me through.

While I waited for the next bus to New York City I was approached by a person who presented themselves to me as homeless. As I engaged this person I could hear the squeak of brakes and the air release that usually happens when a bus breaks or comes to a stop coming from behind me. The Greyhound bus had arrived. I turned my head briefly to the side to confirm that the bus was there.

Once I saw it, I knew I had to make my way there. I didn't want to miss this bus and remain in this unfamiliar community and the location where I knew the federal prison was a few minutes away.

I reached into my pocket and pulled out the little bit of cash that I had. I gave him two dollars. He said thanks and off he went.

Perhaps this was life's way of letting me know I was returning to my life outside the walls. The bus arrived and I watched as stranger after stranger stepped off the bus and went about their journey. Once the driver cleared the bus, he processed whatever he had to process at the small window and made the call for everyone to step in if they were headed to NYC.

I took the steps towards the bus, gave him my ticket, and onto the bus steps I went. One, two, three, four steps. I stood in the aisle of the bus, looked for an empty seat, and decided I wanted a window seat. I took my seat, looked out the window at where I was, and then looked at the aisle as passengers boarded the bus to see who else was getting on, over and over again. I was curious and wanted to see everyone.

Finally, the large door was pulled shut. The bus driver took his seat. We pulled out in reverse and began our travel on the suburban road leading out of that town and heading to the next step in my freedom.

New York City here I come.

24

INTO THE UNKNOWN

Seventy-five miles until I would reach the third leg of my journey back to Hartford. We were headed toward the Port Authority Bus Terminal, close to the heart of New York City. I had been there a few times but never from this direction. It seemed as if thousands of people were in a great hurry to get to either their bus or transition to other transportation nearby.

At Grand Central Station nearby someone could catch a train to pretty much anywhere in New York City or the east coast. There was always public transportation outside of the terminal and thousands of yellow cabs. Whatever the preference of travel, it was available.

I stared out the window with curiosity. Looking at cars below and at different landmarks such as hotels, churches, and other structures I had never seen in New Jersey. As we continued on, I started to see a familiar sign, I-95 North. That was the highway I would travel on my way back home from New York City after I had visited family or had visited the city for fun and entertainment.

After about an hour my surroundings became even more familiar. The most familiar site was that of the thousands of taxi cabs that seemed to indicate we were in NYC. The sights of the cabs were followed closely by the sounds of car horns beeping relentlessly. It was so loud. Trucks honking, cars honking, buses honking, music blaring from cars, police, ambulance, and fire truck sirens going off, planes flying overhead, and trains passing by.

We pulled up to the bus terminal. I had the utmost respect for the bus driver because the narrow city streets were difficult to navigate. The streets were crowded with cars that were double-parked while delivery trucks were focused on unloading contents. The driver managed it well.

The terminal tunnel is located right off a busy street in NYC and the bus seemed to disappear underground. We gently pulled down into the tunnel under the Port Authority Bus Terminal station and we arrived at our gate.

I exited the bus and once I entered the gate area it was exactly how I remembered it. There were people all over the place moving at a frantic pace without tripping over one another as they made their way to their gates or out of the station and into the street.

Although I was not sure where I was headed, I knew I had been there before. I felt confident that I would find my way. Not having moved at such a frantic pace for a while seemed to take my breath away. I felt a heightened level of awareness and excitement.

Awareness is a survival skill I learned from a lifetime of misguided steps. Being keenly aware of my surroundings was just as important as taking a breath. Life on the streets, gang violence, and long days in prison made me fully conscious of my surroundings at all times. It was a matter of life or death. No one could be truly trusted.

Hypervigilance ensures your survival and it becomes ingrained in you so deeply that even silence does not feel safe. I scanned the faces of as many people as possible and did my best to see everything that was happening around me. This was all making me feel tired.

I arrived at my gate to wait for the bus headed to Hartford to arrive. What a relief. I sat with my back up against the wall, not giving anyone an opportunity to sneak up behind me. It was how I felt the safest.

I saw the bus arrive at the gate. I stood up and proceeded to the gate entrance. I waited as each passenger boarded the bus. I once again looked at each face. This time I am looking to see if I recognized anyone. I did not.

The bus driver made his way down the aisle checking the tickets of each passenger and punching a hole in each ticket. Once he was done, he returned to his seat, buckled up, and began his drive toward Hartford.

I could feel my palms sweating as I was en route to the city that I had always called home. My head was filled with thoughts about my arrival. I was quiet and in thought.

What will happen when I see my old city, Hartford? How will I be received and who knows I am headed home? The previous times I had been released from a holding facility, jail, or prison there was no real fanfare or specific reception I received from the community.

To be honest, I felt as if I was returning to a community that did not want me because I was without purpose or direction. I had been going through the motions and "living" each and every day however I could manage.

Once I was released, I'd wander the streets looking for anyone I recognized to let them know I was out and gauge their reaction. How they reacted would determine my next ask.

This is a life skill that I developed while being forced onto the streets. I had to make sure that I could analyze a person quickly so that I would not fall victim to a blindsided attack. I also needed to learn how people responded to my presence and words. All of this was key to making it through to another day.

I learned to ask for help, for a ride somewhere, for a place to stay, or for some money to make phone calls to people whose number I had written on a piece of paper, inside a wallet, or in my pants pocket. I learned to accept "no" in response to a request for a favor.

In some instances, I did not know exactly where I was headed when I was released. I had some acquaintances that I remembered had been helpful and had a little more freedom to allow someone to stay with them even if for just one night. This time, I knew exactly where I would stay, in the arms of my wife and my daughter.

I was reflecting on every single instance where I should have demanded more of myself, remembering that not one of my previous release experiences would equal what I was facing this time.

Being released from federal prison was quite different. The expectations were different.

When I was sentenced in federal court I held a ranking position within the gang, I had been sentenced during a very public trial, and I had become well known in Hartford, across the State of Connecticut, and in some other parts of the country.

I had established a reputation on the streets as a member of a gang. Within the gang, I had been recognized as a major figure. That combination of facts meant that I developed loyal supporters and fierce enemies. Sometimes those two can come from within the gang and those conflicts from the past are not forgotten nor forgiven. Who would be coming for me?

Law enforcement was also aware that a known leader from a major city gang would be back out on the streets. There was no reason for law enforcement to believe that I had changed my behaviors.

In all of my life, I hadn't felt this much pressure from external forces while battling the same from within myself. I knew external factors had challenged me incredibly. It was a newfound internal battle raging that I knew would be the greatest challenge to overcome.

What does change for the good within oneself look like? Who is willing and able to help me when I hit a wall? What skills and talents have I gained that I can pull from to win this internal battle? A battle of pride vs. the need to make better choices. A battle between the desire to fulfill a positive purpose versus developed habits I learned to survive and remain relevant.

Prior to being sentenced, I was working as an outreach and engagement worker for the Institute for Violence Reduction at the University of Connecticut School of Social Work. Professor Michael Borrero led the Institute and provided me an opportunity to work with youth in Hartford who were identified for youth leadership development and violence prevention services.

As part of my role, each week I visited schools in Hartford, meeting with youth in group settings and individually. It was my attempt at preventing youth from making the same choices I had made. It was my way of trying to interrupt the suffering youth may be experiencing because of home and community problems. I was also involved with a youth athletics program for Mi Casa Family Services. I led their football team to an undefeated season. I assisted their basketball team with coaching and I engaged with youth to keep them active and involved in positive activities. I also visited the youth at their homes and in the community as a strategy to keep them engaged in conversations and with resources and support when they needed them.

I had become well known in the community for being able to effectively engage with youth across the city and in other communities across the State of Connecticut. I had my own internal struggles with understanding how to access the deepest parts of my own mind and heart to handle stressors with a positive mindset. I felt that by simply being present for others and using my voice and experience I could affect change in others earlier than I had been able to for myself.

The other challenge in my mind was to be "seen" differently. To be released from the stigma that my life on the streets created for me. Not being distracted by the expectations others had because of my reputation. For the majority of my life, I was known for being active on the streets. I was present at all of the major parties, clubs, and events and involved with the day-to-day actions of being considered popular on the streets.

The pressure of being Smurf was always present. I was expected to spend time on the block with friends and acquaintances. I was expected to continue to drive the gang's conflicts with other gangs and to take risks against my life and my own freedom. I was expected to always show my loyalty to others.

I still had past experiences that I had not healed from and I wasn't sure how to heal from my past pains. I found it difficult to share my true feelings or to be truthful with others. When confronted with my faults, wrongful actions, and behaviors I became defensive.

I knew how to speak of Peace but I had not learned how to create Peace and be in a place of personal, emotional, and psychological Peace. I needed to truly understand what that meant but I had yet to develop the capacity or skills to dig a little deeper within my heart and soul. I was afraid of exposing my feelings and facing the pain. I felt vulnerable. Most importantly, I needed to learn how to dissolve the rage that lived within me that surfaced when I felt it was needed. I needed to learn how to not feel weakness or shame. If I were no longer chosen to act and react with aggression.

I was expected to be a mentor but, in some way, I needed a mentor to help me find myself.

I had dedicated my time while in Fort Dix to writing letters to teens in the community about the "real" prison experience that was riddled with fear, insecurity, vulnerability, and feelings of loss and despair.

The idea of developing a letter-writing project for teens came to me while I was lying down on the top bunk in the dorm I shared with 11 other men. My mind wandered and I reflected on the moments I spent with the youth I mentored or provided support services to.

I remembered how several of the youth testified in open court during my sentencing hearing. They described the positive impact I had on them. I felt as if I had to continue to offer them support despite being incarcerated. My goal when I worked with them was to offer them options and lessons that prevented them from repeating some of my or their mistakes. I wanted to ensure that they were engaged in positive and constructive activities at an earlier stage in their lives than I had.

Writing these honest letters made me feel as if I was continuing the positive engagement and offering lessons based on my experience that would prevent them from ending up where I was at this very moment. The complete opposite of the tough bravado portrayed in films or through personal testimonies of formerly incarcerated men who fear appearing vulnerable, weak, or losing an acclaimed status. I spoke of truth and the harsh reality inside.

I was expected to abide by the release mandates. I was required to report to my federal parole officer regularly and remain free of contact with anyone with a felony conviction, with anyone affiliated with a gang or involved in any criminal activity. I was expected to show proof of gainful employment and pay restitution to any victims impacted by my criminal behavior.

However, my primary focus was to be a dad to my daughter who had lived without me while I was incarcerated. Although I was able to visit with my daughter a few times and talk with her on the phone, my physical presence was missing. I needed to reconnect with my little girl. I needed to be a dad and I had to make up for missed time.

I was overwhelmed. I took a deep breath. I had to surrender. I needed to be the man I felt I could be. This will help me to see a clear path to Peace of mind.

The bus driver abruptly broke the silence. "Hartford, next stop!" We had arrived. He exited the highway from 84 West, onto Asylum Avenue. I saw familiar sights. Bushnell Park, the State Capitol building, and hotels. I had spent nights sleeping in that park, and frequenting this area going unnoticed. I was back in Hartford and I desired to be noticed but in a much different way.

News travels very quickly through the inmates in the federal prison system. There are several means of communication with the outside world. Communication known as "kites" are secret letters that are sent from inside the prison walls to the outside world.

Many times, the kites are written in code that only former prisoners understand. There were also other ways to share the information, like through their loved ones during in-person visits. I am certain there was a message that Iran Nazario aka Smurf was out.

25

THE INTERSECTION

In 2001, I received notice that I had been awarded the "Committed Adult To Children in Hartford Award" (CATCH). A little more than a year after my release from Fort Dix there were those that believed in me. They believed that I was having a positive impact on the lives of youth.

When I was released, I had a raging passion within me to make up for the lost time I spent in prison. I needed to prove to others who had followed my journey and to those who had trusted me that I was the right person to serve our city's youth.

I wanted to believe I was the right person to help prevent their suffering. I had heard that many people who were part of the social services, youth services, and community outreach and engagement communities were disappointed in me for returning to prison.

This was especially difficult to hear because there were those who trusted me and felt that I had betrayed their trust.

I had to be held accountable for the crimes I had committed and that meant having to spend time in prison.

There were those who believed that I had not changed, that I had not become a person with positive goals who was no longer involved in gang activity. Those people were heard speaking amongst each other. They would say that I was only a fraud and faking the violence prevention image because of the money I was being paid.

After receiving the call, notifying me of the award, I felt an overwhelming sense of pride and hope. I thought this award must be due to my work before and after prison.

It was most likely due to my continued efforts to connect and help steer youth in a positive direction from inside the prison. I thought there was no way that I earned this from the time I was out until the present day.

I felt deeply emotional. I wanted to cry because it was a statement to others that I was worthy. They believed in me. I was not going to be dismissed or disregarded as a lost cause. Instead, my efforts were being acknowledged and it gave me hope that I could turn my life around and live a more positive life.

I decided to be a dad to my daughter and I was also hoping I could serve as a father figure to others. Perhaps this meant that I was achieving some success toward that goal.

Despite being the recipient of the CATCH award, I continued my internal battle to remain focused on my goals. I knew that I needed to keep myself as busy as possible with work and by being involved in healthy and positive relationships and activities.

I was an argument away from unleashing my rage again. I had not resolved many of the traumas experienced in my youth and into my adult years.

Triggers might come from any source and could most certainly set me off. I was still relatively young and interested in the nightlife. This meant clubs, bars, late-night parties, and drinking alcohol.

One evening I came face to face with conflict. I decided to spend some time out at a local bar called Piggy's, socializing, partying, and dancing. I have always enjoyed dancing. Everything from poppin' and lockin', breakdancing, housing (or dancing to house music), Latin freestyle dancing, hip hop, rhythm and blues, salsa, and merengue.

While at Piggy's I saw some close friends who were related to my wife. As a song I liked began to play, I reached for the hand of one of my friends and we began to dance.

I felt happy to be dancing and enjoying the evening. While dancing and spinning across the dance floor I begin to feel a sense of negative energy being projected in my direction. Although difficult to explain, I felt as if someone was looking right through me.

I had learned to listen and to be aware of those types of vibes in crowded spaces. I can most relate what I was feeling to a spidey sense like Spiderman has. I scanned the room while I danced and found the source of the energy.

It was a guy I knew of, but not personally. He was a guy from the neighborhood who had joined the Hartford police department. He glared at us dancing while clutching a beer bottle in his hand.

I felt extremely uncomfortable with the way he looked at us. I asked my dance partner, "I notice this person is looking at us with an angry expression, is he something to you? Are you two dating?"

She turned to look at this guy and said, "Yes. Don't worry about him. He's not going to do anything."

I responded, "Okay" but felt as if she was underplaying the seriousness of the moment. I kept myself prepared for any negative action coming from him.

As the song came to an end, I escorted my dance partner off the dance floor and thanked her for the dance. Suddenly, I saw this guy hurrying towards me. He was mouthing words but I was unable to hear over the sound of the music.

I could tell he was angry. He approached me and we stood face to face.

He asked me, "Why are you dancing with my girl?" as he bumped his chest against mine.

I stepped back and responded, "She is like a cousin to me. She is my wife's cousin."

He responds, "I don't give a f***!" and threatens to slap me with the bottle of beer he was holding.

I stepped a little further back and smiled. I did not want to have a fight with him but I was ready to if he charged at me again.

My smile made him even angrier and he charged at me.

A few people that were with him reached in and grabbed him by his arms and asked him to chill. He was trying to pull away from them. I continued to step back in an effort to avoid the fight.

Once I was able to get myself away from him, I decided that I would say goodnight to the people I knew and leave Piggy's to decrease my chances of having any further issues with this guy.

Even though my car was parked in the front lot, I decided to leave out the back to avoid running into this person again.

While I was walking around the building headed to the front, I heard footsteps quickly approaching from the side of the building. Suddenly I saw the same guy running towards me and asking me to put my hands up. He wanted to fight.

We both put our hands up and are in our fight stance. The guys who had held him back inside were once again holding him. I once again smiled and walked around the group and headed towards my car.

I arrived at my car and reached to open the door. I looked up and saw the guy coming around the building and once again looking for me. At this point, I could tell that he was intoxicated and out of control.

He headed towards me. He came around to the driver's side door of my car and got into a fight stance. I leaned his back against my car and set up to fight also.

He stepped back and reached for something from his waist. His stance changed to a stance that is most commonly seen when someone is reaching for a gun.

In my mind, I believed he had a gun. I reached into my waist and pulled out a knife. I was not smiling anymore. I quickly snapped into self-preservation mode. I flipped the switch from a simple fight to, I have to kill him before he kills me.

I flipped the knife open and began to close the distance between us. I wanted to make sure that I could stab him as quickly as possible to end the threat.

His eyes opened wide and he began skipping backward quickly and seemed to revert back to instinct from his training in law enforcement. He yelled, "Knife, knife, knife."

I then realized that he had no gun.

I stepped back as a few dozen people headed in our direction. I knew I had messed up. I opened the door to my car and as I went to sit in, I threw the knife over the car and into some bushes near the street.

I got into my car and sped away. I felt as if I had been set up and now, I was going to be arrested. I drove onto I-84 east and connected to 91 North headed towards my wife's mother's house in Windsor, Connecticut where I was staying at the time. That is where my young son, daughter, wife, and mother-in-law were.

I was headed to them and I knew that I might not see them on the outside of a jail cell for a while.

As I rounded the curve near their street, I could see their house. I felt as if perhaps I may not be in trouble after all. Maybe the police hadn't been called. Maybe this was seen as a situation where guys were just behaving badly while out having some drinks. No one was injured and everyone was still breathing.

As I pulled into the driveway and parked, I saw lights from several police cruisers come on. The Windsor police were waiting for me. I was caught.

I was asked to exit the vehicle. I was placed in handcuffs and searched. I was then placed in the back of a police car and driven to the police headquarters on Jennings Road in Hartford.

As we drove, I asked the officer why I was being taken to police headquarters. He said that there was a complaint made against me but he was unsure what it was concerning.

Once we arrived at the police station I was escorted through the front doors and into the foyer and saw the guy from Piggy's and several other people including some police officers in uniform.

I was taken through a door on the left and placed into a holding cell. I was once again in a cage. I was not sure what was going to happen to me. I had no clue what charges had been filed. What I did know is that once again a split-second decision made after an extended period of time under stress has landed me back in jail.

After some time of waiting in the cell, I heard footsteps approaching and keys rattling. I immediately got flashbacks to the many times I had heard the sound of keys rattling from inside a cell.

The door opened and I was greeted by a high-ranking officer. This officer asked me to step out and began to tell me that I was free to go. I was stunned.

He explained that there were no charges filed or pressed against me and that I could leave. I was speechless. I simply replied, "Yes sir."

He began walking ahead of me and I followed him back through the same hallway I traveled to come into the holding cell area. He opened the door leading to the foyer and said, "Good luck."

I stepped into the foyer not sure about what to think about what had happened. I made a phone call to my wife and gave her details about where I was. I stepped outside and let her know I would be there waiting for her to pick me up.

While standing outside waiting for my ride, I reflected back on the night. I was angry. I was relieved to be free but I replayed in my head various scenarios where I had killed this person. I felt as if I had it would have been justified. I had avoided the fight until I was pinned against my car and felt as if my life was in danger.

I would have been in the right. I also thought about how close I came to losing touch with my kids. Not only my biological ones but the ones who I had promised to serve and save from these experiences.

I was thankful that I had another chance but I was also aware of the fact that I was still very capable of turning on an ugly side of me, a side in me that was deeply caged. This CATCH recognition was wonderful but I felt as if it did not suffice.

What I was feeling was the desire to increase my emotional health and become cognitively capable. I was not sure exactly what that meant and how to get there.

I truly believe that we set our course by our own actions and there are challenges along the way that slow us down.

26

Boathouse

Years later, I stood at a boat house at a ceremony to acknowledge my successful completion of a leadership academy. I peered out a window of a boathouse transformed into a hall for ceremonies. The view was beautiful as it overlooked the Connecticut River. On this particular day, the water was running free under a sunny sky. It was easy to get lost in this view. It is a part of me that I am in love with, my love of nature's beautiful creations and my love of being around water.

I cannot recall where I developed that love of being around or in water. No matter how hard I think I have no memory of where I learned to swim, who was first to expose me to the river or ocean water. I could spend hours in nature.

The only nature that I had known growing up was the park behind our housing complex and the railroad tracks behind that. My brother, cousins, and sometimes friends would run into the tracks and spend hours there throwing rocks to see who had better aim or the strongest arm and looking for grass snakes under the rocks along the tracks.

The only explanation I can offer is that astronomy and numerology declare that I am a nature lover at heart. Perhaps, it is simply how I am designed.

In the distance behind the sounds of rushing waters, I heard the voices in conversations, laughter, and plates clanking as forks hit them while attendees of the ceremony had their breakfast with family members, colleagues, and fellow graduates.

Each cohort of trainees had identified a speaker to share the journey of the group. There was a keynote address and representatives from the City of Hartford congratulated us.

We received our certificates/plaques and just like that it was complete. I was a graduate of the City of Hartford's Youth Development Practitioners Academy 2008 class. Was I now official?

At this very moment in time, there was more going on inside of me emotionally and psychologically than my mind could possibly take in or absorb.

All of the graduates were lingering after the ceremony and I was doing what I do best. Socializing, taking pictures for memories, and posting on social media. I think to myself, *How times have changed.*

It was not long ago that social media was not an option for us. We used beepers and flip phones. I looked around. Something was missing. Family. Something that I had been familiar with. I had no family there to witness my successful completion of this academy.

I escaped into the parking lot and into my car. I placed the certificate on the passenger seat. I was quiet again. Was I more important than when I first pulled up and parked here?

I drove away. Back to reality.

The following fall of 2009 I learned the City of Hartford was having a follow-up to the Youth Development Practitioners Academy (YDPA). The Middle Management Institute (MMI).

The Youth Development Leadership sessions focused on the basics of youth development, team building, engaging the community, building effective relationships with clients, and collaborating with partners to better serve the community.

The MMI was an opportunity for middle managers to become more effective at their roles. Managing teams, budgeting, financial management, cultural competency, conflict resolution, and program evaluation. The tools and skills every middle manager would need to become better leaders of their staff in the process. I thought this was a very interesting concept. A better leader.

There were very few times in my life that I had structure. Now looking back, the discipline imposed on me by my father and mother was not exactly building structure. It instilled fear, sadness, and rage in me. Having to smother my voice and quiet my cries on demand was not building habits that would help me become a better person or teach me skills that lead to success in life.

During this time, I was at COMPASS Youth Collaborative employed as a Program Director for an initiative called Peacebuilders. The purpose of the program is to identify, recruit, enroll, and provide services for youth who are victims or perpetrators of violence or are disconnected from positive social and support circles.

Once again I was challenging my leadership skills as the program's director. I was to lead a group of men and women on this initiative. My personality is that of a high-energy, comedic, understanding, kind, and emotional supervisor.

My hope was that I develop strong, healthy, and productive relationships with the team. This was an effort to build a cohesive unit all looking to achieve the same goals. My zodiac sign would describe me as reliable, practical, ambitious, sensual, and independent. Those are the good traits.

The not-so-good ones are procrastinating, stubborn, possessive, and materialistic, although the materialistic trait is one I agree least with.

Those traits have to be blended in with my desire to be good to people, avoid conflict, and be forgiving. Learning that some of those things are not always practical.

This is where this Middle Management Institute got me to blend these things together. Giving everyone the benefit of the doubt, I know that I will eventually be challenged by those who will see my personality and kindness as a weakness.

During the MMI there is a significant focus on understanding our own personalities. Years ago, when I completed the Myers-Briggs personality test, I was an ESFP. That is short for Extravert, Sensing, Feeling, Perceiving.

During the Middle Management sessions, we focused on leadership/managing and supporting staff, cultural competency, managing change, and motivating

teams, budgeting and financial management, communication skills/conflict resolution, and program evaluation.

Once again, I went through the process. Same behaviors as before with a little
more serious tone to it because at this "level," some members of the group had a
zero-tolerance or interest in distractions.

Seems a little boring if you ask me. I began to feel the pressure of having to
produce documents, assignments, reports, and other projects that were part of
the curriculum.

Telling from the aggressive pace of the upcoming training I knew I had an
uphill battle. Not due to my inability to get through but more due to the place
where I was emotionally.

During this time in my career, I responded to many crisis incidents as a helper
when I needed help myself. I was coming off the most devastating loss of my life,
the loss of my brother. That loss was as painful as the loss of my soul as a child.

Despite my internal battle and bitter reflections on the losses life handed me I
managed to successfully complete the MMI in 2010. Time would not stop and I
could not either. I had goals and aspirations that needed my attention.

27

TURBULENCE

All of a sudden, I was 40. I was not sure that I wanted to turn those numbers around to 04 and claim to be only turning four years old. A funny thing we do as people is fight our aging. As soon as we begin to cross over the 30s, we begin to find ways to decrease the numbers as a way to claim that we are younger or to simply feel better about getting older.

For me, returning to four years old would mean that I would be forced to revisit my childhood. Admittedly I cannot remember, what if I could? I am sure that it would help clear up some of the reasons why I was neglected or abused.

Perhaps it would allow me to see the point when it got out of hand and the Department of Children Youth and Families had to intervene to remove us from the care of my mother.

Remembering 2010 was more difficult than I thought. I searched and searched my memory bank but there was nothing.

Had the impact of the serious head injury suffered after a car accident begun to affect me?

There I was entering a new stage in life and I had to fight through my short-term memory gaps to function, learn what I needed in order to advance in my career, and also fight off some of my bad memories from past traumas.

The 40s is the stage where many would say pre-deterioration begins. When everything begins to feel harder to do, including exercising and changing learned and developed bad behaviors. It is also the stage where you are supposed to consider the future, all of your retirement plans, and when the once dreaded AARP card arrives in the mail.

Sure, I have learned to accept getting older is part of the process, however coming to grips with what it means physically for the majority of us still doesn't sound appealing. Who would have guessed I would have made it to this year, this age, this stage? Off the heels of having been trained to become a future leader, and manager, once again!

Was I truly ready? My face had been in the public eye for many years by then both on television and in print. Sometimes it had been for good reasons and other times for not-so-good reasons. I had been considered a leader for years in the community of youth violence prevention and within the gang. Did I really deserve that recognition? For better or worse I had it.

I spent 2010 celebrating so many of life's natural steps. According to shows and marketing on television, the bible, family, friends, or society, you are expected to follow certain steps and be at a specific place financially, emotionally, and socially by this point. Similar to what the trajectory from elementary school to college is supposed to be for all of us.

This year had several weddings, the birth of children for people close to me, and trips to celebrate the end of the single life for one (a wedding). I was also in transition from being a rescuer to my mom and to being a decider of my marriage. The workplace was just as fragmented.

As I mentioned previously, I was expected to be a leader. This was scary for me because that meant that I was supposed to have control. How much control did I really have?

Consider that title LEADER. Coming from my past I understood it to mean that you bow down to no one. At this time in my life that was far from the truth.

I had to answer to those who were above me. I was held accountable for producing results and outcomes for the funds that contributed to my salary.

The stubborn man in me showed himself regularly especially when I was not wanting others to see my deficiencies or when I felt as if I could not perform to the expectations.

After all, this man here didn't fold, he fought through and needed no one to survive. He was a dreamer, creator, and socializer. To me, process, policy, and procedure suffocated the joy out of life and made me feel that life could not be spontaneous or fun.

This taught me that responsibility was going to be present forever. To me, it meant that I couldn't breathe.

I would put up incredible fights and mount a serious defense when confronted with my shortcomings. I never wanted to nor was I allowing myself to take accountability for the failure to perform the "boring" and unnecessary part of my job.

Writing reports, presentations, documenting my efforts, or even submitting time sheets, blah... *why?*

The fact was that internally I was very aware that I had a very difficult time remembering information. I also knew that I had never developed any habits for writing. I do not remember a time when a parent, family member, or friend sat with me and helped with homework or read me a book.

I felt as if I didn't understand the assignment and that I would look foolish once the information I had written was presented. Not knowing how to effectively write or how to develop the type of thoughts to support the information they needed added another level of pressure and anxiety. So I would choose the one thing that I could control. An outburst.

Anything to deflect the true issue. It was easy for me to disregard a request because once I made up my mind to not do it, there was nothing that would change my mind. I was that stubborn bull. I would just put it aside, and consider it unnecessary and a waste of time.

Perhaps that was frustration, shame, and pride at play. After some time, I felt embarrassed when I was not able to figure things out. My charisma and charm began to wear thin on those who were responsible for reporting our results and proving that we had met the outcomes promised to those who were paying for our work to be done.

It was so difficult for me to retain the information I needed to do better. It just didn't matter to me; it had no meaning. Why couldn't I just say what I did and that be enough? Why couldn't I just share awesome stories, heroin stories, or dangerous stories?

I could just captivate the listeners and not have to worry about paperwork. I did not possess the discipline in my habits or my thinking to give paperwork and accountability the importance they deserved. I wasn't an office guy, I was a gang prevention, violence prevention, and outreach person. Why should all that writing stuff matter?

If I didn't know it now and had "made it" this far, why would I have to do it and learn it now?

Although every day felt like I had to force myself up when thinking I would once again be asked to not just do work but provide evidence of the work completed, I liked the feeling of being in workspaces like the University of Connecticut School of Social Work and the Hartford Housing Authority.

I enjoyed the feeling of safety, belonging, and structure that came with being in a space where I was seen as someone valuable.

I enjoyed the money too. These were not volunteer opportunities as I had been involved with in the past. Between 1993 and 1995 my path within the gang was changing. I was not just a member or soldier. I was starting to develop into a leader. Someone with a voice and authority.

This afforded me time to speak at meetings and made it possible for me to make suggestions on the actions the gang should take in the community. I became the spokesperson for the gang. Being assigned that title meant that I could speak to anyone interested in speaking with gang leadership on their behalf.

It was that appointment as a spokesperson that landed me my first interview on television. It was with none other than Mr. Lew Brown also known as "Downtown Lew Brown" from NBC CT.

The interview was held on the street on a frigid cold night. We prepared for the interview and just chatted a bit. Lew, was straight to the point and appeared very comfortable standing on the street in the Frog Hollow neighborhood.

I was pretty nervous. I had no media training and I was not really sure how this was supposed to go, what questions I would be asked, or even what to say. But I had been identified as the voice for the gang so I had to complete the assignment.

I wore a black beanie-style hat and a brown leather jacket. I spoke about the dangerous drug ecstasy that would change the behaviors of young people in our community and embolden them to commit crimes.

Lew knew the community very well and wasn't the least bit surprised by what I was sharing. He grew up in the city and understood the many challenges facing those who lived there. I had seen Lew on television for many years reporting on the many violent crimes that had taken place in the city.

From that interview, I earned a following and gained the interest of some leaders in the community who were interested in working alongside the gangs to prevent violence. This was one of my roles at the Hartford Housing Authority under the leadership of Mr. John Wardlaw.

I enjoyed the feeling of being clean when I was at the office. I had professional clothes that I could wear and it felt good. My "professional" attire wouldn't necessarily be considered professional in the normal sense. It was plaid shirts, clean/neat jeans, timberland boots, and many times a baseball-type hat (known as a fitted hat).

Another seemingly small item to some ended up being a huge item for me. The way in which professionals spoke. It was a different language from what I was used to. Especially in boardrooms.

Data this, analysis that, human development, etc. As we discussed strategies for reducing the levels of violence and crime across the city of Hartford and at the housing complex aka "The Projects."

There were many differences between the lifestyles that I led. On one hand, I had to survive the "streets" and on the other, I had to assimilate into my professional surroundings.

Speaking differently, thinking differently, behaving differently, and learning differently. All of this was a balancing act within my head. There was no way that I could allow my newfound professionalism to make me weak on the streets.

Who would take my spot in the gang, who would challenge me and my reputation? What was happening in the community that I was missing? Would I be a target of another gang and be forced to take action on behalf of the gang that I belonged to?

This new version of me was incredibly difficult for me to adapt to. In many ways, I felt as if it was a matter of life and death. That is the balance that I referred to previously.

Adapting to the work environment was a little easier than adapting to the realities of the threats I faced due to the perception that I was no longer loyal to the gang or to the streets.

The first few weeks on the job were challenging as it would be for anyone beginning a new experience or job. There was a grace period as I was learning the ropes of the job. I was asked to work at the housing complex that many of my gang brothers and sisters called home and even in other housing authority properties where my enemies lived. This compounded the difficulties of adapting to my new role at work.

The greatest test of my new role came from some of the residents of the A-Side of the housing project known as Charter Oak Terrace. COT, as it was known to us on the street, was split into two sections. A-side and D-side.

For many years these two sides were in conflict with each other. I don't know the history but during my time as an employee of the Housing Authority, I knew that A-side was the claimed territory of the national gang and D-side was claimed by the local gang.

Each day I had to report to the office. I had to be aware of my surroundings. I was a rival and I was on their turf. The management offices and the parking lot for the Housing Authority were separated from the housing units by a chain-linked fence.

On many occasions when I arrived, left for the day, or went about my work day in and out of the office I would run into members of the national gang. Some days they would yell things at me, other days they would throw up their gang signs, and other days they would just look my way.

From time to time, I would have other members of the gang accompany me at the office to help conduct outreach in the target communities with youth who were in need of support or to attend meetings related to employment opportunities for young men and women who lived in the housing complex.

One day while traveling to a section of the North End with one of the members we noticed a vehicle behind us that appeared to be following us. After I moved from the slow lane to the travel lane on the highway, I noticed the vehicle behind us also changed lanes.

I shared this with my passenger and he turned to look at the vehicle. Through the rear-view mirror, I noticed the passenger reaching out his window. In a matter of seconds, we heard gunfire. I stepped on the gas and accelerated to over 80 or 90 miles per hour.

The car behind us accelerated and the passenger fired again. We both ducked slightly in our seats trying to become less of a target than if we were sitting straight up.

I dipped the car at a high rate of speed into the fast lane and the car behind me followed. For several exits, I was swerving from lane to lane avoiding any possibility of being a steady target for the passenger shooting at us.

At the fourth exit, I was able to swerve in front of a semi-truck in the slow lane on my left. I cut the truck off and he slammed on the horn and broke. I was able to make the exit ramp and the car chasing us could not make it. We escaped with our lives and took a deep breath. We continued looking behind us making sure they had not found a different path to reaching us.

We continued on to our destination. We both understood this was possible and were grateful that we had been paying attention. We were not sure who they were but that could be the case on any day of the week. Someone I had never met could be the person to end my life.

I had to control myself and not allow anything to distract me from the work. I was a target and could be attacked at any moment.

I had to present myself in a different way while I was at work and in my normal way when I was off work. I had to survive both roles. I could not afford to lose either the job or my connection to the streets.

In order to get by and keep my job I did what I would do on the streets. I used my charm and charisma so that others would feel compelled to help me. I believed they felt they were helping a friend.

I was not a very capable reader or writer so I pushed things aside that required that. It put me in a bind more than once because I was late on assignments often. Joking around, being silly, and using words that I had just learned on the job got me by.

I could do a lot of talking but when the real work was required, I failed miserably.

Once I began to understand the importance of completing tasks, I began to take pride in what I was able to complete. Even though my completed written tasks would always be met with many corrections including many grammatical errors. I was given some credit for the progress I had made.

In many ways, I was a project, perhaps research, to those who gave me opportunities. They took a major risk on a high school dropout, convicted criminal, and high-profile gang member who was still very much involved with the day-to-day actions of the gang.

But within their circles, they were seen as trailblazers, and risk-takers and regarded for taking on this challenge.

In more circles than not they were also seen as coddlers and supporters of gang involvement and criminal behavior.

One anonymous reader of the *Hartford Courant* who read the article announcing that the Housing Authority had hired me wrote, "This guy (referring to me) should be taken somewhere and shot." He did not think I deserved the salary I was being paid. This person also wrote, "There are those who are not convicted criminals who deserve the opportunity at the job he was hired for."

I was not deterred and continued on. Many years would pass before I completely bought into learning anything new but this was at least a start.

During the time when I was working, my brain was busy and focused on work. I didn't have to worry about where I was going to sleep because the money I was making allowed me to rent an apartment.

One thing that I have come to learn about myself is that I believe that I can adapt to any situation. Perhaps all of the lived experiences with trauma, abandonment, abuse, neglect, homelessness, and uncertainty had permanently designed me to make it work somehow. Adapt and keep on.

Just as I had learned to mask my pain and fear as a child, I had learned to put on the show I needed to as I grew older and the challenges I faced were different.

I believe that the key was survival instincts. I figured out 1 plus 1 equals 2. That if you wanted this, you had to do this (with some bending of the rules). I had a very difficult time quieting my thoughts. I had to keep my life outside of work present in my thoughts, I had to return to it every day. I also had to keep my head in the game in the office if I was going to keep the job.

I had many years of practice with transition (although not the best training) and it was paying off somewhat here.

As an abused child who was threatened with physical harm if I spoke of my torture to anyone, I had learned how to present as if nothing was wrong to protect myself.

As a homeless teen, I learned to say what was necessary to someone to convince them to help me. I also learned the incredible skill of reading people's true intentions and feeling their energy. I became resilient through fear.

I was just focusing on the experience and I hadn't had that before. Overcoming the challenges wasn't an easy process. It wasn't like an overnight thing, it was a slow drip, a long process to get away from what I experienced every day.

I hadn't had a safe space to think, rest my apprehensions, or relax my hypervigilance. Having this time to be at work and being in a different space helped me see that quiet is possible.

Those moments of pause from chaos are actually a pretty sweet deal.

When it was quiet, I learned how to think better and healthier. It supported my ability to focus.

When you learn how to develop goals and how to take steps to achieve those goals it does something to you internally. I believe it allows you to see beyond the moment. It gives you a sense of possibility.

It is not without fear of the unknown but it does give you a new perspective and suddenly noisy spaces and chaos are not as attractive.

One of the things that was clear was that I had to leave my job every day and return back to my reality and there were two completely different worlds. I started to figure out the best way to balance my work world and my street world. I needed to spend more time in this quiet environment, this other environment, this more productive environment, than I was spending in the other more violent, more chaotic environment. This was helping.

I began to make better decisions, smarter decisions on who I associated with and for how long, what to expose myself to, and what to consider healthy for me. I had to understand that positive decision-making was a skill I needed.

I started to realize all of that. Not by knowing the textbook definition but by what I felt. I was feeling better about choosing to do positive things with my time. Going back to my life on the streets was not as appealing as it once was.

Once I started to understand that, I started to realize that I needed to be able to think clearly, and critically about the decisions that I was about to make, spend more time on myself, and work on myself. I needed to adopt this mindset.

I had to practice what I had learned at work. Not just at work but actually doing more thinking about it when I was home.

For the first time, I began thinking about going back to school. For the first time, I was thinking about actually reading about the career that I wanted. For the first time, I was using some of the words that I was hearing in my new environment with people around me.

I felt like I wanted to learn. If I was to expand my knowledge, awareness, clarity, and vision I had to have the desire to do better in all parts of my life.

I was able to overcome some of the challenges when I started to realize the risks that I was taking. I had to apply actions and thoughts that could help me avoid costly mistakes.

No more frequently turning to drinking alcohol because I had a responsibility. I started to develop accountability.

I fought tooth and nail against being accountable when my mentor was working on teaching me how. For once I felt bad (after a while) for getting to work late. I felt as if I owed somebody something.

This responsibility I was given was greater than me.

I realized I had to do something different in my life when I was able to spend more time at the UConn School of Social Work.

The more I experienced new people the more I realized there was more to be seen and done than what I was seeing and doing.

28

INDIANA

I was able to get a taste of doing something very different when I flew out to Indiana University to speak in front of several thousand students attending a conference.

They were looking for inspiration and I was chosen as one of the people that could offer them that with my story. They needed someone to speak with those in attendance about the dangers of gangs and the risks associated with being a member of one.

This was the first time in my life that I had been to any place outside of my bubble. That bubble included Hartford, New York, New Jersey, and Puerto Rico to visit family.

Corn and barley fields appeared to surround the vehicle I was in. The drive to Indiana University from the airport allowed me to just take in the sights and be in awe of a new place. I do not remember any structures or landmarks but it sure was different being there.

I arrived at the university and was in awe of the size of the campus. They had a massive stadium that hosted football games. I had never seen anything like that. I was greeted by the organizers of the event and they provided me with instructions on what I would be doing and when I would be presenting.

I was then directed to a building that would serve as my hotel or sleeping quarters while I was there. It was a single unit in a student dorm. Once again this was a first-time experience for me. It was surreal to me.

The next morning the phone rang and it was one of the organizers on the phone requesting that I head down to the conference area for breakfast. As a kid from my city and with my lived experience, I had never known anything like this. I never imagined I'd be experiencing something like this.

I made it to breakfast and there were hundreds, perhaps a few thousand people walking around and eating breakfast. They were mostly youth accompanied by adults wearing badges to identify them. Most of the youth wore identifying t-shirts for their group.

I was just taking in the sights and trying to figure out what to do. Where do I go? How do I behave? Where do I sit? Who do I talk to?

I got my breakfast from a buffet-style line and took a seat with several strangers. I said, "Good morning." People looked up from eating their food and nodded or said, "Good morning." We exchanged information with each other for a little while. We spoke about things such as where we were from and what group we represented.

Breakfast was over and I headed back to the dorms to relax before I had to head back to the conference space.

The phone rang again and it was the organizer explaining that they were ready for me to join them for my presentation. I get myself organized and begin my walk to the conference space.

I walked in and was absolutely overwhelmed by the number of people who were present in that space. A sea of people. Mostly young students from schools around the country. I was escorted to the stage and seated next to a couple of people who were also expected to speak.

After a few introductions and welcoming comments, I was introduced. That was my cue to get up and head towards the podium. I was somewhat nervous. It was the first time that I was going to share my story about my life living in poverty and gang membership with many strangers.

I arrived at the podium and faced the crowd. There were more people than I could see. I looked towards the back of the room that seemed to be so far away.

Having a podium allowed me to rest my hands on something to prevent me from moving around too much. I tend to be very animated when I talk and I sometimes wave my hands when I am making a point I am passionate about.

On the face of the podium were the words "Youth & Unity Rebuilding Our Community." It was a message directed at the members of the audience. If they united, they could build a better community.

I wore a light blue sleeveless button-down shirt with my red and blue beads which were mandatory necklaces members of the gang had to wear to show their membership to whoever we came across. On my head, I had a handkerchief made up of two handkerchiefs sewn together. One side was red and the other was blue. The knot tying it together was to the front to communicate the message of a bond between the colors.

The beads and bandana-style headgear were all part of the role and symbol that allowed us to represent our membership openly.

Once I was done with my remarks, I rejoined the others seated on stage. I received very warm applause from the audience.

I returned from that trip feeling a sense of pride and inspiration. I was hooked.

I was hooked on the feeling of being valued by others because I had life experiences that I could share to help others avoid my mistakes.

I was hooked on the kind treatment by those who had afforded me the opportunity to be on this trip and to serve in the role that I was serving.

It felt amazing to look out into a large audience and see faces of wonder and admiration. I didn't need to fight or behave irresponsibly to get attention.

It felt great to share my story and it felt healing to have it recognized and appreciated. I wanted to feel this again and again. Storytelling became a form of therapy.

Before the presentation, I had a feeling of uncertainty, anxiety, and awe. I was not sure how I would be received or how my message would be understood.

I was encouraged to just let it flow and be myself. In the end, I felt pride and accomplishment. I had managed to overcome all of the jitters and shared my journey of gang life and the prison experience.

The experience was a challenge to my fear of telling my truth and sharing my vulnerabilities. This was not something that I practiced growing up. On the streets sharing these things was seen as going soft or could even lead to the loss of my "man card."

This unwritten rule made me feel as if sharing what frightened me, what pain I'd been through and the struggles I had with life was less than manly.

That perhaps was the greatest self-defeating lesson I learned. Never let them see you sweat or look weak.

In reality, everything strong is in being connected to your emotions and finding productive and positive ways to embrace all of one's terrors and pitfalls.

29

BROKEN VOWS

Perhaps the reason 2010 was such a blur was due to my battle with my wife at the time. We were at the end of our relationship. It was a period of our relationship that was filled with turmoil, arguments, fights, and frustration.

There were moments of attempted reconciliation that were mostly considered as a way to stay connected to someone I had become used to or to a situation that was familiar. The love that had united us was no longer the same and the fight to end it was sometimes bitter.

Relationships with women have always been difficult for me. I did know love but not commitment. Commitment meant that I was opening myself up to be hurt. That I would be vulnerable and that a person would see the real me. Not the charmer or the person who was confident in his ability to be a tough guy. I felt as if I should be free to be who I was and to do as I wished. Interestingly enough I did not truly know who I was.

My first relationship with a woman had failed. It had led to hurt, pain, loneliness, and abandonment. That relationship was with my mother. I refused to allow another woman to make me feel that way again. I created drama in relationships when I felt I was getting closer to women. I masked the fear of falling in love with acts of self-harm and rage-filled tantrums.

I would storm out of places, and engage in arguments for things I made up or perceived as being disrespectful to me. Honestly, I just never wanted to be vulnerable to being hurt again.

This behavior contributed to so many of my challenges and encounters with the police. The irrational thinking that every woman was out to hurt me made it impossible for me to engage in honest relationships. I had allowed my pain and fear to determine my actions.

I had unresolved feelings of loss and trauma and my coping mechanisms were putting up a wall of violence, threats, emotional outbursts, and self-destructive behaviors.

For many years I had subjected my wife to my bad behavior. The lies and bad acts were all created to guard me against truly accepting love into my heart.

Many years before the end of our relationship I had realized that I was hurting my relationship with my wife and negatively impacting the young life of our daughter.

I had been arrested a few times before my relationship began and I had dropped out of school. That negatively impacted my ability to find opportunities for work or to make progress in my life. After the arrest for the demonstration at the hospital, I made sure to do better.

I secured a job working for a maintenance company and did my best to stay away from the streets. I did what I could to sustain the family that I had. I still could not figure out a way to get away from what I was connected to on the streets.

My duties at the work site included cleaning out abandoned apartments and preparing apartments for future renters. Every day I would head out to the back alley of the building located on Washington Street to dump old furniture and trash left behind by former tenants.

On the street behind that alley, there was a wooden fence limiting access between the two buildings. During one trip to the alley, I noticed several guys moving in the backyard behind the fence. I was always aware of any movement around me. I needed to make sure that I was not too comfortable in my workspace because I could get caught off guard by my enemies.

I could hear them talking from behind the fence and then noticed the colors they were wearing. Black and gold. The colors of a national gang.

They were behind the building waiting to see if they could confront me. I quickly slipped back into the building and climbed the stairs to the second floor.

I looked out the window and confirmed they were "posted" (waiting) there until I came out to the alley. The street I worked on was mostly in the national gangs-controlled area.

I used a phone in the management office to call a few of the guys I knew to come and get me and to make sure that I made it out safely. Once they arrived, I exited the front door, jumped into a waiting car, and headed home.

Several guys were waiting out front in a car and immediately pulled out from their parking spot and began following us. The driver of the car I was in stepped on the gas, ran several lights, and headed toward Capitol Avenue.

They continued chasing us down Capital Avenue and onto Broad Street headed north. We pulled into the parking lot of an insurance company that allowed us to cut across to Sigourney Street. Once we entered that area, they stopped chasing us.

If they continued chasing us in that direction, they would have been in another local gang's territory and would most likely have had to deal with the guys hanging out on the street. It could be a costly and deadly decision. They retreated back toward where they came from.

I arrived home grateful to be safe and knowing that I had to arm myself in the future while I was at work if I was going to feel as if I had a chance to survive.

While staying engaged in this circle of violent incidents and the gang lifestyle I continued to be missing from many times where it was important that a father be present for their daughter. At night when she cried, or when my wife needed a break so she could rest or study for her college classes.

I would come to the house after having been out drinking. I would be loud and inconsiderate. Making all kinds of noise and disrupting everyone's rest and quiet time. This was causing tensions to rise between my wife and me resulting in our daughter having to listen to us fighting.

Sometimes I would come home after a fight bloodied and acting like a madman. My wife would fear for her safety and my daughter would be sad that her daddy had a boo-boo.

I began arming myself with knives and guns to protect myself and them from my enemies on the street.

One evening while we were all home, I saw the tires of a car slowly moving on the driveway that led to the rear of our building. We lived in a basement-level apartment and the driveway could be seen from our windows.

That car was "creepin'" (slowly moving or laying low to not be spotted). I was in our bedroom at the time and I was always on the lookout for anything that seemed suspicious. This caught my attention and I followed the car through every room in the apartment.

It turned out they were members of the neighborhood gang and they were looking for me. I lived in an area that was closest to the territory they claimed as theirs. I recognized the car from the neighborhood. I grabbed a weapon and prepared myself to engage them if they made it to my apartment door or if they looked through my windows.

I watched as they parked in an empty parking spot and waited for a while. Eventually, they exited through the other side of the driveway. Even though they had left, I could never relax.

This continued to build up the levels of anxiety at home and eventually, my wife decided it was time to leave this place.

My actions and behavior had eroded the trust in my ability to keep them safe and to tend to my duties and responsibilities.

My actions were normal for me. It was my lesson as a child. Chaos ruled. Uncertainty and desperation must be present at all times in order for us to survive and take action.

So, I created it. Although I was employed, I had not abandoned those lessons and believed this was how I was. My mind was fixed this way. I wanted it and felt it was necessary for me to function.

I had no other lessons on how to be a different kind of man or person. I worked because something inside of me thought this is what a man is supposed to do. He works to take care of his family. Other than that, I was not responsible for the mental, physical, or emotional well-being of my family. No one had made sure those were fine in me.

I had promised myself to not expose my children to trauma but with every action I took in honor of the gang or to feed my addiction to violence I did the exact opposite. Every time I left the house accompanied by my family they were at risk of being innocent victims of violence due to my actions and decisions. I would protect them with my life but they needed protection because of me. I so wanted to be a role model to my children and make them proud as a father.

I believe the desire to be a "family man" came from two experiences in my life. One was the missing family element in my life as a child. Being shipped from one home to another. The sadness I felt having had my brothers and sisters separated.

The other was what I was exposed to physically. It made me angry and violent but it also made me think that I did not want to do that to my children. I wanted to feel that I was safe in a space with the people who were my family. I wanted some stability.

I believe that along the way I saw what I believed to be good families and felt happy to see it. I also believe that when I was younger my aunts and grandparents stepped in to show me what family bonds could be like.

I really love the traditions that I experienced with my family in Puerto Rico. Those are pieces of what formed my need to be a family or to have one but I was still connected to members of the gang, I was connected to the lifestyle of gang membership violence, war with other groups, late-night drinking and not having a plan.

Watching my back not only from law enforcement, enemy members of other gangs, and even some members within the gang I was a part of who apparently wanted to elevate their position within the gang.

In order for that to happen sometimes, they have to discredit you or try to do whatever they could to prove that they were more worthy than you were of a leadership role.

I also had to consider those who had been victims of the gangs. They were those additional enemies we had developed because they felt hurt and angry due to our actions against them.

When you hurt somebody, you can't assume they forget simply because you moved on.

My wife and I were at the end of our relationship. Nearly 17 years had passed and we were done. We had many good times and two beautiful kids. In the end, I was at fault for the failed marriage. I had yet to be free of my fear, insecurity, rage, and deep-rooted pain and it cost me.

30

A Wish Granted

It all began as a usual year does, whistles, screams, hugs, and desires for a successful/blessed new year.

Screams and hugs of a different kind would replace the hopeful joy-filled ones of a New Year's celebration.

The year that crumbled the foundation of my family would soon take place. It was also the year that turned things from cloudy to clear for me in my head and heart.

Cold frigid Connecticut makes it difficult to visit those you have lost in the cemetery. The grounds in January and February are frozen solid, snow-covered, and unforgiving.

I spent days visiting my beautiful big brother in this climate, accompanying my sickening mom on her tear-filled visits. January was the month he was taken from our lives.

Even if January was a blazing hot summer month anywhere else it will always represent the bitter chill that goes through me when I remember hearing, "I am sorry, we did everything we could to save him, however, he didn't make it, he's gone."

This was going to be my first full year on my own after my split from my wife of almost 17 years. I was going to focus on my children's well-being and on proving that I could be a good dad even when I did not live with them all of the time.

I had received word that my mom's health was deteriorating. She had been diagnosed with cancer. This news changed the way I planned my every day. I had to plan for visits with my mom in Boston Massachusetts so that I could see her as often as possible to provide her whatever support I could in dealing with her sickness.

I spent many hours traveling from Connecticut to Massachusetts. I felt as if I had to be there for her and make sure that she knew that she could depend on me to provide her with some care.

The two hours there and back allowed me time to process how the visits would go and time to decompress from the experience of caring for her. I felt sad for her. I knew that she had been a smoker and drug user for many years but I didn't desire for her to suffer in the manner she was.

She was battling esophageal cancer. Doctors expressed how unlikely it was that she would be able to survive it. She was scared and I could see it in her eyes, hear it in her voice and feel it in her heart when I hugged her.

She was not ready to die but did not have any control over what would happen next. As I reflected on the visits on my way back home, I often thought about how the passing of my brother had crushed her spirit.

I thought about how unfair life can feel at some points. Having lost my brother in 2008 I was now faced with the 99% certainty that I would be losing my mom three years later.

I don't believe she ever recovered from receiving the horrific news of my brother's death due to homicide. We all struggled with the loss and needed time to heal from the pain. She never really regained her will to heal.

My experience and journey with my mom had been one of ups and downs. Her actions and lifestyle of drug use made it impossible for our connection to be a normal mom-and-son relationship. I found myself creating distance from her as I grew through my twenties and thirties.

I did not see her often between those years of my life. I was on a path filled with violence, gangs, uncertainty, feeling lost on the streets, serving time in prison, and doing my best to navigate all of that. It was the same time period where I was also straddling two worlds.

I was surviving the best way I could. I had been married, had a child, started going back to school, got a job, purchased my first home, obtained a license, and began to understand that I could do something positive with my life.

She missed all of those moments. The good and bad. The ugly and sweet. The tender and hurtful. The fear and hope. All missed. I resented that. I was angry and hurt on the inside and I had not reconciled that with her.

I had been aware of my mother's on-and-off struggle with drugs from the age of 12. That is when I began to notice behaviors from her that made me realize that something was not right with her. There were moments when she would be overly excited and others when I would watch her fall asleep almost standing upright.

I would come to learn that at the moments when she was overly excited it was due to cocaine and when she could not keep herself awake it was due to heroin. I felt so confused as a child because I could not understand what she was doing and why.

This on-and-off battle, mood swings, and changes in behavior were frustrating and embarrassing. It filled me with desperation, depression, anger, and bitterness. Those feelings remained within me for many years and I didn't know how to ease them or rid myself of them.

I remember hearing my mom and other family members refer to a daughter my mom had with a boyfriend that she had lost custody of. I had heard the talks about how much pain she felt losing her as a result of an investigation by DCF. She was devastated to learn that she had been adopted by a family and would no longer be able to see her.

During several tearful conversations, I also learned that the drug use was in part happening due to the emptiness she felt in her heart for having lost her daughter to the system.

Several years prior to mom's diagnosis I had begun to believe that I could find this person she was missing in her life. My sister. Someone I did not ever recall meeting. I was interested in finding her. I wanted to see what she looked like. I wanted to see who she lived with. I wondered if she remembered us.

I asked my mom if she could give me any information about her. Could she provide any records from her birth or any other things that she could remember that could assist me in finding her? Due to her off-and-on battle, she could not. She had lost most of her possessions which included documents and pictures of her children.

She asked me to reach out to her ex-boyfriend who had fathered my sister. I was able to make contact with him. I sat at his kitchen table and asked a series of questions. He was able to provide me with her name and approximate year of birth. Neither one of them had very clear memories of any other information related to their daughter.

I used the information that I had received to approach DCF and request permission to make contact with her. My request was denied due to the fact that I was not a parent and needed permission or rights of guardianship transferred to me in order for any action to be taken.

I convinced my mom to transfer parental rights to me. I went back to DCF with a notarized letter from my mom detailing that I now had the parental rights to submit a request for information on my sister.

I was told that they could not share any information on her or her whereabouts. They could put a note in the record that I had been looking for her and wanted to meet her. If she ever contacted them to learn about her birth mother and siblings, they would share my information and leave it up to her to reach out if she so desired.

I said I understood.

I shared this information with Mom and she appeared to have a slight glimmer of hope but remained skeptical that she would ever see her again.

A few months went by and I received a call from an unknown number. I did not answer the call. I saw a notification come in that whoever called had left a voicemail. I continued doing what I was doing at the time and decided to check the message later.

That evening I accessed my voicemail and confirmed there was a message. I struck the number 1 on the telephone keypad and began listening to the message.

A voice I had never heard before spoke. The caller stated they were from DCF and were calling to speak with Iran Nazario. The caller provided a number to call and an extension where I could reach them.

It was late in the day when I listened to the message so I was sure that I would not reach anyone. I felt a sense of excitement because I knew that DCF would only be calling regarding my inquiry into my sister. I thought about the voicemail for a while that evening. I was not sure what I would hear.

Maybe there was no information available? Maybe she was not interested in meeting anyone? Maybe something had happened to her and she was no longer around? Or maybe it was just a procedural call to get more information from me?

I called my half-brother and told him that someone from DCF had called me and that I would let him know what they said when I spoke to them. He was always very interested in learning about his sister and mentioned her every so often.

The next morning, I called the number and typed in the extension when prompted. I was able to connect with the DCF representative. I was absolutely thrilled with what I was told.

My sister had checked in to see if someone was looking for her. Due to that action on her behalf, DCF was allowed to share my contact information with my sister and she could reach out when and if she was ready.

I was advised that there was no guarantee she would reach out or that she would even check back in with them to inquire about someone looking for her again.

I hung up the phone and my mind raced with thoughts of her reaching out and calling to make a connection. I thought I had to share this with her siblings, her father, and my mom. I thought for sure this would bring joy to the family and in some way inspire them to get more involved with the process.

As I shared the information with my siblings, I received mixed reactions. I believe that it was hard for them to wrap their brains around the possibility that our sister would finally be in our presence. My update was met with cautious optimism and uncertainty.

Surprisingly her father and my mom had similar reactions as the brothers and sisters. It appeared they did not know how to respond. It felt like an "Oh that's nice dear" moment. Almost as if they believed my efforts would not pay off. They were not as excited as I was. In my heart, I felt this was progress.

Perhaps their minds and years of not knowing would not allow for them to be excited about a simple possibility.

A couple of weeks went by and there was no word from either DCF or her. As it usually happens, I continued on with my life and tucked the possibility of making a connection with my sister in some space in my head.

Suddenly my phone rang. I looked at the screen and saw it was a call from an unknown number. Perhaps because I had tucked away the possibility of receiving a call I answered. That is something that I would not have done before if I saw an unknown number on my phone screen.

I said, "Hello."

I heard a soft voice on the other end. The caller said, "It's me, your sister."

I was sitting in my car at the time. I pressed the phone tight up against my ear, felt myself getting a hot flash, and felt goosebumps all over the back of my neck.

I said, "Hi, how are you?"

It was the call I felt would come and it had finally happened. I had so many questions for her. I wanted to know so much but I was not sure how to process what was happening. It felt so strange to be talking with her. It never crossed my mind that this person on the other side of the call was a fake or that this was a cruel prank.

For some reason with only her voice on the phone, I could feel our connection as kin.

I explained to her that there were several people that wanted to meet her. She explained she was not ready to take that step. We spoke for a short while and she said she would call me back sometime in the future to talk some more.

I hung up the phone and sat in the car a little while longer trying to figure out what to do next. I had to tell Mom. I felt victorious. I was smiling from ear to ear.

This news would most certainly turn my mom's heartache of having lost her into pure joy.

A major part of me had been searching for my sister with even more determination after my brother was murdered. I cared deeply that my mother was suffering so much due to the loss of my brother. I watched as she fell deeper and deeper into a state of depression. She mentioned that now she would never see two of her children again.

Although my heart was broken and I was operating as an injured healer for her I felt as if finding a way to bring some good news to her would make it easier to heal from her feeling of pain.

I drove out to Boston Massachusetts to deliver the wonderful news to her in person.

"Mami, I spoke with my sister."

She was lying in bed and her eyes burst wide open.

She asked, "*En serio?* (Are you serious?) But how? When? What did she say? Where is she?"

All of these questions spilled out of her in rapid fashion as she worked her way up to a seated position.

I gave her all of the details of how we became connected and shared some of our conversations.

Her next question was, "Does she want to see me?"

I responded, "She is not ready to do that yet." She was surprised and for a few moments had to grasp that fact. She was asking why. After I calmed her down a little, I explained that I would be the one to make the connection but only after she was ready. She agreed and asked me to tell her she said hello.

In November of 2008 in a town right near the Connecticut-Massachusetts border, I finally met my sister.

We went to a small local place she was familiar with and I was thrilled that she had followed through on her decision to meet in person.

She asked me many questions and I responded with as many questions as she asked. I stared into her eyes and face and it was obvious that she was my mother's daughter. The similarities in facial features were clear.

We spoke for over two hours about many things. I shared the passing of her brother and she expressed her condolences. We continued talking as we walked away from that space and told us until next time.

As I drove away from there, I realized just how important a moment this was. I realized that I had met my sister who I had not seen since we were young children. She was real.

After the visit, I stopped in to see some family in Lawrence, Massachusetts. I spent the night there and then traveled to Boston in the morning to tell my mom in person about the meeting with her daughter.

When I told my mom she began to cry. I explained that she was real and that she looked a lot like her. She called out to God and said thank you. She was in total shock and felt a sense of relief. She hugged me tight and said thank you.

She then immediately asked, "When can I meet her?"

I responded, "I don't know yet."

From the look on her face, it was clear she didn't understand.

I knew that was how she was feeling so I explained that she should give her some more time. She reluctantly agreed.

Two weeks later after a few more conversations the moment that mom had been waiting for since I could remember the mention of my sister had arrived.

Mom was finally going to meet her daughter.

We met in Wethersfield, Connecticut. The moment was filled with tears of joy for Mom and moments of curiosity from my sister. They embraced regularly mostly due to my mom reaching out to grab and squeeze her. In my family when we got together, we embraced often and were very affectionate with each other in a loving, kind way.

In my heart, as I watched them embrace and look at one another I was hopeful it would mean healing for Mom and reconnection for my sister. I was filling my heart with something joyful to help heal the pain from the loss of my brother and perhaps also mend some old wounds from my childhood.

Several months passed and my sister and mom had connected on several occasions. By the summer of 2009, my sister had met other family members and her birth father. Things seemed to be going well.

There was direct communication with family members and I had been developing my own relationship with my sister.

Despite the meetings and time spent together something wasn't quite right with Mom. She was getting sick frequently and visiting hospitals with regularity. She was being prescribed more medications to help deal with her symptoms.

I was fearful that she was relapsing back into a dependency on drugs. This time over-the-counter medications. I did not want to see that again. I remained connected to her as much as I could from over 2.5 hours away.

31

FORGIVENESS

M om had several sisters in the area that helped to care for her and make sure she would follow up on appointments.

One afternoon I received a call from one of her sisters informing me that Mom was in the hospital and that she was going to be kept there for an extended time. My aunt requested that I go to the hospital to speak with her and the doctors. I went there the next day.

I arrived at Brigham and Women's Hospital and reported to the front desk to provide her name to the front desk attendant. I was given the room number and floor where Mom was being treated. Based on this information I realized it was cancer.

At this point in my life, I had seen many commercials sharing information about the many cancers that existed or that one could be diagnosed with. I wondered what cancer mom was battling and what stage it was in.

The hospital floor she was on was like any typical hospital wing. Sounds of monitors beeping, the footsteps of hospital staff moving from room to room quickly, and the voices of other visitors muffled by the hospital room doors.

I arrived at her room and made my way in. I was surprised to see how much her health had deteriorated since I had last seen her. Unfortunately, I had seen my mom appear frail and very sick before due to the drug use and the impact drugs had on her physical appearance when she had been fully addicted to it.

I was sad to see her that way but there was not much I could do. I made sure to let her know how sad it made me feel to see her that way. I would ask her to check in to a drug addiction services center for help. I could not force her to go.

Despite her condition, she appeared optimistic and comfortable. She had been in hospitals many times for a number of medical issues associated with her lifestyle of drug use. Perhaps she believed this would also pass, that she would be treated and eventually be released.

The nurse entered the room to check on her and introduced herself. She mentioned that the doctor would be in shortly. I mentioned to her that I was her son and thanked her for checking in. A short while later the doctor came in, introduced himself, and asked Mom how she was feeling.

She said she was feeling okay.

The doctor asked to see me in the hallway and provided me with an update on her condition. The diagnosis was esophageal cancer and it was at stage 4. The diagnosis was grim and the outcome most certainly was death.

The doctor walked away and I remained standing there soaking in the information he had just shared with me. It was almost certain that she would not be walking out of this hospital.

I walked back into the room and didn't really mention anything. I looked at her and thought, does she really understand how serious this is? On the surface, it did not appear to be the case.

As the weeks went by, I became her representative and legal guardian. That afforded me the right to speak with doctors about her health and receive updates about any progress with the cancer treatments.

Being the older brother I charged myself with being the connecting tissue through all of this while at the same time living my life. Through the months and months of treatment and visits to the hospital, I shed many tears.

This was my reality for the foreseeable future. Is this part of the growth process? Is this the lesson of maturity we all must face at some point in our lives? It is a cruel one.

Months of going through the expectations and maintaining a steady course passed. Her condition worsened to the point where the doctor informed her that there was nothing else they could do. They mentioned that all they could do at this point was to keep her comfortable until the cancer ran its course.

It was during this time that I began to see a significant crack in the smile my mom had. The optimism and calm were replaced by fear and extreme sadness. I had only seen my mom afraid one time in my life. I am sure that she was afraid on many occasions but I just could not see it on the outside.

When I visited her she would cry during almost the entire visit. She was on heavy drugs to keep her comfortable so she would fade in and out. When she would come, she would cry and ask questions about her other children and other family members.

She would also ask if she had been a good person and a good mom. I would answer yes.

I had come to terms with the fact that I was abused, neglected, and left to fend for myself years before. I decided to forgive my mom for what she had done to me during my childhood. I realized during one of my last prison stints that a major reason for my rage, anger, sadness, and self-destructive behavior was because of the resentment I was harboring inside for my mom.

I've been charged with crimes and served time on numerous occasions. The majority of these charges and prison sentences involved acts of physical, emotional, and psychological violence. Punching through walls, kicking through doors, slamming objects, reaching for edge weapons, cursing, punching myself in the face, cutting myself, and using hurtful and menacing words to ensure that I had power and control. Striking my victims with physical blows or with any instrument or weapon I could find. I exploded with rage. My impulses would overcome me and I wanted to cause the most damage possible.

All of this felt normal. These actions allowed for my fears of love and loneliness to be kept at bay from others. I could not show weakness. I was taught from childhood that you overpower anyone who attempts to disrespect you or not do as you wish.

These actions continued to land me back in jail or prison. These actions continued to sink me further and further down into depression and anxiety. I continued to destroy relationships with people who loved me and continued adding to the list of enemies.

I had to fight my emotional insecurities and my lack of impulse control in order to prevent myself from ending up back in jail. I had to stop.

My aha moment struck me a few days after my son was born. Mom happened to be in the area and wanted to visit with my son who was at the hospital being cared for after being born prematurely.

I met Mom outside the hospital and we walked toward the elevators to the Neonatal Intensive Care Unit. While we were in the elevator Mom began to give me advice on how to care for my son. I began to feel my heart rate increase. I listened carefully but her voice appeared faint. I was beginning to only hear a murmur over my own thoughts.

I was saying to myself, *how dare you give me advice on how to raise and care for my son? After everything that I experienced due to your actions? How dare you?* All of the embarrassment, rage, disappointment, and unachieved potential for most of my life due to all of the anger I was harboring started to boil to the surface.

I believe that most of these thoughts were in my subconscious. I did not spend every waking second thinking about my childhood. It was in those times of quiet that it came to mind.

Sometimes I would be watching TV or having a conversation with someone, or just walking the streets, and something would trigger my past and my experiences.

Suddenly I felt like I exploded. I said, "MOM!!!! Stop talking!!! What are you telling me? That I don't know how to raise my child?" I stated that I had raised my daughter without her help and that I didn't need her advice.

She attempted to say something and I was filled with even more rage. I told her, "If you say anything else I will punch you in the face."

She leaned back in surprise and shock. Her eyes welled up with tears and she said, *"Esta bien mijo* (okay my son), *te entiendo,* (I understand), *disculpame,* (forgive me)."

Although I was shaking with fury, I felt bad. I had lashed out. I was worried about my son's health and only wanted her presence, not her advice.

Before the elevator arrived at our floor, I said to Mom, "I am sorry. I wouldn't hit you. Let's just focus on seeing my son." She said, "Okay."

Walking toward the NICU doors I felt as if I were sick. I was shaking and had cold chills. This incident impacted me horribly and triggered those physical reactions in me.

If I did not forgive and understand my mom and why she was the way she was I would not survive. I had to go through the same process with my dad. I felt less sadness for him than for my mom but I was still very angry and hurt because of how I felt he mistreated me.

On May 3, 2011, Mom was no longer able to fight. Cancer didn't win but her soul was determined to release her of the pain and suffering. I was in the room when she passed. Her last question, before she went into a frantic scream, was, "Do you forgive me?"

I remained strong so that she could see me in control and could be confident that I was clear in my response. "Yes, Mami, I do forgive you. I forgave you a long time ago. I am sorry you went through what you did in your life and I forgive you. I don't blame you. I believe you loved me and I am grateful for our time together."

We both cried together and I could feel her slipping away. Until next time, Mom. I rested my head on her chest and just embraced her for a while. Tears streamed down my face.

I stepped out of the room to see members of the family waiting. There were a large number of family members in the family room and many more on their way. Mostly her sisters and their kids. They were really close. This hurt. They knew from my tears that she was no longer with us.

The screams and hugs that celebrated this new year now had to be what we use to release pain and comfort one another.

I was really looking forward to at least one more birthday celebration with my mom and one more memorial birthday celebration for my brother. It wouldn't be.

Instead, it would be spent planning the funeral and transport of my mother's body to her birthplace and land of Puerto Rico.

Mother's Day would be replaced with a mother's worst nightmare as we delivered the sad news to Abuela (Grandma). Her beloved daughter was on her way to be laid to rest on Mother's Day weekend.

In my family (at least for the older generation and those raised in Villalba, Puerto Rico) the ceremony was always the same. We would bring the person who had passed into the living room of the home where everyone could come to pay their final respects.

Having been to a couple of funeral services as a child I had very blurred images of exactly what happened there.

I do remember running around outside with my cousins while the adults prayed with one another for the soul of the deceased. I remember chasing the chickens and just talking to my younger relatives about other things.

I also remember being yelled at by one of my aunts for not being more respectful to whoever it was that was being remembered.

This time it was different for me, I arrived with the body. I arrived at San Juan Airport. I was on one plane and my mom's body was on another.

The airlines have a system for the transport of the deceased. The funeral home director in Villalba would be responsible for picking up her body and transporting her to the funeral home for preparation before the viewing at the home in the pueblito of Jobito.

Her sisters took care of combing her hair and preparing her makeup. While all of this was taking place, I was reconnecting with family who I had not seen for a while and sharing stories about my life and theirs. I met new family members who were born since my last visit. There were so many family members there, many who I did not really know. I was grateful they were here to lend support to one another.

As the night fell, I could remember that people were mostly in good spirits while they waited for my mom's body to arrive. Then it happened. The hearse started climbing the narrow hill leading to our little pueblo (town), slowly creeping up and finding its balance. Eventually, they arrived at the back door of Abuelita's house and they began to unload her.

That's when the pain once again was made clear. Screams that tore at us began echoing through the mountains in our pueblo. Hugs, tears, fainting, and raw emotions. She was there in the living room of the house. It seemed like forever and so many people came out to pay their respects, including my father, his girlfriend, and my youngest sister.

I spent the time receiving condolences and having conversations.

Taking Mom away from the house once the services were over was the most difficult to watch. Her sisters were having such a difficult time seeing her being taken away.

Everyone got ready and started following the hearse to the cemetery where she would be finally laid to rest. The cemetery had these beautiful, larger-than-life stones and many of the lots included more than one relative or person.

After climbing a hill for a very long time we arrived. We went through the process and just like that, it was done. Mom was resting along with Grandpa.

Once we began the walk back, people began dispersing and I found myself for a little while alone. I reflected as I walked down this beautiful mountainside turned cemetery.

I gathered some people in a group and we stopped off to grab a slurpy-style refreshment. It was really hot out. I was now returning to the pueblito where it all began. Mom was free from her pain and I was at Peace knowing she believed I had forgiven her.

When I got back home, I realized that I had lost my brother and mother. The two people I most associated with my childhood and most of my life. I was truly the only remaining part of that trio. I had made them part of my conversations for so many years and could count on hearing from them from time to time.

That would no longer be the case. I would play the old voicemails they had left on my cell phone or watch a video that included their laughs and smiles. It was part of my reflection and grieving process.

Time ticked away and I dove further and further into my work as a violence prevention and crisis responder. I knew that violence had taken away my brother and mom in different ways. My brother was gunned down and my mother never recovered from domestic abuse and self-torment.

I had become a wounded healer, giving everything I had to prevent others from having to succumb to the pain that violence causes.

A few months later the matriarch of the family was also gone. My abuela who I had just visited and shared the sad news of mom's passing away in May had died on November 23rd.

I was called back to Puerto Rico.

I was not sure how this trip would go. I knew there would be some similarities to what happened just a few short months ago.

This service and coming together to honor her memory had a different feel to it. There were feelings of fear, a fear of what would happen to the family bonds now.

Who does the family turn to as the staple of the bloodline? The bearer of the history of the family, the strength we lean on?

I struggled to understand how so many pieces of my life fell apart in such a short time. Like turbulence on a plane, it was all out of my control. I was forced to just sit there and deal with it.

My abuela was always the same with me. Loving, kind, honest, and supportive. She didn't care about anything she had heard from others.

She always wanted to hear how my life was going and what I was up to. She always encouraged me to seek forgiveness for what I had done in my life and to be forgiving to those who had done me wrong.

She was also straightforward when she had to tell you about yourself, mincing no words when she thought you were wrong for something you had done or said. She demanded respect and made sure I understood that.

I would sit on her front porch which faced the homes of other family members strewn along the mountainside of our little pueblo. Her little house was the first house that I visited when I went to Puerto Rico.

She made sure I was well-fed and cooked up all of the traditional Puerto Rican dishes she knew I'd enjoy. She took care of me and I never felt alone with her.

I believe her influence on me was a reason why the seed of forgiveness had been planted in me and was possible for me to access.

Her ceremony was the same as Mom's. We walked her to the same lot where Mom had been laid to rest just six months earlier. She would be buried alongside her husband and my mom.

Once the ceremony was over and the vigils had taken place, I once again had an opportunity to be alone. I walked up a very steep mountain. I was high enough to see most of the pueblos that neighbored ours.

While standing there I could see my abuela's house in the distance. I thought, *What now? What ties me to this place? Who do I come to visit first when I arrive?*

After some time spent there on my own, I realized that I was at Peace. I had come to pay my respects. I had benefited from my abuela's love, and now she was in heaven alongside her husband and daughter. She was resting in Peace.

32

The Ascent

I was back in New York City in a room that was very similar to those I had seen in the Godfather mafia movies of the 1970s. It was in a cigar shop in the middle of Manhattan tucked away inside a typical New York City skyscraper. There was no way to tell that space was there unless you were a member of the cigar shop or were invited to attend a meeting or event there.

I had been working in the community helping youth learn some of the actions they could take to help prevent incarceration and violence in their lives. As I mentioned before I had opportunities to participate in professional development training.

These opportunities allowed me to travel to a number of states across the country where I met professionals in the human services field and other social service providers.

Networking during training sessions, conferences, and meetings of professionals in the social services field was important to building connections, finding common practices, and gaining support for my efforts.

I had a story to tell and wanted to make sure that as many people as possible heard my story.

Sharing my story has become another mechanism for healing from my past trauma. The more I shared the story the more I realized I was gaining control over it and the more I realized where I needed to focus my internal work.

To be honest I was only working on the surface of my emotions. I would share to a point and was not truly in touch with the true depth of the work that would be required to achieve a level of Peace within me.

I had developed many bad habits that despite the feelings of accomplishment and progress would still come to the surface during times of high stress, uncertainty, challenge, and conflict. When I felt pinned or backed up against a wall, I would lash out to ensure that I was not being bullied or smothered.

It could be something as simple as not knowing how to pronounce a word correctly or being corrected on information that I felt I knew. I hated feeling foolish, I hated being wrong. It meant that I was not worthy or could be dismissed. *Not today!* I would say in my head.

Shame controlled that part of me. I had felt shame many times due to the behaviors of my mom when she was under the influence of drugs, or when my dad would forcefully shut me down with violence or threats of a beating. As an adult, I adopted the mentality that I would not be shamed.

When I felt shame, it was like having a 100-plus fever that I could feel on my neck, in my ears, and on my forehead. My hands would get sweaty, I could feel myself begin to sweat over my body and my heart rate would increase significantly. I was ready to defend my pride and ego with aggression. What I was really feeling was that I was inadequate.

Being this protective of what I felt were my weaknesses had served me well on the streets. I survived because of it. I could survive this professional space using those behaviors that while very destructive had proven to be successful. Surviving was the measuring stick. Not thriving.

On one of my trips to a conference, I met a woman from a New York City-based youth program. She wanted to learn more about my work in Connecticut. We exchanged contact information and promised to keep in touch.

During my professional growth period, I was advised to create a LinkedIn professional networking page in order to build my connections and increase my professional reach. This space is where I could go to expand my personal brand while also learning about work others were doing to have an impact on the lives of those who they served.

One day while I was posting an update on my LinkedIn page, I noticed the message icon was red indicating I had a message in my inbox. I clicked on the mail icon and saw the photo of the person I had met from New York.

She was reaching out to inform me that I was being considered for an award for my work in the communities in Connecticut. She wanted to interview me to learn more. I responded to her message and said thank you. I recorded her number and called the next day. We spoke for a while and she said she would be in touch with a decision at some point.

I was pretty surprised that she would reach out to me all the way from New York to discuss a nomination I received for an award. Why had I come to mind? What was it about my work that was important enough to receive recognition from another state?

Several months later I received an email congratulating me for being awarded the "El Award" by El Diario La Prensa Newspaper in New York. This was an award dedicated to "a select group of Latinos who faced challenges but never lost track of their goals."

What I learned during a conversation I had after I received the email was that the awards selection committee had called numerous people in my home state to ask about my work and impact. It was decided that I was worthy of the award. I never learned who they spoke to but was truly surprised that I was chosen.

I was invested in the work of doing my best to save young lives and to help steer them on a path of positive progress and purpose but others were also doing the same. Perhaps they saw something in me or heard something that appealed most to them.

This recognition was only several months removed from the passing of my Abuela, the passing of my mom, and only a few short years from the passing of my brother. My challenges were still very much in my face.

I had developed the ability to accept my reality. I was navigating the world I existed to the best of my ability. I had understood that most of my immediate family foundation was gone.

Experiencing my trials and tribulations as a child developed my capacity to absorb painful blow after painful blow. I learned to continue doing what I could to survive. To "just keep swimming" as the famous Dory in *Finding Nemo* would say.

Days of hunger, moments of injury, and times of darkness and uncertainty all contributed to developing the mindset of doing whatever you can to get up and fight. No surrender.

These moments were not without intervention from others who (perhaps not even realizing it) had planted seeds of hope, clarity, motivation, or encouragement in my head and heart.

Despite my challenges with recalling some of my childhood and other experiences in my life, I have vivid memories of two occasions when I believe seeds were planted although I was not ready to water them at that time.

I was working at Century 21 Department Stores in Brooklyn, New York. On this particular overnight shift, I was done stacking clothing racks and storing shelves early. It was approximately 4:00 am.

I left the warehouse and hopped on a train headed toward home. I arrived at my stop in Brooklyn, New York, stepped out of the train station, walked up the stairs, and turned the corner onto the street.

It was a dark and cold night, no one was around on the platform, in the station, or on the street that I could see.

As I turned the corner to head up the block towards 6th Avenue I felt as if someone grabbed my shoulder. It felt like a tap.

At that time, I was about 215 pounds and had just been released from prison a few months before.

I was still a very angry kid (although I was in my early 20s) and my defenses were always up.

I turned around wondering who was touching me. I was ready to engage whoever it was in physical violence and aggression.

Once I made contact with the person who had touched me, I realized I was looking at an older woman.

I was confused as to why this woman would touch me. Especially at this time of the morning with no one else around. In my head I spoke the words, *What are you? Crazy?*

She looked me directly in the eyes and said in Spanish, *"Tu tienes un llamado de Dios* (you have a calling from God)."

I was not in a position or a mindset to believe in God or any of that. When I was growing up, I had been an altar boy at a church in Hartford. I went there with my mom. I learned as I got older the reason she was taking me there.

She was not taking me there to spend time with me. Instead, it was so that I could be occupied or taken care of while she ran the streets. I spent time there and I still did not really get close to God so when this woman said that I had a calling, I did not accept it and kept on walking.

But like Jade Ivy stated in a poem, "Once is a mistake, twice is a coincidence, three times is a pattern." This wouldn't be the last time someone would approach me to let me know that my life had a purpose.

This cigar club filled with smoke and dimly lit was like no other place I had ever been in. I felt out of place but was intrigued. I carefully observed the behaviors of folks who were huddled up in groups smoking cigars and having conversations. I was making sure not to stare.

I was dressed in a suit and tie with black shoes. I'd rarely dressed like this but this was required for the award ceremony.

I never made a connection with those who were in the room with me. I was introduced to some but beyond that, there was not much conversation. I sat at a table by myself for a while until the ceremony began.

I was called up to receive my award and received warm applause. Once I returned to the table, I heard a few congratulations, and just like that, it was over. Shortly after that, I headed out and started my trip back home.

Although I was grateful for the recognition, I honestly did not know if it was significant or not. I did not feel as if it changed my life or made me a better person. I had no one there from my family or friends to celebrate with. It felt strange but at least I could add it to my resume and share it with those who were close to me.

Perhaps I was not paying attention to the rumblings of what was happening around me. I would come to realize that others were.

This award, although not connected to anyone I was in direct contact with, would set off a chain of events that would highlight just how much impact my efforts were having on the community I served.

I would go on to receive four additional awards between 2012 and 2014. New York, the State of Connecticut, and the City of Hartford proclaimed me a role model whose contributions to underserved populations and communities had a positive impact.

My confidence began to grow and I began to believe more in myself. Being recognized by my community, peers, and leaders of other organizations meant that I had value and meaning. That others believed in my abilities and that I had earned their trust.

My reputation for many years in most professional and community circles was of a gang member and convicted criminal. I had earned those titles with every action that I took that resulted in an arrest or violent incident.

Getting to the point of being honored with recognitions and awards was a slow, painful self-evaluation. At every point in my journey, I had to fight the urge to fall back into my learned and practiced bad behavior.

Transforming my thinking from negative to positive would require challenging myself to stop and think before I respond to any stressor or perceived emotional threat. I had to develop stimulus control.

In 1996 after being indicted for a number of federal crimes I had been evaluated by a social worker from the court who advised that I begin to see a counselor. I was not insured nor did I have the financial means to afford a therapist.

I was making enough money to pay bills, and my debt and to cover the basic needs of food, shelter, and clothes.

I was directed to the services of a pastoral counselor in West Hartford, Connecticut. Seeing a counselor was now a requirement from the court. It had to happen prior to adjudicating the case.

I remember walking into a counseling office for the first time in my life. It was a quiet space, very quiet. The pastor sat across from me. We had a very lengthy conversation about my life.

I was able to learn a lot about him and met with him for several weeks. I started to realize that I was angry with my parents for the treatment of me as a child and how much that treatment had led me to be who I was. I was diagnosed with "stress impulse disorder," meaning that as I became stressed, I would impulsively hurt someone, or myself. I was not in control of my impulses or my behavior and adding alcohol to that accelerated that violent behavior. Acceptance of my bad behavior by others, uncertainty, feelings of fear, feeling dumb or illiterate, and my life experiences made me even worse.

Seeing a professional therapist to discuss my feelings and share my experiences was one of the reasons why I feel like I was able to start looking at my challenges from a different viewpoint.

I had to see my circumstances, challenges, and current state of being in a different way. I had to look at what I was doing to contribute to keeping things as they were or making them worse.

I had to consider each step and action I took and assign it a consequence. What was going to happen if I did this?

I had to look at where the opportunities to make things better were. I was not very skilled at seeing opportunities and building an action plan to take advantage of those opportunities.

I also had to look at the actions of those who I associated with and calculate what consequences I would face for them.

I had to balance my mindset and manage my emotional responses to anything going wrong or not as I wanted.

This was a challenge for me.

I questioned the purpose regularly of thinking differently. *Why was it impor-tant? Who cares?*

Everything had to be considered.

I had to do my best to not take any comments or actions from others personally. Why should it matter?

It was a second-to-second fight in my head. I had to fight against what I had learned in order to survive.

It was scary to believe that I was not in control and that I should not simply do as I knew or as I've always done.

After many trials and failures, ups and downs this new way of thinking did help. It afforded me the opportunity to be taken a little more seriously as someone who was in transition and capable of changing bad habits to be better and to do better.

New thinking allowed me to care about consequences, not only for me but for anyone in my life. I learned that my actions, words, and thoughts could also hurt others around me.

New thinking also allowed me to listen with positive intention and to listen to understand.

I spent nearly a year visiting with the pastoral counselor. I would say the impact was average.

Based on all of the trauma that I had experienced in my life and the bad habits I had created I knew I needed more time to develop new healthy and positive habits.

I believe that the therapy at least awakened a new way of processing my feelings and actions. It allowed me to pause and take a moment to compose myself before I made any decisions based on an emotional response.

Before this, all of the decisions were made with little thought. If I felt it, I did it.

In the long term, I feel as if I developed the capacity to see a new way of processing information and reacting to that information.

This would allow me to see my everyday experiences in many different ways. As time passed, I made many decisions, good and bad. They all included a little more processing than in the past.

Hence the good and bad.

Before this new way of thinking it was all bad.

Every time there was a minor or major decision to make it was made from a space of emotion.

That was trouble since I could go from a smile to an evil hate-filled grin in milliseconds.

By even taking one minute to process I could either make sense of my decision or not. I was still very much stubborn and dependent on my ways to get by.

Having another option for my emotional trigger response was helpful but it would take much time to engrain this as part of my strategy to respond more positively and progressively.

My ability to reduce negative incidents in my life allowed me to focus more on the good that had happened in my life.

I could be more relaxed and could begin to set goals for myself. It made me be more present for those who were in my circle of friends and family. Less chaos and emotional breakdowns afforded me the trust of others.

For many years I had wanted to help young people overcome their challenges and avoid prison or the call of the streets. I felt now that I had a little more control over my negative emotional responses that I could do a better job of helping others.

I became someone that others believed was worthy of being a permanent part of their lives. I had made such gains that several friends honored me by asking that I serve as Padrino (Godfather) to their children.

I would take on the responsibility of caring for someone's child in the event they became ill or worse. If no other immediate family was able to care for their child, I would be asked to step in.

When I was in my early twenties, I had been asked to be a Padrino by a few young people that I worked with at Mi Casa Family Services. Mostly teenagers who I mentored and supported through their daily challenges in school, at home, and in their community.

I was very new at that type of work but I cared about their well-being. I just wanted them to feel the support and happiness I had not felt at their age.

I was silly and open to being funny. I was also very charismatic, friendly, and honest with them and made sure to always actively listen when they spoke. I believe they asked me to be a Padrino because they felt I cared.

I even had one young person ask me to serve as a Padrino to her. Although this was a responsibility that I took as seriously, I was not exactly sure of all that it entailed. It would end up being something that shaped into more like a distant relative or absent dad.

We were all so young, what exactly did we know?

My hope in this second chance is that I can live up to this responsibility to be what is expected of me.

When I entered my teens, I made myself a promise that if I was ever blessed with fatherhood, I would be a great father. I never did realize the true impact of that promise.

I learned that I loved being a dad or someone children could depend on to provide them with support, love, and kindness. I learned that those things were different than what I thought they were during the times I was on the streets or experiencing my hardships.

Support means that you are present, available, and reliable instead of adding to the pain, supporting the negative risks, and cheering on the destructive violent behavior.

Love means that you protect them, spend time with them, seek to understand them, nurture them, and never physically injure them.

Love does not mean that you demand they do as you wish, that you threaten them with violence when they do not behave as you expected, or that you only value that person when they can benefit you.

Kindness means that you listen to learn and help if needed, that you value them, and that you step in when they are doing wrong and challenge them to do right.

Kindness was not providing them a place to live only to torture them as payment for your favor. Kindness was not stepping in when needed only to punish them to make a point.

Kindness was not providing material things while stripping someone of their dignity, self-worth, and identity with physical and verbal abuse behind closed doors.

I submerged myself completely into the work of helping youth. I felt as if it was my best opportunity to improve the lives of those who were from the same communities where I had spent so much of my time. The place where I had shed so many tears, experienced so much heartbreak, caused so much suffering, and experienced some of my darkest moments. I felt I could change that for other young people.

In 2007 I received "My Precious" (as Gollum would call the ring in *The Lord of the Rings*), the "Fathers are Key" award. It was awarded to those in the community who worked with youth and became a father figure for them.

On the agenda speaking that night were Walter "Doc" Hurley, educator, veteran, athlete, and founder of the Doc Hurley Scholarship Fund that helped raise money for youth athletics in Hartford, and Michael Eric Dyson, writer, minister, and scholar. These were two men who had positively impacted the African American, Black, Hispanic, Latino, and other communities across the country. I was there with giants who were known by many. I was extremely proud to be among them and to be honored for my work. I was most excited that my children were there to see me receive the award.

At the time the Fathers Are Key Award meant that I was doing what I had promised myself as a teenager. I would be a good father. I had to be a nurturer. I had to be present. I had to be dependable. I had to be patient. I had to show affection, and love, and help to provide my children with basic needs so that they could thrive.

What I had not realized is that I was also offering that fatherhood to more than my birth children. I was seen as a father figure to boys and girls throughout the City of Hartford.

I felt for many years that I had a fire burning inside of me. That fire was fueling my determination. I was focused on working to improve my professional abilities. To help improve my skills to perform my work better.

I could not afford to fail. I remembered where I came from, what I had been through, and what I hated about my bad behavior and I had challenged myself to not return to my old habits.

33

THE CHOICE

The scent of melted candles, spilled alcohol, marijuana smoke, car exhaust, and the sounds of music began to fade as I began to walk away from where my brother's street memorial was taking place. I slowly regained awareness of where I was. I felt each step I took as I walked away from this corner that would forever bring me painful thoughts.

As I headed towards a waiting vehicle, my childhood friends were looking at me intensely, waiting for my answer to the offer to seek vengeance and revenge by those memorializing my brother on this makeshift memorial site. They would follow my decision. After some silence, I responded by saying, "Respect! Thank you, I'll hit you up (I'll be in touch)."

I walked away from the memorial site and got into the back seat of the car, feeling as if I was abandoning my brother's spirit. I felt like there was nowhere I could go that would be a good space to heal my pain or ease my rage.

We drove off.

The guys decided to drive me back to my home in Windsor. For the entire drive, I was deep in thought. I reflected on everything about my brother's life, our lives together, and how I would resolve this situation I was faced with. I regretted not being there to protect him. I always had his back. I felt as if I had let him down.

I had felt this same feeling many years earlier. My brother had been incarcerated for drug and violence-related crimes. One day on the drive home from visiting family in New York, I had a sudden jolt of pain across my temple. I began to feel as if I had a headache. I was not sure what was happening but I knew what it was that came upon me suddenly.

Less than an hour later I found out that my brother had been injured in prison. Someone had hit him in the face with an Old Spice cologne bottle stuffed into a sock.

The impact of the blow had crushed his eye socket and caused damage to his cheek. After being taken to the hospital doctors determined that due to the injury sustained from the blow to his eye, he would be permanently blind in his right eye.

The news shattered my heart into a million pieces. I immediately began to sob uncontrollably. I could not contain my pain. I blamed myself for not being there to protect him. I felt that if I had been there, I would have stopped whoever was targeting my brother. I would have hurt that person severely or attempted to kill that person for challenging or attacking my brother. I carried that feeling of guilt for many years. I felt as if I owed him my protection after all he had done to protect me as a child. In this instance, I felt as if I had failed to keep my promise to keep him from harm. I felt helpless.

I recalled my last conversation with Smokey on New Year's Eve 2007. I called him as the traditional ball dropped in New York City yelling "Happy New Year, wooooooooooo hooooooooo!" I expected to hear loud music in the background, voices cheering and slurred speech from a little too much of his favorite drink, Hennessy. Instead, I was met with a subdued and calm voice and no noise coming from the background.

I was surprised, so I stepped aside from where my crowd was and asked, "Yo Smoke, where ya at?"

He responded, "I am at home chillin' with my girl. I am keeping it low-key and taking it easy."

I was shocked! My brother knew how to party and when I was with him, there was never a dull moment.

Still surprised I said, "Well then, Happy New Year, my brother. Stay safe, and have fun. I love you."

He responded, "I love you, too."

I hung up and remembered sharing my call experience with someone who was in my crowd, still surprised about the call but happy to know he was safe and just relaxing.

I knew I would ask him in the future, "Why did you decide to be low-key?"

A few days after the New Year, my call with Smokey was still heavy on my mind. I was working at a youth service and afterschool program as the director of a community outreach and engagement project, targeting youth who were perpetrators or victims of violence. We would work in every corner of the city on helping to prevent violence and decrease the incidents of retaliatory violence among youth. I needed another person to join my team and help with this effort. I felt as if my brother was ready to.

That Saturday I picked up an employment application and called him. I simply said, "Yo my brother, I have a job for you! I need you to help me do the work that I do."

He said, "Yo, I'm down."

I said, "Cool." We made plans for him to come see me on Monday, January 14, 2008, and complete the employment application.

He was shot that next morning and died before I could ever hand him the application. Looking at that application laying on the passenger seat of my car, I realized that he died stepping in to break up a fight.

He died a Peacebuilder.

I decided.

My brother died believing in me and he died with me believing in him. We believed that we could stop the violence. I wasn't going to let him down.

Did I want to press my luck or gamble with my life again by choosing violence? I would most likely attribute most of my brushes with death or greater prison time to fate or luck.

Luck played a role in my life when I was not killed after being beaten by five neighborhood teens and an adult. Luck played a role when my father or mother did not kill me.

Luck played a role when I was in my car accident and did not die. Luck played a role when I was in a fight that included knives and I was cut. Luck played a role when I was chased in a car and shot at on two occasions.

Luck played a role when I was in spaces and shootings broke out and I was not hit. Luck played a role when someone told me they were sent on a mission to kill me but could not find me. Luck played a role when I was drugged at a local bar and had someone there to save me. Luck has been present in many of my life experiences.

I could no longer rely on luck. I believed in working hard and considering the consequences of my actions, and I believed that my purpose in life was to serve others and help interrupt some of the sufferings of as many people as physically possible. I believed in creating my opportunities and in my potential to choose what was in my best emotional, physical, psychological, and professional interests.

Whatever I decided to do next would be the most difficult decision in my life. I had experienced the justice system. I had been on the other side of the law and had learned how to function within that space. I could return to a life of violence and prison and no one would blame me. I would be celebrated by some.

I had seen the system working against me from the inside. I knew of many injustices within that system. Men in prison whose time served did not reflect a proper consequence for their heinous crime, while other men were sentenced to far too many years for a crime that did not match the years they were given.

I knew in my heart that the person who murdered my brother would one day live a life outside of prison bars but even with the possibility of a life sentence, he would still live. My brother would not.

His daughters, granddaughters, his family, his girlfriend, and his brother would never enjoy his company again.

I had been numb since the moment I learned that my brother lay fighting for his life. That numbness turned to extreme grief and confusion. It then turned to a heavy desire to see him, to confirm what that doctor had said outside those double doors of the operating room.

After I saw my brother, I was crushed. I felt lost. As the minutes ticked by, I was not really thinking about much. I was just feeling the pain and replaying the vision of seeing my brother on that stretcher.

I began to battle between revenge and justice. I had learned who was responsible. I knew where to find him, and I had the resources to end his life and the lives of anyone who was with him.

At the time my brother was killed, I was expanding my work in community violence prevention. I had been to many scenes like the one I was in where mothers, sisters, brothers, children, grandparents, friends, colleagues, girlfriends, boyfriends, and spouses had received the terrible news that their loved one was murdered.

I held many of those grieving, angry, and crushed individuals in my arms. I talked many of them off ledges or used all of my grip strength to hold them back and prevent them from attacking a hospital worker or anyone who they felt would make their pain go away. I had the experience of watching people with deep faith and conviction decide to not respond with violence.

Being a witness to that response taught me that there was another way to respond to being broken. I saw firsthand how those individuals were able to move through emotions and the reality of the moment sooner. They were able to allow their lives to continue although they were pained.

I was serving as an example to so many youth and leaders in the community, my staff, and my children. Having responded with violence in the past led me to prison or to some level of loss. I felt I wanted a different solution. I felt I wanted the Peace I was asking others to find or to practice.

That made it possible for me to resist the old me and stand up to my inner beast. I chose progress, Peace, and a positive solution before. My brother died knowing me as a Peacebuilder.

I had learned to understand the consequences of a negative, violent response. To dig deeper into my feelings and be rational with my thinking. Weigh the options and decide the path to take.

One path would lead to loss, continued pain, and seclusion, and the other path would help mend my pain while affording me the opportunity to continue on my path to Peace.

My ultimate goal was to be well. It was to be present for my children and my community. I had made such gains and I could lose it all in that matter of a mere second. I needed to see where this life would allow me to go and what I was capable of.

I had learned through my life experience, my work, and my professional training that negative actions reaped negative consequences.

I had learned that this response would be immediate in releasing some pain but everlasting in introducing new pain.

I had witnessed many others respond to pain and loss with vengeance and, in every instance, the instant gratification led to a lifetime of stress, consequence, continued violence, and suffering.

I learned that a negative response fueled the ever-revolving cycle of my community's suffering. Through my work, I had become tired of the pain and developed a level of compassion beyond my understanding.

Victims of violence needed me to help them grieve and heal. Perpetrators needed me to help them understand why their actions were wrong. Both needed someone to help them find ways to better their lives and heal their wounds.

Many times, I found myself in the crosshairs of both groups and witnessed how sad, frightening, and full of pain these violent incidents were. I had learned to find no joy in a violent response.

I learned to enjoy the safety and positive outcomes of solving my emotional pain or stressors through mediation, self-control, and accountability.

The expectation was always to respond with violence because it was the known manner for how someone responded to the killing of a loved one. Especially if you were part of a gang, and grew up in some of these communities across the city.

Violence was met with violence, force with force, and pain with pain. Many of my friends or people I knew were committed to preserving their reputations, egos, or status.

Crying was a sign of weakness if it was not followed with violent action. It was the right thing to do. It was a coping mechanism. It was the fair thing to do.

To be considered someone who was soft was not acceptable. Even if you were killed you had to go out fighting.

The murder of my brother was the perfect example of when no positive solution was possible. Death or serious life-changing injury was the answer.

The hate must be immediate. The desire to hurt is right alongside that. There was a sense of power and respect in responding with violence and speaking with rage-filled words. It made others believe that you cared about the person who was killed.

I grew up watching many fights that took place because it was expected. No measure of control, a system for a violence-free resolution, or advice to let it go.

Most were judged or awarded based on how much damage they could do with either their knuckles or with a weapon. We were built to break anything that we felt shamed us, disrespected us, or hurt us.

In many ways, we were also taught to do the same to even those who loved us and who we loved. If they shamed you, disrespected you, or hurt you, they'd be punished physically and everyone would understand.

Growing up I spent time in every single neighborhood in the city for one reason or another and through that journey, I met and befriended many.

Although my childhood and adolescence created noise in my mind, I always treated others with respect and kindness. Any conflict or violence that I created, although there is no excuse, was because of the influence of alcohol, a bruised ego, or a desire to overpower a rival group.

Throughout my life, I have come across many who remind me of something I have done for them, a time I stepped in to defend or fight for them, a time I helped them move something, a time I told them they were beautiful and made them feel beautiful, or sang to them, or taught them how to box or breakdance.

And, there were moments when I was visiting Hartford after working on the construction site in New Hartford when I would give people money or buy them food. I may have had the physical weapons to fight the bad fight but, my heart desired to be good to people and to connect with the souls of others.

There was a time when I felt no shame for being arrested or acting in a violent way in front of anyone.

I shared the stories of my wrongdoings as if I were telling a tale, looking for a reaction or response. But telling the story is all a part of the process.

Many of those who I knew on the street were very familiar with the revolving doors of incarceration. Many had friends or family members who had been incarcerated so it was not shocking that someone would be.

Poverty, segregation, exclusion, lack of resources, blighted neighborhoods, lack of equity, and rampant illegal substance distribution coupled with violence. All pieces of my fractured childhood.

These conditions forced me to grow up with a survivor mentality. Survival of the most powerful, the best fighter, most violent, aggressive, largest crew or gang, the biggest, and the ones with most weapons.

I was trained to respond to aggression with aggression. This was the perfect recipe for minor situations to escalate quickly.

This all became all too normal and we either moved away to escape it or stayed in the house all day to avoid it, were blessed enough to have a family that focused on keeping us out of the mess, or were fortunate enough to skate by untouched.

Everyone wanted to live so without the resources and support you created your own safety. This meant having weapons or finding others to be by your side with the same mission as you.

You must crush your threat, competition, foes, and those who perpetrated anything deemed disrespectful against you by any means necessary.

I believed life was living by the minute. No plan for the future that included school, savings, retirement, or anything to plan for the later years of life.

Life was supposed to be a fight for survival each day, filled with many periods of fruitless partying, sleeping with women, and fighting with anyone who crossed you or you had a disagreement with.

Life was watching your back all day from enemies, police, or strangers in the community who were just as hurt as you were and were looking to release some of that pain by way of violence or some type of conflict.

Life was a day-to-day test of your will and luck. Each day you made it was a win. That win was masked with a sense of toughness and the belief that you were somehow invincible. That invincibility was the reason no one killed you the day before or why you were able to avoid being arrested by police.

When others see you involved in all of those acts of self-sabotage, violence, and irresponsibility and they celebrate or accept you, how else would you know differently?

In order to know the difference, I had to experience it, witness it, learn it, and put it into practice.

The phrase practice makes permanent comes to mind when I think about the many days and nights I spent convincing myself that my life would be better off without violence, conflict, self-destructive behaviors, excessive drinking, and wasting time on trivial things that led to nothing good.

I had to understand that needing help was okay and asking for it was true bravery, rather than being ashamed or embarrassed by it.

I had hurt myself on so many occasions when I became upset. I had ended up on the streets, ousted from where I lived, arrested for my actions, and increased the number of enemies I had and the number of victims I had victimized.

This all became toxic and counterproductive to what I had begun to believe was necessary for me to succeed at achieving the goals set for myself.

I needed to look at myself a little bit more seriously and do the hard work of being able to reflect on what I was doing to myself by allowing my bad habits to take the lead in how I responded to stressors.

This was not the time to simply toss aside all of the strategies, techniques, habits, and action steps that I had learned and practiced. My capacity to make positive decisions had been developed. To hit rock bottom again would most certainly spell disaster.

My head felt as if it was heavier than usual. Although the car was moving, the sights and sounds of the ride to Windsor were in the distance. I felt as if I was in a fog. I needed to regain a clear mind so that I could communicate what I was thinking and feeling to my friends in the car.

I took a deep breath and it was painful. My chest felt stuck. I was holding on to pain and had been taking shallow breaths for hours. I felt the bones in my chest and shoulders pop like fingers on hands when someone cracks their knuckles.

As my head rose up from the deep pocket I felt it was in, I broke the silence in the car. I said, "Yo."

One of the guys quickly turned towards me and asked, "What's up?"

I looked my friend in the eyes with tears in mine.

My eyes were swollen, red, and puffy from crying.

I asked my childhood friend for the card I had passed along to him at the hospital and called the detective from the Hartford Police Department. I gave him the information about who was responsible for killing my brother so that they could arrest him and let the justice system deliver justice, not revenge, for my brother.

I chose Peace.

—•—

ACKNOWLEDGMENTS

I credit those who stepped in and provided me guidance, opportunity, support, and honesty for instilling in me the principles to reach my goals and develop the capacity to believe a peaceful life was possible.

Steve Warner, for seeing me when I felt I had become invisible to everyone. For opening your home to me and teaching me the lesson of hard work and seeing things through until they were done correctly. You gave me a safe space when I needed it most.

Kathy Nazario, for teaching me about inner strength, patience, true love, forgiveness, and fighting for what you love. Thank you also for being the wonderful mother you are to our two children.

John Wardlaw, for teaching me about investing in something despite facing opposition from others who did not understand the reasoning behind your decision. You took a chance on me and allowed me to begin my career in youth and community service. I've loved the work ever since and there are so many others who are healthier, safer, and more successful today because you opened the door to me.

Michael Borrero, you taught me the one word that has remained with me from my early twenties. Although I did not understand it nor did I know how to apply it in my life. That word was accountability. In your world, it means to be reliable and responsible. In short, keep the promises you make and show up when expected. You taught me the importance of evolving intellectually and offered me many chances to prove myself. You became my role model and my most consistent supporter early in my career and planted the seed of possibility in my life. You taught me that one person can make a difference.

Father Lou Paturzo and Father Jim Ahern for your advice and support with no expectations. Your words are spoken many times at the right time and with the purpose of helping me think through my decisions. You were out on the streets with many of us who were lost and fighting to find acceptance, healing, and love. You never wavered in your support and encouragement to be good people.

Joe Muniz, thank you for stepping in when I was facing years in prison for actions I engaged in while on the streets. My freedom today has allowed me to be available to my children, my clients, and my community. Thank you for affording me a second chance to achieve my purpose.

April Goff Brown and Lew Brown for thinking outside of the box for how to best positively impact the lives of youth who were deemed disconnected or at a high level of exposure to adverse risk. You chose me as your employee because you believed that I was the right person for the job and believed that I possessed something special that would allow me to help youth in the community make better choices. You then embraced me as a friend, a close family member and now I am your bonus son. You gave me love, advice, and hard feedback when I needed it and you always believed in my abilities to be a better person. Your loving home is now mine to visit to feel that love every person needs.

Jose "Chelo" Mendez, my young friend. As a child, you wanted to keep me safe. You took risk after risk to ensure that I wouldn't go hungry. You took risks to make sure that I had a warm place to sleep and never saw me as a burden. Your brotherly love was genuine and your admiration of me came from a place of pride. Your made-up language made it impossible to confuse who was calling on the phone or who was calling my name out on the streets. "Smurfy, Queeeee Passaaaaaa" became our brotherly greeting. I will always be grateful for the mercy and love you had for me. May you rest in eternal Peace.

To my stunning, brilliant, compassionate, loving, and determined wife Jacquelyn Santiago Nazario, for first challenging me to believe I was capable of achieving my goals and reaching my dreams. For teaching me about healthy habits, and better ways to protect myself against self-destructive thoughts and behaviors. For embracing my fears, pain, loneliness, and doubts with love, kindness, understanding, and encouragement. For paying attention to what caused me stress and stepping in to teach me how to breathe and relax through it. For instilling in me a love of learning. For your unwavering support of my aspirations and for keeping me afloat when times of challenge arrived. You were present for most of my darkest moments and brightened up my spirit with your care, sympathy, shoulder to cry on, and for being there to provide me with whatever it was I needed.

To my children. You have blessed me with your existence. Your lives have enriched mine and have introduced a level of love that perhaps I would not have known. Every dream you had, every stumble, every question, every bright spot, every aha moment, every time you needed comfort, and everything else I witnessed with you has allowed me to know the depth that love can reach. I am better because you exist and all I've wanted is that you live up to your potential, that you care for yourself, that you are a good person to others, and that you live healthy, successful, and peaceful lives. You are each a piece of my heart.

Finally, to every person who gave me a place to rest my head, every teacher who never turned their back on me, and every employer who by hiring me told me they believed in me. Thank you. You contributed to my blessings and in a special way gave me moments of reprieve, safety, inspiration, motivation, structure, education, and support.

—·—

ABOUT THE AUTHOR

I ran Nazario is the Founder, President, and CEO of the Peace Center of Connecticut. The mission of the Peace Center is to engage in partnerships to build action for achieving Peace in our communities.

Through his work, he continues his pursuit of Peace for the community where he grew up.

He is a Peace advocate, trainer, motivational speaker, and consultant helping communities, organizations, institutions, and schools improve their program and services and the impact those programs and services have on their clients, students, communities, and stakeholders.

Iran began his career as a volunteer in 1993 helping youth overcome their challenges, serving the community, and building networks that would help prevent violence throughout the City of Hartford, Connecticut, and throughout the country.

For over 25 years he has worked in the program management, gang prevention, youth outreach, engagement, and community support field. He is an expert in gang prevention and mediation with a proven impact on the management of staff and programs.

His career has included leading programs at the Hartford Housing Authority, University of Connecticut (UCONN) School of Social Work, Urban League of Greater Hartford, Mi Casa Family Services, Hispanic Health Council, the City of Hartford, Hartford Public Schools and COMPASS Youth Collaborative.

Working in partnership with the Hartford Police Department in June of 2015 Iran was "badged" by the department to serve as a community/law enforcement partner. In this role, Iran is to serve as an intermediary in citywide crisis situations under President Obama's My Brother's Keeper Initiative.

Iran is the recipient of numerous awards for his contribution to improving the lives of residents in the Hartford community and across the country.

Iran is the co-author of the poetry book *Bullets into Bells,* which describes the impact of gun violence across the state of Connecticut. With his memoir *Rage to Peace*, he hopes to inspire readers to embrace positive change in their lives.